The Politics of Platform Regulation

Oxford Studies in Digital Politics

Series Editor: Andrew Chadwick, Professor of Political Communication in the Centre for Research in Communication and Culture and the Department of Social Sciences, Loughborough University

Apostles of Certainty: Data Journalism and the Politics of Doubt
C. W. Anderson

Using Technology, Building Democracy: Digital Campaigning and the Construction of Citizenship
Jessica Baldwin-Philippi

Expect Us: Online Communities and Political Mobilization
Jessica L. Beyer

If ... Then: Algorithmic Power and Politics
Taina Bucher

The Hybrid Media System: Politics and Power
Andrew Chadwick

News and Democratic Citizens in the Mobile Era
Johanna Dunaway and Kathleen Searles

The Fifth Estate: The Power Shift of the Digital Age
William H. Dutton

The Only Constant Is Change: Technology, Political Communication, and Innovation Over Time
Ben Epstein

Designing for Democracy: How to Build Community in Digital Environments
Jennifer Forestal

Directed Digital Dissidence in Autocracies: How China Wins Online
Jason Gainous, Rongbin Han, Andrew W. MacDonald, and Kevin M. Wagner

Tweeting to Power: The Social Media Revolution in American Politics
Jason Gainous and Kevin M. Wagner

When the Nerds Go Marching In: How Digital Technology Moved from the Margins to the Mainstream of Political Campaigns
Rachel K. Gibson

Trolling Ourselves to Death: Democracy in the Age of Social Media
Jason Hannan

Risk and Hyperconnectivity: Media and Memories of Neoliberalism
Andrew Hoskins and John Tulloch

Democracy's Fourth Wave?: Digital Media and the Arab Spring
Philip N. Howard and Muzammil M. Hussain

The Digital Origins of Dictatorship and Democracy: Information Technology and Political Islam
Philip N. Howard

Analytic Activism: Digital Listening and the New Political Strategy
David Karpf

The MoveOn Effect: The Unexpected Transformation of American Political Advocacy
David Karpf

News Nerds: Institutional Change in Journalism
Allie Kosterich

Prototype Politics: Technology-Intensive Campaigning and the Data of Democracy
Daniel Kreiss

Taking Our Country Back: The Crafting of Networked Politics from Howard Dean to Barack Obama
Daniel Kreiss

Media and Protest Logics in the Digital Era: The Umbrella Movement in Hong Kong
Francis L. F. Lee and
Joseph M. Chan

Bits and Atoms: Information and Communication Technology in Areas of Limited Statehood
Steven Livingston and Gregor
Walter-Drop

Digital Feminist Activism: Girls and Women Fight Back Against Rape Culture
Kaitlynn Mendes, Jessica Ringrose, and Jessalynn Keller

Digital Cities: The Internet and the Geography of Opportunity
Karen Mossberger, Caroline J.
Tolbert, and William W. Franko

The Power of Platforms: Shaping Media and Society
Rasmus Kleis Nielsen and
Sarah Anne Ganter

Revolution Stalled: The Political Limits of the Internet in the Post-Soviet Sphere
Sarah Oates

Disruptive Power: The Crisis of the State in the Digital Age
Taylor Owen

Affective Publics: Sentiment, Technology, and Politics
Zizi Papacharissi

Money Code Space: Hidden Power in Bitcoin, Blockchain, and Decentralisation
Jack Parkin

The Citizen Marketer: Promoting Political Opinion in the Social Media Age
Joel Penney

Tweeting is Leading: How Senators Communicate and Represent in the Age of Twitter
Annelise Russell

The Ubiquitous Presidency: Presidential Communication and Digital Democracy in Tumultuous Times
Joshua M. Scacco and Kevin Coe

China's Digital Nationalism
Florian Schneider

Networked Collective Actions: The Making of an Impeachment
Hyunjin Seo

Credible Threat: Attacks Against Women Online and the Future of Democracy
Sarah Sobieraj

Presidential Campaigning in the Internet Age
Jennifer Stromer-Galley

News on the Internet: Information and Citizenship in the 21st Century
David Tewksbury and Jason Rittenberg

Outside the Bubble: Social Media and Political Participation in Western Democracies
Cristian Vaccari and Augusto Valeriani

The Internet and Political Protest in Autocracies
Nils B. Weidmann and Espen Geelmuyden Rød

The Civic Organization and the Digital Citizen: Communicating Engagement in a Networked Age
Chris Wells

Computational Propaganda: Political Parties, Politicians, and Political Manipulation on Social Media
Samuel Woolley and Philip N. Howard

Networked Publics and Digital Contention: The Politics of Everyday Life in Tunisia
Mohamed Zayani

The Digital Double Bind: Change and Stasis in the Middle East
Mohamed Zayani and Joe F. Khalil

The Politics of Platform Regulation

HOW GOVERNMENTS SHAPE ONLINE CONTENT MODERATION

ROBERT GORWA

Oxford University Press is a department of the University of Oxford.
It furthers the University's objective of excellence in research, scholarship,
and education by publishing worldwide. Oxford is a registered trade mark of
Oxford University Press in the UK and in certain other countries.

Published in the United States of America by Oxford University Press
198 Madison Avenue, New York, NY 10016, United States of America.

© Oxford University Press 2024

Some rights reserved. No part of this publication may be reproduced, stored in a retrieval system, or
transmitted, in any form or by any means, for commercial purposes, without the prior permission
in writing of Oxford University Press, or as expressly permitted by law, by licence or under terms
agreed with the appropriate reprographics rights organization.

This is an open access publication, available online and distributed under the terms of a Creative
Commons Attribution – Non Commercial – No Derivatives 4.0 International licence (CC BY-NC-
ND 4.0), a copy of which is available at http://creativecommons.org/licenses/by-nc-nd/4.0/.

You must not circulate this work in any other form and you must impose this same condition on any acquirer

Library of Congress Cataloging-in-Publication Data

Names: Gorwa, Robert, author.
Title: The politics of platform regulation : how governments shape online content moderation /
Robert Gorwa.
Description: First edition. | New York, NY : Oxford University Press, [2024]
Identifiers: LCCN 2024009078 (print) | LCCN 2024009079 (ebook) |
ISBN 9780197692851 (hardback) | ISBN 9780197692868 (paperback) | ISBN 9780197692882 (epub)
Subjects: LCSH: Online social networks—Law and legislation. |
Online social networks—Political aspects. | Social media—Law and legislation. |
Social media—Government policy.
Classification: LCC K564.C6 G67 2024 (print) | LCC K564.C6 (ebook) |
DDC 343.09/944—dc23/eng/20240316
LC record available at https://lccn.loc.gov/2024009078
LC ebook record available at https://lccn.loc.gov/2024009079

Contents

Acknowledgments ix

1. Introduction 1

Part One FOUNDATIONS

2. Governance by Platforms: Definitions, Histories, Concepts 13

3. Regulating Platform Companies: A Cross-Domain
   Policy Overview 29

4. Explaining Government Intervention in Content Moderation 53

Part Two CASE STUDIES

5. 'What Is Illegal Offline, Should Be Illegal Online':
   The Development of the German NetzDG 77

6. After Christchurch: Diverging Regulatory Responses
   in New Zealand and Australia 95

7. From Coast to Coast: State-Level Platform Regulation
   in the United States 114

viii CONTENTS

Part Three   LOOKING FORWARD

8. Platform Regulation and the Majority World   147

9. Conclusion   165

Appendices
  A. Methods Appendix   171
  B. Regulatory Context Appendix   187
Notes   203
References   211
Index   235

Acknowledgments

My work on this book unfolded in two more-or-less discrete stages, from 2017–2021 and then again in 2022–2023. As commonly noted in these kinds of acknowledgment sections, it truly does take a village—and actually, upon further reflection, at least a medium-sized, if internationally dispersed one. I'm thrilled to have an opportunity to finally thank the huge number of friends, teachers, mentors, colleagues, and family members who have been part of this first major stage of my academic journey.

The project began as a doctoral dissertation, which I researched at the Department of Politics and International Relations at the University of Oxford. A huge debt of gratitude goes out to my patient supervisors, Lucas Kello and Thomas Hale. In Oxford, I also benefited from the time, wisdom, and collaboration of many incredible people, including but certainly not limited to Timothy Garton Ash, Corinne Cath, Jamie Collier, Florian Egloff, Monica Kaminska, Nahema Marchal, Karma Nabulsi, Vicki Nash, Rasmus Kleis Nielsen, Carl Öhman, Anton Peez, Ralph Schroeder, James Shires, Max Smeets, Duncan Snidal, and David Watson. Special thanks to Vicki Nash and Taylor Owen, and for the time and insights offered to this often clueless grad student by extremely generous folks like Elizabeth Dubois, Blayne Haggart, Robin Mansell, Fenwick McKelvey, Abraham Newman, Thomas Poell, Nick Srnicek, Nic Suzor, Damian Tambini, Natasha Tusikov, and Heidi Tworek.

I was very fortunate to receive financial support for my studies from the Social Sciences and Humanities Research Council of Canada, the Mackenzie King Scholarship Fund, and the Canadian Centennial Scholarship Fund. I also am grateful for the additional assistance provided by St. Antony's College and the Department of Politics and International Relations at Oxford, as well to the many research projects that helped keep me fed through RA work. Many thanks are due here to Phil Howard and the Oxford Internet Institute, Taylor Owen and McGill

University/the Centre for International Governance Innovation, Rasmus Kleis Nielsen and the Reuters Institute for the Study of Journalism, and Nate Persily and Robert Reich at Stanford University.

The book you are now reading is a substantially revised and updated version of my initial dissertation, defended in September 2021. The work of expanding, editing, and excising material for this book was conducted at the WZB Berlin Social Science Center, which I was incredibly lucky to join as a postdoc in fall 2021. I'm hugely thankful for my great colleagues there, especially Martin Krzywdzinski, Samantha Gupta, Eileen Jahnke, Jeanette Hofmann, Julia Pohle, Thorsten Theil, Sana Ahmad, Sonata Cepik, Torben Klausa, Dieter Plehwe, Florian Butollo, and the many other GAP/POLDI/Fairwork/DIGI members. Special thanks to Clara Iglesias Keller.

More generally, I would like to raise a glass to Naomi Appelman, Chinmayi Arun, Jef Ausloos, Pranav Bidare, Elettra Bietti, Hannah Bloch-Wehba, Robyn Caplan, Jennifer Cobbe, Brenda Dvoskin, Niels van Doorn, Nicolas Friederici, Bharath Ganesh, Tarleton Gillespie, Doug Guilbeault, Amélie Heldt, Joris van Hoboken, Tomiwa Ilori, Shagun Jhaver, Julian Jaursch, Christian Katzenbach, Matthias Kettemann, Kate Klonick, Daniel Kreiss, Seth Lazar, Paddy Leerssen, João Magalhães, Shannon McGregor, Paloma Viejo Otero, Christopher Persaud, Jonas Pentzien, JC Plantin, Julian Posada, Sarah Roberts, Jat Singh, Philipp Staab, Jill Toh, Michael Veale, Matthias Vermeulen, and Stacy Wood.

I was able to hone the final version of the book through invited presentations at a number of great institutions in Europe and beyond. Thanks in particular to event organizers at FAccT 2022, the Institute for Information Law at the University of Amsterdam, the European Law School at Humboldt University Berlin, the Department of Media and Journalism Studies at the University of Groningen, the Digital Politics Network at Uppsala University, the Centre for Digital Governance at the Hertie School of Governance, and colleagues at the Technical University of Munich and TUM Think Tank. Special thanks to Richard Traunmüller for giving me the 'third C.' Additional thanks to folks at the European Commission's Observatory on the Online Platform Economy, the US-EU Trade and Technology Council, the Centre for Internet and Society Bengaluru, the Mozilla Foundation, Yale-ISP, NYU Law, Science Po Law, and FGV Rio for inviting me to speak at more general happenings that I was able to draw upon for this work.

While researching additional material for publication, I made great use of the Center for Democracy and Technology's fellows network. My thanks to Dhanaraj Thakur and Emma Llanso, as well as to the many busy people who made the time to be interviewed for this project, helped me connect with prospective interviewees, or assisted my work in any other ways. Additional thanks to Janine de Vera for research assistance at the WZB in 2022–2023.

This book could not have happened without the guidance of Series Editor Andy Chadwick and Oxford University Press's Angela Chnapko. A huge thanks to you both for your patience with this first-time author, and for your keen advice and insights as to how to make this a substantially stronger project. The open access publication of this book was facilitated by funds provided by the WZB and the Leibniz Open Access Monograph Publishing Fund. My deep gratitude here again to Martin Krzywdzinski, Samantha Gupta, and Britta Volkholz for helping make this possible.

Finally, and—of course—most importantly, I'm enormously indebted to my family. Dziękuję za wszystko. Bardzo Was kocham. And Zo? Thank you for everything.

1

Introduction

On the 8th of January 2021, the President of the United States had his Twitter account suspended. After years of using Twitter to spew vitriol and misinformation that energized his voting base, cannily influencing media coverage and shifting domestic policy debates, President Donald Trump posted a tweet that Twitter's 'Trust and Safety' staff read as the final straw. Trump's apparent call to violence during rioting at the US Capitol in Washington led Twitter—quickly followed by Facebook, Stripe, AirBnb, Shopify, and a few other technology companies with connections to the Trump campaign—to suspend his widely followed and influential accounts, and to begin cracking down on the social and commercial online activity of his followers (Dellinger, 2021).

For many commentators reflecting on the decision, the episode signaled a pathbreaking moment for the exercise of private power in the twenty-first century (Roose, 2021; Jennen and Nussbaum, 2021). Here was an extraordinary demonstration of the ability of new, powerful multinational information gatekeepers to influence not just public discourse, but also democratic transitions and elections, 'deplatforming' someone who would be—for a few more weeks at least—sitting at the helm of a US-orchestrated and dominated global order.

Whether or not Twitter felt finally empowered to act given that Trump appeared to be on his way out, their decision shows how much, and how rapidly, the theory and practice of *platform governance* has changed in recent years. After all, only a few years earlier, most social networks were still largely portraying themselves as 'neutral' platforms that merely facilitated public discourse via their services, rather than profoundly shaping it. In a 2020 interview, Facebook CEO Mark Zuckerberg had repeatedly rejected the argument that his company should make what amounted to high-stakes political decisions over the acceptable bounds of speech or action online, infamously stating that Facebook should not become a global rulemaker and 'arbiter of truth' (McCarthy, 2020). Staff at Twitter were similarly known for referring to their policies on user-generated content as aligning with the "free speech wing of the free speech party" (Halliday, 2012).

The Politics of Platform Regulation: How Governments Shape Online Content Moderation. Robert Gorwa, Oxford University Press. © Oxford University Press 2024. DOI: 10.1093/oso/9780197692851.003.0001

Despite these claims, a wide range of technology companies with assorted business models had, in fact, for years been developing intricate socio-technical administrative infrastructures for exactly the kind of rulemaking and enforcement that the Trump takedown rendered visible. The largest publicly traded platform firms facilitated access to user-generated content—the videos, images, and text uploaded by ordinary people, creators, and media organizations in multiple countries. To police this content—and pacify advertisers, regulators, and other stakeholders—these companies had established policy teams that created rules on illegal or potentially unsavory content across a dizzying array of issues from hate and harassment to copyright and child safety (Arun, 2018; Gillespie, 2018; S. T. Roberts, 2019). This form of private speech and behavior governance, often termed 'content moderation' or 'trust and safety,' had emerged slowly since the global rise of internet intermediaries in the early to mid-2000s (Wagner, 2013; Klonick, 2017; Caplan, 2018) and, in the 2010s, increasingly become a site of intense government interest (Gorwa, 2019b).

Almost exactly two years after Donald Trump took to Twitter to type his last message as US President, the European Commissioner for the Internal Market, Thierry Breton, published a meme from his verified personal Twitter account.[1] The post alluded to an argument, increasingly popular among policymakers in Europe, that the platform economy had become an under-regulated 'Wild West' that desperately needed government intervention. Sharing a video with footage from the Italian director Sergio Leone's legendary trilogy of Westerns starring Clint Eastwood, Breton wrote that "A new sheriff is in town—and it goes by the name DSA"—in reference to the sweeping new Digital Services Act (DSA) regulation that had been developed in 2020–2021 by the European Commission. The goal: to create a wide-ranging set of standards for how technology companies operating user-generated content platforms in Europe would need to report upon, audit, and design their content moderation frameworks.

The DSA might be seen as akin to a General Data Protection Regulation (GDPR) for the space of online content regulation. It is a complex piece of legislation with global political-economic repercussions, and its implementation and enforcement—and the ensuing knock-on effects—similarly promise to have major ramifications on how hundreds of millions of people, if not billions, engage with the tools and spaces they use daily to communicate, learn, work, and play. While the DSA is probably the most sophisticated regulatory framework to emerge in this policy area to date, it is not the first state-led intervention seeking to reframe how industry governs the politically or socially harmful content on their services.

In May 2017, the German Bundestag passed the 'Network Enforcement Act' (NetzDG), which included reporting requirements, transparency provisions around platform decisionmaking, and other rules that firms would need to follow when handling complaints about potentially illegal content in the country. Since then, related policy initiatives have been proposed by lawmakers on every continent, including in countries like Australia, Austria, Brazil, Canada, France, India, Malaysia, Nigeria, Singapore, the United Kingdom, the United States, and others. If platform governance was once largely the purview of business, something that consisted of 'secret rules' and invisibilized, behind-the-scenes policymaking (Gillespie, 2018; Suzor, 2019), recent years have demonstrated a multitude of government efforts not only to thrust this corporate activity into the light, but also, crucially, 'take back control' over facets of these increasingly important structures of public-private global rulemaking. How, why, and where exactly is this happening? Why now? And how do we best understand the vast array of strategies being deployed across jurisdictions to tackle this issue?

1.1 The Politics of Platform Regulation

This is a book exploring how governments around the world are seeking to regulate the policies and practices of harmful content governance being developed by the technology companies that operate popular platform services. In other words, and depending on one's disciplinary jargon of choice, it is a book about how governments are increasingly intervening in the transnational realm of 'content moderation,' 'trust and safety,' or 'platform governance.' I call this process—of government actors seeking to shape the design, architecture, policies, and practices developed by platform companies around the capabilities, uses, and affordances of their services—*platform regulation*.[2]

In particular, this book is about the *politics* of platform regulation: the policy drivers, political dynamics, and institutional characteristics that shape the development of platform regulation in different jurisdictions. My interest is primarily in advancing our understanding of *how*, *why*, and *where* platform regulation emerges. In the following chapters, I seek to do so both theoretically and empirically.

1.1.1 CORE ARGUMENT

I begin by presenting a conceptual toolkit for thinking through government-led regulatory change in the platform realm. Although this space and other interlinked policy areas are often presented as a discrete policy field with unique dynamics (for instance, due to high degrees of technical complexity and the apparently 'disruptive' pace of technological development), I argue that platform regulation has become merely another (albeit increasingly important) space of transnational political contestation in the global context. The successful development and adoption of platform regulation in certain jurisdictions is, in my view, primarily shaped by the relatively banal realities of ordinary domestic politics in various political systems, as well as their occasional interlinkages with international and transnational political forces. In particular, the book highlights the importance of theorizing a host of policy dimensions that have been largely underdeveloped in the emerging interdisciplinary literature on digital platforms, including elections (and their timing), the role of motivated local or transnational policy entrepreneurs, the procedural quirks embedded in different legislative structures, and the legal constraints of international trade agreements or regional 'single market' harmonization projects.

In contrast to much work in this burgeoning field of study, my approach is not informed primarily by a legal tradition, or by media studies, communications, and related fields of scholarship that have long been interested in understanding the social, cultural, and political impact of major firms in the internet economy. Instead, my theoretical framework draws mainly upon political science work, in particular from the subfields of transnational regulatory politics, global governance, and public policy studies. Drawing on this literature, I develop a tripartite typology of platform regulation strategies: *contesting, collaborating,* and *convincing.* I conceive of these as a menu of ideal-type strategies that government actors consider during a policy episode in an attempt to meet their goals, ranging from institutionally complex and costly efforts to layer new rules on top of existing industry practices (and 'contest' the status quo) to softer, informal strategies where governments exert pressure on industry to change their policies through personal relationships, established channels of complaint, or other related tactics ('convincing' other actors within the regulatory status quo).

The book then offers an original theoretical model for helping explain variation between these strategies across different policy episodes and contexts. This 'demand-and-supply' framework for technology policy development suggests that the decision of a government to intervene and regulate a platform company in a certain way, the strategy that it will choose to do so, and the likelihood of its success are all influenced by two overarching factors, which I call *political will* and *the power to intervene.* Through these categories, I bring in a series of insights from the global regulation literature on the preferences and motivations of political actors to demand policy change, and the institutional features and linkages that condition their ability to meet that demand. Concretely, the book suggests that a number of political factors—salience shocks due to crisis events, effective forms of policy entrepreneurship, the extent of executive power, the character of institutional veto points—appear to be especially important for understanding the development of platform regulation and explaining its adoption in certain jurisdictions and not others.

1.1.2 EMPIRICAL APPROACH

The bulk of this book is given to applying this conceptual framework through in-depth description and analysis of the actual development of platform regulation. I examine key international 'policy episodes' that occurred between 2015 and 2023, with a focus on debates relating to how user-generated content platforms dealt with online hate speech, violent extremist content, and disinformation.

I focus on three case studies: the development of the NetzDG in Germany from 2015 to 2018, New Zealand and Australia's diverging responses to the Christchurch shooting in 2019–2020, and the efforts of Texas and Florida to regulate platform moderation immediately following the 2021 US Capitol insurrection. I also engage with ongoing developments in China, India, Brazil, and beyond, discussing a varied set of policy episodes that range from the first international occurrence of harmful-content-oriented platform regulation to the eventual reverberation of these types of policies 'back home' for platforms in the United States.

These deeply researched case study chapters draw primarily upon two new bodies of data. First, I conducted more than 75 interviews from 2019 to 2023 with stakeholders in industry, government, and civil society working concretely in the platform policy debates in question. Second, I used freedom of information access (FOIA) requests to create a new archive of internal, deliberative policy documents touching on the development of platform regulation in my case study jurisdictions.

At the core of this empirical approach is an effort to examine the politics of government-led technology policy development at a micro-scale. Qualitative interviews with key players (e.g., parliamentarians, firm employees, civil society) allow one to get a deeper understanding of not only the way that platform regulation emerges, but also the important juncture points and 'roads not taken' that underpin the regulatory episodes that are assessed in depth in this book. Internal government documents obtained through FOIA requests made by myself, as well as other journalists and activists, allow one to get further insights into the procedure and politics lurking 'behind the scenes' of new regulatory proposals. These methods help me explore questions like: who exactly drove the effort to develop a new regulatory initiative, what kind of political and institutional constraints did they need to navigate, and what did the fight to implement the

6   INTRODUCTION

initiative (if there was any) look like? More information about the case selection, the interview process, and my FOIA strategy, including the way I formulated, analyzed, and publicly archived these primary documents is available in Methods Appendix A.

1.1.3 WHAT THE BOOK IS NOT

Due to its core questions of interest, and its combination of a regulatory politics-oriented conceptual framework with empirical research, this book is quite unlike any platform studies scholarship that has preceded it. Nevertheless, I have bene-fited enormously from the wide range of interdisciplinary work that continues to be produced on issues closely interlinked with the subject matter I discuss in the ensuing pages. Before we move forward, I wish to offer a few disclaimers about the scope, limitations, and ambitions of this project.

First, this is not a book about the ways that platforms govern, shape, or regulate the behavior of their users around the world. My central focus is not directly on the processes of design, rulemaking, and enforcement being itera-tively developed everyday by platform firms of all sizes, nor on all of the interest-ing socio-political and commercial dynamics that might shape those processes. It is not, for example, about the relations between advertisers and other business stakeholders and platform firms, the movement of trust and safety personnel across different firms and in between industry and government positions, or the role that civil society engagement and campaigning is having on the entire ecosystem. I am minutely focused here on *government-led* efforts to intervene in these systems. For work that more deeply examines governance practices in and around the platform firm, I would recommend the excellent and ongoing writing produced by a range of scholars that include Robyn Caplan, Stefanie Duguay, Brenda Dvoskin, Tarleton Gillespie, Kate Klonick, Shannon McGregor, Courtney Radsch, Sarah T. Roberts, Sarah Myers West, and others.

Second, this book does not seek to provide a detailed legal analysis of the cen-tral developments of platform regulation in the global context. I am grateful for the many technology law and policy academics that have spent countless hours reading the text of crucial legislative proposals in this domain and interpreting not only how they work, but also where they may fall short. For those interested in the specific provisions and implications of many of the policies discussed in this book, I can recommend the work of academics like Chinmayi Arun, Christoph Busch, Evelyn Douek, Eric Goldman, Joris van Hoboken, Tomiwa Ilori, David Kaye, Clara Iglesias Keller, Daphne Keller, Matthias Kettemann, Jeff Kosseff, Aleksandra Kuczerawy, Paddy Leerssen, and the many others cited throughout the case study chapters.

Third, this book is not a normative analysis of platform regulation, or a how-to guide as to how make it better. Whether that be conceived more narrowly in terms of its actual impact on reforming platform business models and practices and achieving positive reform for users, or more transformatively, in terms that conceptualize the aspirational effects that platform regulation should have on human rights, justice, and democracy, my approach here has been intentionally limited to an analysis of the development (rather than implementation and enforcement) of new policy frameworks. There is a wealth of research and activism that is engaging in these debates, seeking to ensure that platform regulation not only respects human rights, but ideally also could be harnessed for broader aims of social justice. A limited list of this work might include writing from folks like Naomi Appelman, Caroline Are, Ruha Benjamin, T.J. Billard, Hannah Bloch-Webha, Jennifer Cobbe, Marwa Fatafta, Rachel Griffin, Jameel Jaffer, Rebecca Mackinnon, Spencer Overton, Javier Pallero, Felix Reda, Barrie Sander, Nic Suzor, Katrin Tiidenberg, Michael Veale, and Jillian York.

1.2 Outline of the Book

With all that in mind, I hope that the book will still have much to offer for the broader interdisciplinary audience interested in platform regulation and online content regulation more specifically, and in technology policy and the governance of complex, privately developed socio-technical rulemaking systems more generally. The book is structured in three parts.

1.2.1 FOUNDATIONS

Part I features two review chapters that lay out an overview of platform governance and platform regulation both as academic fields of study and as active spaces of policy engagement.

Chapter 2, 'Governance by Platforms: Definitions, Histories, Concepts,' seeks to provide a comprehensive survey of the relevant literature that this book contributes to, discussing emerging work on governance in digital media, political communication, and 'internet studies' circles, as well as the larger body of relevant scholarship in global governance that deals with corporate actors. I hope that it can serve as a reference chapter for those looking for a cohesive conceptual literature review on platform governance.

Chapter 3, 'Regulating Platform Companies: A Cross-Domain Policy Overview,' seeks to tackle the same questions but from a policy standpoint, outlining key trends in platform regulation broadly conceived. It briefly pushes beyond the realm of user-generated content to also address issues relating to data protection, competition law, and labor regulation. The chapter reviews the range of emerging ways that the rule-making activities of platform firms with different business models are increasingly being subject to government rulemaking, oversight, and intervention.

Part I concludes with the main theoretical framework for the book, Chapter 4: 'Explaining Government Intervention in Content Moderation.' The chapter outlines the aforementioned three-part typology of platform regulation (convince, collaborate, and contest), and presents the book's 'demand-and-supply' model for explaining variation across these three regulatory strategies.

1.2.2 CASE STUDIES

Chapters 4–7 provide the core of the book's empirical material, applying my conceptual model via a process-driven analysis of the development of platform regulation in four jurisdictions.

Chapter 5 focuses on the fight to impose standards for how platform companies conducted their online content moderation in Germany from 2015 to 2018. The chapter discusses the origins of the German NetzDG in an ostensibly failed effort to establish a co-regulatory, collaborative framework that would voluntarily affect how platforms received, handled, and acted upon user complaints around hate speech and other forms of illegal content in Germany. It outlines how German policy entrepreneurs, motivated by electoral and other factors, built upon this effort to develop new domestic rules for platform firms active in the country—despite not only significant opposition from industry and global civil society, but also the institutional constraints of a European Union set up to prevent exactly this sort of regulatory fragmentation.

Chapter 6 discusses the diverging regulatory responses of Australia and New Zealand in the aftermath of the March 2019 Christchurch attack. These cases provide an example of two neighboring countries with close social, economic, and political ties, seeking to respond to the same event—and achieve the same stated policy goal of regulating terrorist content on major social media platforms—with two very different strategies. This in effect offers a policy experiment that helps shine light on the politics of pursuing a contested or collaborative platform regulation strategy.

In Chapter 7, I turn to the United States—a crucial jurisdiction as the home of many of the largest globally active platform companies. The chapter explores how state-level policy entrepreneurs, bolstered by a rising and revisionist coalition of conservative anti-tech interest groups, were motivated by Trump's deplatforming to try and shift the platform regulation status quo in the United States. I examine how these actors used state-level legislation as a way to bypass federal-level gridlock, and worked against significant institutional constraints and industry resistance to enshrine—if only temporarily—a contested platform regulation strategy into Texas and Florida law.

1.2.3 LOOKING FORWARD

In Part III, I look beyond these in-depth case studies to demonstrate the applicability of the conceptual framework developed in the first section of the book.

Chapter 8 looks beyond Europe, North America, and Oceania to provide a snapshot of the platform regulation landscape in three crucial countries for the future of global platform politics: China, India, and Brazil. Drawing on the work of researchers and civil society in these regions, I show how the 'demand-and-supply' model I have developed—and the general politically-oriented toolbox I offer throughout this book—can be used to glean interesting insights into the emergence and adoption of various platform regulation initiatives in a range of political contexts.

The concluding chapter summarizes the findings of the book overall, outlining some potentially promising paths for future work, reflecting upon the book's methods and research design, and offering a short final note on a few important policy developments on the horizon.

Part One

FOUNDATIONS

2

Governance by Platforms

Definitions, Histories, Concepts

How and why do platform companies govern their services? When Mark Zuckerberg sat in his Harvard dorm room and first began developing a creepy 'hot-or-not' app to allow students to rate each other for attractiveness, he probably didn't think that he was sowing the seeds of an empire—one that would eventually require him to create a sprawling private bureaucracy that would shape what billions of people around the world could say and do online (Gillespie, 2018). Similarly, when Pierre Omidyar set out to create a simple auction service that would allow World Wide Web users to bid on their old knicknacks, he didn't initially think that he would need sophisticated systems of reputation management for buyers and sellers, or that his company, eBay, would need to develop detailed rules about prohibited goods and behavior (Lehdonvirta, 2022).

The systems that technology companies have developed to govern their services developed over time, in an ad hoc manner (Klonick, 2017). These systems—which involve design decisions, interfaces and architectures, rules and policies, and rule-enforcement procedures that shape how interactions on a platform are organized, structured, and regulated—are the outcome of a heady cocktail of commercial and political motivations. Business sense instilled firms with a desire to prevent fraud, to assuage advertisers, avoid lawsuits, and to build a specific brand distinguishing them from competition (Gillespie, 2018; Suzor, 2018). Political pressure from policymakers, civil society, and concerned publics motivated firms to act in ways that would minimize the illegal, unsafe, or otherwise potentially harmful impacts and uses of their products (Gorwa, 2019b; York, 2021).

What are the key moments in this story of 'platforms as governors' of online and offline life? And before we get there—what precisely are platforms, any-way? These are large, book-length questions which cannot be comprehensively answered in a single chapter, especially given that the main focus of this study

The Politics of Platform Regulation: How Governments Shape Online Content Moderation. Robert Gorwa,
Oxford University Press. © Oxford University Press 2024. DOI: 10.1093/oso/9780197692851.003.0002

is not on the internal development of systems of content moderation and other governance mechanisms by tech companies, an important topic well covered in existing work (Gillespie, 2015; Caplan, 2018; S. T. Roberts, 2019). Nevertheless, this chapter will look to set the stage for the rest of the book's analysis by exploring some of these historical and definitional questions.

I begin with an overview of the digital 'platform' as a concept, tracing how the term has risen to prominence since the 1990s, expanding to involve a combination of technical, economic, and political assumptions. This first section then offers a working definition of two key terms—*platform* and *platform company*—that will be used in the rest of the book. The following section provides an overview of the various interdisciplinary literatures that outline how platform firms engage in governance. In particular, it discusses how platform firms with different business models can all be said govern generally along three broad lines—through their design, rulemaking, and gatekeeping. The chapter concludes by identifying some key emerging institutional and organizational trends in how platform firms, facing growing public and policy pressure internationally, have begun governing their services more exhaustively.

2.1 What Is a Platform?

If we look historically, the earliest usage of the term platform in its technologically associated current sense likely began in the 1990s in California, as software developers began to conceptualize their offerings as more than just narrow programs, but rather as flexible 'platforms' that enabled code to be developed and deployed. A 1995 pamphlet published by Sun Microsystems described operating systems like Linux, Mac OS, or Microsoft Windows as platforms (Bogost and Montfort, 2009). The broad use of the term did not take off, however, until the early 2000s, when a new crop of technology entrepreneurs found the old notion of a flexible computational 'platform' particularly compelling in the so-called 'Web 2.0' era of user-generated content. Mark Andreessen, a technology entrepreneur who created the Mosaic and Netscape web browsers, outlined platforms as follows:

> Definitionally, a "platform" is a system that can be reprogrammed and therefore customized by outside developers—users—and in that way, adapted to countless needs and niches that the platform's original developers could not have possibly contemplated, much less had time to accommodate.
>
> (Andreessen 2007, quoted in Bogost and Montfort, 2009, p. 4)

That first notion of platform as a data-driven infrastructure remains key today (Plantin et al., 2018). Nevertheless, as more and more of these generative online services were founded in the early 2000s, economists honed in on the ways that various platforms profited by bringing multiple parties together. Platforms were defined here as technologies or services that mediated interactions and relations between two or more parties, with their core feature being their effective identity as *multi-sided markets* that created network effects (Rochet and Tirole, 2003). For instance, early work on the digital economy noted that the providers of 'credit card platforms' had to get both businesses and users to buy in, whether by purchasing or leasing the credit card terminals for their stores or choosing to use the specific type of credit card when making purchases (Evans, 2003). In another example, the makers of operating systems for personal computers had to balance the needs of third-party developers that would make applications that worked on those operating systems with those of the consumers that would eventually purchase them. Business could usually make most of its profits on only one side of the market: in the credit card case, this meant subsidizing consumers while hitting retailers with transaction and hardware fees; in the case of operating systems, companies issued incentives to developers while making money off of consumer sales. And crucially, as the number of end-users on platform grew, the more attractive it became to everyone—not just the end-users, but also to the 'complementor' actors involved (Gawer, 2014).

Alongside this economic notion of the platform came a third, political conception. As technology companies began branding themselves as technical and commercial 'platforms' that facilitated access to certain services, the term also became central to the idea that as intermediaries or middle-men, platforms embodied a distinct form of laissez-faire public responsibility. The media scholar Tarleton Gillespie has written extensively on this genealogy, noting that YouTube press materials began in 2006 to refer to the service as a "platform for people to share their videos around the world" (Gillespie, 2010, p. 352). Facebook CEO Mark Zuckerberg actually initially referred to his product as a 'utility'—reflecting his goal to provide an understated service that was a generally useful and essential part of people's everyday lives—before being told to re-brand as a 'platform' and 'community' by company lawyers, who warned that utilities were tightly regulated in many countries and that Zuckerberg's language bore regulatory risks for the company in the long term (A. Fisher, 2018; Hoffmann, Proferes, and Zimmer, 2018). The contemporary usage of the word platform, therefore, cannot be separated from the legal landscape that major American technology companies had to navigate. In a shift from the early technical dimensions of the term (platforms strictly understood as programmable computational infrastructures), from the 2000s onwards the term gradually became broader, more strategic, and more political. As Gillespie writes, "Platforms [became] 'platforms' not necessarily because they allow code to be written or run, but because they afford[ed] an opportunity to communicate, interact or sell" (Gillespie, 2010, p. 351).

2.1.1 IN DEFENSE OF PLATFORMS: DEFINITIONS

Overall, 'platform' is an imperfect and ambiguous term, one that rolls of the tongue of some while confusing others. Part of the issue is that the word is often used differently in various academic communities (Andersson Schwarz, 2017), and it doesn't help that it has become a buzzword often deployed carelessly both in the tech community and in policy circles. While ongoing conceptual debates among academics about the boundaries of the term have yet to be resolved, some, like the writer and journalist Ben Tarnoff, have voiced their mounting frustration with the wide variety of services and businesses—some of which seem to have almost nothing to do with one another other than some nominal digital component—all being grouped under the 'platform' umbrella. "The word isn't just imprecise; it's an illusion," writes Tarnoff, a term "designed to mystify rather than clarify" (Tarnoff, 2022, p. 75). In his view, public and scholarly discourse would be improved if the term were abolished. Despite these sorts of critiques, I believe that the word shouldn't be discarded wholesale just yet. If used carefully, it can shed light on a few important dimensions of today's digital policy landscape that other competing terms do not adequately capture.

In this book, I think it is enough to generally understand a platform as a *digitally enabled product that mediates relationships between two or more parties, usually featuring technical elements that allow third parties to build upon it or interact with it.* This definition has three notable aspects: (1) it acknowledges technical features while noting that contemporary platforms are at their core *products* designed to generate profit for the companies that operate them; (2) it acknowledges that platforms are not simply neutral, and that "a platform is a mediator rather than an intermediary" (Van Dijck, 2013, p. 29); and (3) it acknowledges that platforms are multi-sided markets that structure relationships between a number of different actors. No other competing definition (from the 'online mall' that Tarnoff favors, to the range of other generic terms like 'information service' or 'intermediary' that are often also used) captures all three of these elements, while also potentially being flexible enough to account for the wide range of digitally-oriented business models that we see in the global economy of today.

2.1.2 PLATFORM COMPANIES ARE COMPANIES

Today, digital platforms seem to be everywhere. A report prepared for the European Commission in 2017 suggested that there were more than two hundred relevant platform companies operating in Europe (Fabo et al., 2017). By 2020, an explanatory memorandum published by the Commission in a proposal for new platform-related regulation was arguing that there were more than ten thousand (European Commission, 2020). Where did all of these services come from?

Clearly, digital platforms don't simply emerge into the void, fully formed. Platform services are created by *platform companies*: the technology companies that own and operate platforms. This is a straightforward but powerful insight. Multinational platform companies like Alphabet own and operate many different platforms (e.g., Google Search, YouTube, Google Cloud Services). These different platforms have not only varying business models, but different political characteristics and features. Some, like what certain media scholars and media economists have termed 'user-generated content platforms' (often also called 'social networks,' with examples including YouTube, Instagram, and Twitter/X) orchestrate complex online environments, building out not just intricate public-facing interfaces for content ranking, recommendation, and delivery, but also increasingly sophisticated bureaucratic underbellies designed to police the 'digital public spheres' that they create and manage. Other platforms, for example cloud platforms like Amazon Web Services or Microsoft Azure, are more traditionally conceived services, providing business-oriented software access and computing power on demand, with fewer visible forms of platform mediation.

It is common to refer to all of these different platform companies simply as 'Big Tech.' But there are many examples of smaller, yet still potentially impactful platform businesses across various sectors and industries. Companies like Netflix and Spotify have begun to exert a global influence on cultural production (Nieborg and Poell, 2018). Firms like AirBnb, Uber, Lyft, and its local antecedents (Didi, Bolt, Ola, Grab), as well as service-provision services that are more clearly grounded within local economies (such as Gorillas, Delivery Hero, Uber Eats, Swiggy) are smaller in terms of revenue, usership, and market capitalization than the global tech giants, and yet can still become important political actors with an effect on public life (Seidl, 2020; van Doorn, 2020a). They may displace traditional businesses, actively lobby policymakers and shift political incentives on the ground—all the while designing their apps and implementing policies that have a significant impact on the lives of their workers (Collier, Dubal, and C. L. Carter, 2018; Culpepper and Thelen, 2019).

Additionally, there are the Chinese giants, companies like Alibaba and Tencent, which more clearly fit the 'Big Tech' archetype and operate marketplace, messaging, cloud, and user-generated content platforms, but are still often not part of a discourse focused squarely on Google, Apple, Facebook, Amazon, and Microsoft ('GAFAM') in the United States and Europe (Lei, 2021; Zhang and Chen, 2022). These companies create highly popular services that often serve as 'super apps' (Steinberg, 2020) integrating a range of functions (financial services, social networking, communication, transport, entertainment), and exhibit a distinct form of content governance due to their close collaboration with Chinese government actors.

Not all platforms are run by companies. Other business models exist, including alternative, community organized, not-for-profit, or decentralized platform services, which have proliferated in the past years (Scholtz and Schneider, 2016). These services, from the legendary and long-running Wikipedia to newer federated social networks like Mastodon or PixelFed, provide a vital challenge to the status quo, and show that technical infrastructures can be effectively deployed by non-profits, co-ops, or otherwise self-governing entities (Muldoon, 2022). As of right now, however, these initiatives—many of which seek to embody the lost ideals of the early web—remain relatively niche, generally unable to overcome the network effects and venture capital-lined pockets of leading platform firms. In practice, when we talk about platform rulemaking and governance in the global context, we are usually talking about what the biggest multinational enterprises do (See Tables 2.1 and 2.2).

Table 2.1 **Breakdown of broad platform categories, and the platform types within these categories.**

Platform Category	*Platform Types*
Marketplaces	E-Commerce, App Stores, Online Labor Markets
Communication	Peer-to-Peer Messaging, Feed-Based Social Networks, Bulletin Boards
Entertainment	Copyrighted Content Streaming, User-Generated Content Streaming
Information Retrieval	Search, Wiki
Business-to-Consumer Software Services	Consumer Cloud, Payment
Business-to-Business Software Services	Internet Infrastructure, Enterprise Cloud, Enterprise Payment
'Locally Tethered' Services	Accommodation, On-Demand Transport, Food Delivery

Table 2.2 **More exhaustive list of platform types, with examples.**

Platform Type	Examples	Core Business Model
E-Commerce	Amazon, Alibaba	Transaction Fees
App Store	Google Play, Steam	Transaction Fees
Online Labor	Upwork, MTurk, Fiverr	Transaction Fees
Peer-to-Peer Messaging	WhatsApp, WeChat, Telegram, Signal	Varies
Feed-Based Social Network	Facebook, TikTok, Instagram, Twitter	Advertising
Bulletin Boards	Reddit, 4Chan	Advertising
Copyrighted Content Streaming	Netflix, Prime Video, Spotify, OnlyFans	Subscription
User-Generated Content Streaming	YouTube, Twitch	Advertising
Search	Google, DuckDuckGo	Advertising
Consumer Cloud	Dropbox, GDrive	Subscription
Payment	PayPal, Klarna	Transaction Fees
Internet Infrastructure	Cloudflare, Dyn	Subscription
Enterprise Cloud	Amazon Web Services, Microsoft Azure	Subscription
Enterprise Payment	Stripe, Visa	Transaction Fees
Accomodation	AirBnb, Booking.com	Transaction Fees
On-Demand Transport	Uber, Bolt, Ola, Lyft	Transaction Fees
Food Delivery	Uber Eats, DoorDash, Swiggy	Transaction Fees

2.2 How Do Platforms Companies Govern?

Thinking of platform companies as *companies* provides a starting point from which to conceptualize their political effect and impact. Helpfully, there is a long lineage of political science and international relations scholarship grappling with the governance problems posed by powerful private actors, which was catalyzed by a wave of concern about the influence of corporations in global affairs in the 1970s (Vernon, 1977; Strange, 1991). However, outside of a few narrow exceptions, there has been little work extending this tradition to understand the governance impact and power of today's tech giants (Srivastava, 2023). Nevertheless, there is a growing body of work in the interdisciplinary spaces of 'internet studies' and 'platform studies'—largely a combination of media studies, communication, digital sociology, law and technology, cultural studies, and organization scholars—that has looked at the tech sector more closely, and can teach us about the different ways in which platform firms govern. A first group of researchers has focused on the way that social networks, search engines, and content hosting-services govern at a social, political, and cultural level through their design decisions and rulemaking. Another has looked more broadly at the governance being conducted by other types of platform companies, including online marketplaces, ride-sharing and local service delivery platforms, among others.

2.2.1 COMMUNITY VS. COMMERCIAL: THE EVOLUTION OF CONTENT MODERATION

Online communities began to slowly emerge and thrive even before the widespread adoption of the World Wide Web in the 1990s. From bulletin boards operated by companies like CompuServe to distributed discussion forums like Usenet, early virtual spaces where people could upload and share their own content (predominantly text) revealed the important political and gatekeeping role played by those who set the rules in the space. What kinds of topics were on board—politically, ethically, culturally—for users to dial in and discuss? What exactly were the boundaries of legitimate behavior in these spaces, and what would be considered spam, hate, or harassment (Brunton, 2013)?

These questions became key for researchers interested in how online communities created sets of rules, fostered norms of common understanding and acceptable behavior, and how they embodied varying types of democratic culture and political organization through their governance (Kraut and Resnick, 2012; Fiesler and Proferes, 2018). Early platforms were, in many cases, significantly influenced by volunteer members of that community. These trust and safety systems varied, from the smaller boards that were led by a single founder who would write the policies for participation, to larger forums that had multiple volunteer sysadmins or *moderators*. Early forms of platform governance could be sophisticated. The tech law scholar James Grimmelmann noted that governance in an online space should be understood on a spectrum, ranging from the 'soft' architectures that structured interaction with that space (such as menus and interfaces, pseudonyms, and rating or ranking mechanisms) to the 'hard' interventions (like content or user removal) developed by community managers to curb harassment and set positive norms around beneficial participation (Grimmelmann, 2015).

These moderators, and the systems they built, were essential to the communities' success. Well-functioning moderation infrastructures, according to

Grimmelmann and others, helped make Wikipedia and other sites of 'peer production' actually productive, leading to constructive debate, communication, and collaboration, rather than chaos, trolling, and chicanery (Grimmelmann, 2015). And moderation did not just exist on early social networking sites: as economic sociologists studying the evolution of popular online marketplaces have noted, these soft and hard governance systems (reputation management, reviews, product safety and fraud investigation teams) were key to the commercial success of platforms like eBay when contrasted with the more anarchic and unpredictable marketplaces (e.g., on Usenet) that preceded them (Lehdonvirta, 2022).

In other words, a range of scholarship has argued that platform governance has been a crucial component of the growth and viability of the digital economy in the past two decades. That said, this governance is not always homogeneous, and there are various ways in which it can be implemented. In particular, the policy and design decisions that make up these governance systems can either be made bottom-up by the community itself, or top-down, by the service owners and operators (Schoenebeck, Haimson, and Nakamura, 2020). In the 1990s and early 2000s, the status quo for early social networks was volunteer moderation (Chandrasekharan et al., 2018). But as they became more commercialized and grew in size to have millions of users, problems of scale, practicality, and reliability combined with a profit motive to lead today's major platforms away from an early reliance on volunteer moderators. While some large sites, like Reddit (approximately 430 million users as of 2023), have retained the predominantly community-organized moderation model—clustering into forums called 'subreddits' which have their own specific rules and volunteer moderators who evaluate user reports (Squirrell, 2019)—the big user-generated content platforms of today are run by sprawling multinational enterprises that have largely adopted top-down governance models.

In this type of platform governance, the rules of the road—the crucial systems that "facilitate cooperation and prevent abuse" (Grimmelmann, 2015, p. 47)—are created in house, traditionally by legal teams composed of US-trained lawyers.[1] These rules consist of detailed explications of what exactly should be considered a violation of a platform's policies, with frequent carve-outs and exceptions that are like scars illustrating the outlines of previous controversy. Facebook, for instance, has a comprehensive sexual content policy that involves a ban on female nipples, except in the context of breastfeeding or political protest (exemptions that are the result of many years of campaigning by motivated Facebook users as well as feminist advocacy groups; see West, 2017), various strict definitions of how and what genitals may be depicted in art or in imagery, and even rules around pantomime, prohibiting, for instance, "Implied stimulation of genitalia or anus, defined as stimulating genitalia or anus or inserting objects, including sex toys, into or above genitalia or anus, when the genitalia and/or the activity or contact is not directly visible."[2]

If someone makes a complaint (a report, commonly termed a 'flag') about a photo they see in their Facebook or Instagram feeds, this then generally goes to a human moderator, who like the sysadmin of yesteryear, looks at the post and makes a judgment about whether it violates the rules of the road (Crawford and Gillespie, 2016; Seering, Kaufman, and Chancellor, 2020). In a marked contrast to the salad days of the early internet, however, more often than not, this moderator is not even directly employed by the company in question. Instead, a user flag triggers a global supply chain of outsourced contract labor (Ahmad and Krzywdzinski, 2022), with the content eventually being screened by a sort of call-center employee for the internet age, often located in a country where labor is comparatively less expensive.

To distinguish the dynamics of this type of moderation from its 'community' predecessor, digital media scholar Sarah Roberts coined the term 'commercial content moderation,' emphasizing its industrial, outsourced, and profit-driven nature (S. T. Roberts, 2018). Vital research and journalistic investigation has highlighted the often poor working conditions facing these moderators, who are generally given only a few dozen seconds per image to make difficult decisions, often paid a pittance, and provided with inadequate support for what can be really psychologically taxing work, especially when it comes to looking at some of humanity's most grotesque and disturbing images and videos (S. T. Roberts, 2019). Labor exploitation is commercial content moderation's original sin: a real travesty, given the profit margins made by leading firms, and the centrality of this 'trust and safety' work to the viability of platform's user-generated content business model (Gillespie, 2018).

Intertwined with this globally networked human labor lies an opaque, yet increasingly important, socio-technical assemblage of automated systems for content detection, classification, and enforcement. Every single piece of content, be it text, image, video, or audio uploaded by ordinary users to a major user-generated content platform—such as your Instagram or your teenager's TikTok—is 'fingerprinted,' scanned, and compared by firms against massive databases of hash-fingerprints of illegal content. These predominantly have been used to combat the spread of copyrighted content, as well as more evidently problematic material like child sexual exploitation images and terrorist videos (Gorwa, Binns, and Katzenbach, 2020). They have become crucial for governance at the scale of the modern platform economy, where millions of uploads and shares are made every day. Firms are also continuously iterating on other types of automated content classification systems, including those that try and proactively detect violations of their standards before they are reported (Shenkman, Thakur, and Llansó, 2021). While the scope and scale of these efforts vary, virtually all platform companies—from those that operate cloud storage platforms like Dropbox or peer-to-peer communication applications like Zoom or Telegram, to those operating vast marketplaces like Amazon or those facilitating transportation or service delivery services at a more local level—have had to establish 'community operations,' 'trust and safety,' or 'compliance' teams ensuring that the behavior of those on their platforms is kept within legal and commercially advantageous grounds.

Today, this is effectively how all of the major user-generated platforms active around the world develop their policies and moderate content. Whether they be an established global player like Instagram or YouTube, a rising challenger like TikTok, or an ostensibly niche service like Pinterest, all companies that reach a significant threshold of usership need to develop systems for *setting rules* around what users can upload/share/comment/interact with, *detecting* content that might be breaking those rules, and 'actioning' content and *enforcing* potential violations by removing it, downranking it, or taking other actions.

These processes are far reaching and often not fully visible. As the legal scholar Evelyn Douek has quipped, "everything" is increasingly falling under the purview of this platform governance status quo (Douek and Weaver, 2023, n.p.). App stores, encrypted messaging apps, internet infrastructure providers: all of these services are making governance decisions, setting rules and policies that can have a global impact (See Table 2.3). Platform companies may insist that they don't want to become 'arbiters of truth' building and maintaining political, socio-technical, and bureaucratic governance infrastructures. But in reality, they already have.

2.2.2 STRUCTURAL GOVERNANCE BY PLATFORMS: GATEKEEPING, DEPENDENCY, AND NETWORK EFFECTS

Naturally, technology companies that run either consumer or business-facing content-oriented platforms are not the only ones that matter from a political perspective. Depending on the various types of platform services they provide, different technology companies will exhibit different flavors of governance

Table 2.3 **Today's commercial platform governance status quo (especially applicable to marketplace and social media platform types).**

Governance Role	Task	Actor Group
Standard Setting	Community Standard Development	Industry
Detection	Flagging, Automated Detection	Industry / Public
Enforcement	Human Moderation, Expert Systems	Industry

depending on their business models, business strategies, and other contingent and sector-specific factors. Intuitively, the way that Amazon governs third-party retailers need not necessarily have the same dynamics as Apple's interactions with the vast transnational supply chain it has established to manufacture its products. Similarly, service platforms like Uber or Deliveroo interact with the workers, businesses, and individuals using their systems in ways that may have certain similarities to other platform types (ranking mechanisms, reputation management), but otherwise also have unique characteristics (Cutolo and Kenney, 2021).

That said, all large consumer-facing platformized companies will have trust and safety departments and some sort of policy staff. While these teams may create rules that govern conduct on their services, potentially engaging in forms of human and automated content governance similar to those discussed earlier in this chapter, platform companies also seek to govern by facilitating network effects, shaping interactions with complementors, and serving as gatekeepers (Srnicek, 2016; Cennamo, 2019; Van Dijck, Nieborg, and Poell, 2019). In particular, platform companies in various sectors have developed forms of governance premised on controlling third-party actors, mechanisms that entrench the central position of platform firms in economically important networks, and strategies that facilitate the creation of dependent relationships between the platform firm and other social and economic stakeholders.

Platforms that are predominantly commercial—profiting from business models that are not advertising-centric—often derive power and economic success from being the central architects of a multi-sided market. As work from organizational scholars, as well as political economists interested in platform firms has demonstrated, these platforms create various "'regulatory structures' that dictate the terms of interaction between workers and employers, buyers and sellers, clients and contractors, creators and viewers, and advertisers and consumers" (Rahman and Thelen, 2019, p. 179). These involve contractual relationships like terms of service and non-compete clauses (Suzor, 2018), as well as processes of procedural review and control, as in the case of Apple's App Store, which reviews apps uploaded by developers before they can be sold or shared (Cowls and Morley, 2022). Whereas major marketplaces conduct content governance by deciding whether or not certain products or sellers are unsafe, fraudulent, or otherwise problematic, they are often also important gatekeepers, able to shape seller (and buyer) behavior by preferencing certain products or offering promotions and sales on certain items (Täuscher and Laudien, 2018; Athique and Kumar, 2022).

Service-oriented platforms in the 'gig economy' or 'sharing economy'—what Woodcock and Graham (2020, p. 7) call locally or "geographically-tethered" platform firms that operate primarily at the municipal level—also govern through their design, gatekeeping, and network effects. These types of platforms commonly make governance decisions that affect workers (Krzywdzinski and Gerber, 2021; Wood, 2021): determining worker routes, setting targets for delivery/drop-off times, and building incentive structures that have a major impact on worker scheduling, time-management, and autonomy. For the end-user opening the app on their phone, locally tethered platform applications also involve systems of visibility management (Rosenblat, 2018). The platform controls what is promoted—or not—to certain parties, based on data like location, as well as more holistic profiles with predictions about individual behavior. They can deploy design nudges, such as 'ghost car' icons that make consumers more likely to order a car that they think is right around the corner (Knibbs, 2015; R. Davies and Bhuiyan, 2022). The platform can hide listings of apartments in certain neighborhoods, and decide how to present crucial information to users; it can shape the technical features and physical access to their application programming interfaces and other computational infrastructures, using policy and design decisions to try and prevent competitors from breaking their network effects.

All of this should be unsurprising: on platforms, everything is architected. Across business models and platform types, platform companies govern in a wide range of ways. Whether one considers granular forms of rulemaking and enforcement or much broader, strategic design decisions and incentives that impact those that rely upon or use the platform, today's platform companies are important political—as well as economic, social, and cultural—actors.

2.3 Key Trends in Platform Governance

What platforms do—and how they do it—can change rapidly, in response to public pressure, scandal, or the mercurial whims of a new billionaire owner. The way that platform companies govern has evolved substantially over the years, and new, unforseen developments are always on the horizon. Nevertheless, there are a few overarching trends poised to further shape the future of this landscape moving forward.

The clearest is that platform governance is consistently becoming more pub-licly visible and politically salient (Alizadeh et al., 2022). From Elon Musk's ill-fated Twitter takeover (and the apparent rapid dissolution of important trust and safety teams at the company) to the 'deplatforming' of major celebrities and politicians, the role that certain companies play as important political and cultural gatekeepers has been thrust into the spotlight. Mainstream news organi-zations are covering previously niche issues, such as Apple pressuring companies to change their platform policies by threatening removal from what is effectively one of the two marketplaces for mobile apps in the world (Nicas, 2021a). From coverage of audio streaming and podcasting companies to internet infrastructure providers, it is now not uncommon for news stories to illustrate the private rulemaking and enforcement power of the numerous technology companies that citizens and businesses around the world rely upon.

Alongside this wave of public attention, some of the most existential critiques of the global platform governance status quo have been able to gain more oxygen. A set of audits performed by contracted third parties have examined the way that the policymaking of platforms like Facebook has failed vulnerable groups around the world (Sissons, 2022). These reports bolster the longstanding argument made by civil society groups that companies have historically underinvested (both in terms of automated systems and other resources, as well as in terms of expertise, staffing, and on-the-ground expert engagement) in low-income regions and countries marked by conflict (Kaye, 2018; Arun, 2022). These arguments build upon previous accounts documenting the opacity, arbitrariness, and lack of due process that underpin much of private platform governance (MacKinnon, 2013; Suzor, Van Geelen, and Myers West, 2018; York, 2021). Nevertheless, despite the increase in critical writing about the topic, and the growing number of wide-reaching efforts to imagine something better, these broader structural issues remain largely under-addressed in today's mainstream discussions of the potential issues with platform governance in various sectors.

Another general trend relates to the growing use of automated systems to enforce platform rules at scale. Whether it be the use of automated classifiers seeking to detect potentially 'suspicious' behavior on marketplaces, or the use of automated flags that will report content with certain keywords for human moderator review on a social network, more and more companies are relying on technical systems to police a wide range of platforms. Some of this might be considered 'Fake AI' (Kaltheuner, 2021), blustery developments that hide behind the purported flashiness and technical sophistication of the 'Artificial Intelligence' label but actually involve no more than the usual human labor traditionally relied upon for commercial content moderation. For example, certain taxi and transportation platforms, under pressure from local officials to screen drivers more thoroughly for public safety reasons, have asked their workers to upload images of themselves before every shift, which are ostensibly screened in an automated fashion but in actuality are often manually reviewed by a human content moderator (Boland, 2021). This sort of subterfuge, directed towards investors, the public, and regulators, is likely to continue.

However, there are other emerging and important forms of platform governance that do in fact involve complex socio-technical systems for feature extraction, content detection, and content matching at scale, as in the case of the 'hash-databases' now being deployed by many firms to detect copyrighted, violent extremist, and potentially sexually abusive content. In an era of increasing public attention paid to—and government scrutiny of—platform rulemaking, firms have been ramping up their reliance on automated tools in an effort to meet the demands placed upon them by governance stakeholders at scale (Gorwa, Binns, and Katzenbach, 2020; Cobbe, 2021). Company executives have consistently pointed to their purported technical innovations in trust and safety when speaking with policymakers, and their promise that AI systems will be able to do this work better and faster has been a consistent, problematic, refrain.

A third important trend is what might be called governance hybridization. Private platform governance is steadily becoming less of a purely private affair, as leading firms are now seeking to involve other governance stakeholders—civil society groups, academics, government representatives—in their policy development and enforcement processes (Gorwa, 2019a). This is happening not only to help improve these processes, and to comply with public demands, but also to help outsource some of their responsibility to third parties (Caplan, 2023).

To take one of the most notable examples, Facebook CEO Mark Zuckerberg published a long essay titled "A Blueprint for Content Governance and Enforcement" in the winter of 2018. In it, he claimed that he had "increasingly come to believe that Facebook should not make so many important decisions about free expression and safety on [its] own," and as a result, would create an "Oversight Body" for content moderation that would let users appeal takedown decisions to an independent body (Zuckerberg, 2018, n.p.). The company then proceeded to spin up this new quasi-independent institution (initially dramatically dubbed 'the Supreme Court of Facebook'), investing millions of dollars in staffing, servicing, and promoting it (Douek, 2019; Pallero, 2020). It recruited academics, journalists, activists, and former politicians to well-paid positions advising the company on its content decisions and policies.

Although the Oversight Board was set up by a single firm, there are other emerging organizations, like the Global Internet Forum to Counter Terrorism (GIFCT) or the WeProtect Global Alliance, which have become crucial actors in platform governance across the tech sector. These entities combine features of a policy network (with summits and meetings bringing together public officials with tech industry leaders) and a standard-setting organization (developing protocols, best practices, and tools that can be shared by member firms), managing key technologies like GIFCT's shared industry hash database of extremist content.

In this sense, platform governance is becoming a tad more multistakeholder—but interestingly, through these kinds of new institutional venues, and not the traditional legacy institutions of internet governance and internet standards development. Instead, initiatives like GIFCT are voluntary organizations run and organized by industry but with varying levels of government and civil society steering and involvement. These developments don't fit neatly within traditional understandings of co-regulation (as they aren't legally encoded or mandated in national law) or self-regulation (as they aren't pursued totally independently from governments and other governance stakeholders), and remain difficult to study due to their opaque nature and sensitive links to public safety and national security issues.

3

Regulating Platform Companies

A Cross-Domain Policy Overview

The stakes for platform regulation are considerably lower when nobody uses the platforms in question. But the leading globally active platform firms have grown significantly in the last decade, and with each additional user comes more responsibility. As various platform services have taken on roles closer to that of quasi-public digital infrastructure—one that is becoming a significant part of the political, economic, social, and cultural fabric in many parts of the world—it may not be surprising that platform governance issues have correspondingly also attracted more and more attention from policymakers and the public. In recent years, a wide range of jurisdictions have seen the introduction of new policy initiatives seeking to influence, shape, or constrain how different platforms with different business models operate. What are the main contours of these developments in the global context?

A growing number of researchers across the social sciences are seeking to follow this complex, multifaceted policy debate, but there have yet to be any comprehensive, large-scale efforts to track these policy developments across a large set of jurisdictions. Part of this is an issue of scope: because different types of platform services can have significantly different business models, it is not always clear where to delineate the boundaries of potentially relevant policy frameworks, especially when trying to parse through large amounts of pre-existing regulation affecting telecommunications, the media industries, transportation, accommodation, and other established 'legacy' sectors. And the platform economy often simultaneously implicates a range of complex policy fields, from privacy and data protection law to competition policy and workers' rights.

Given that a comprehensive synthesising overview of how technology companies across a diverse range of sectors have been regulated in various international jurisdictional contexts in the past 30 years is out of scope for this project (and something that would be best left to historians), I wish to further set the

The Politics of Platform Regulation: How Governments Shape Online Content Moderation. Robert Gorwa, Oxford University Press. © Oxford University Press 2024. DOI: 10.1093/oso/9780197692851.003.0003

scene by providing a brief—and by no means exhaustive—historical analysis of some of the most important platform-oriented regulatory efforts, specifically as they pertain to three of the platform types laid out in the previous chapter: marketplaces, feed-based social networks, and 'locally tethered' service delivery platforms. In particular, I focus on those that are making a difference in big markets, are serving as precedent for policy efforts in other jurisdictions, or are potentially being applied with extraterritoriality by platform firms and thus having a de-facto transnational impact.[1]

3.1 Data Protection Regulation

In her rich history of the legal, technical, and institutional foundations of today's digital economy, the legal scholar Julie Cohen identifies the development of web-based tracking protocols by researchers at Netscape in the 1990s as a critical moment in the pre-history of the eventual emergence of platform-based tech business models (Cohen, 2019). Since then, the 'cookie' and other related technologies have allowed for businesses to follow users around the internet, unleashing not only a rich bounty of commercial possibility but also eventually catalyzing public and policy concern about both corporate and government surveillance of individual behavior. The first data protection frameworks, which set out rules for how the personal data of and about citizens could be handled, originated in Europe in the pre-internet era, and set the foundations of a European approach concerned with "control over personal data, autonomy, and 'informational self-determination' " (Veale, 2019, p. 87). In the 1990s and 2000s, European data protection and privacy law was more about setting the fundamental 'law of the land' which would affect how all sorts of private and public entities could use people's personal information. For example, the European Union's lesser-known data protection framework, ePrivacy [Directive (EU) 2002/58], governs online tracking in general, across the internet ecosystem.

Data protection regulation did not occur in a vacuum, of course. Since the 1990s, many countries developed and refined privacy and data protection rules, and these policies were from the onset subject to international contestation and negotiation, given their potential impact on international trade. Farrell and Newman (2019a) note that the European Commission was able to negotiate a privacy exception into the 1994 General Agreement on Tariffs and Trade process (the major multilateral treaty signed by more than 120 countries that led to the creation of the World Trade Organization), ensuring that the United States would not be able to later challenge EU data protection law as a protectionist barrier to trade. A few years later, the Safe Harbour Agreement of 2000 was made between the European Union and the United States, giving American firms a mechanism through which they could obtain 'adequacy' with European data protection rules, permitting them to legally transfer data to the United States and still comply with European law (Weiss and Archick, 2016).

As major platform companies grew in the late 2000s, however, they began to attract more direct scrutiny for their data handling practices and potential privacy violations in the United States, Europe, and beyond. In 2011 and 2012, the US Federal Trade Commission signed agreements with Google and Facebook following an investigation into potentially misleading privacy policies. These 'consent decrees' committed the firms to implementing a privacy program, with simple audits to demonstrate compliance mandated for the subsequent 20 years (Gray, 2018). In January 2012, the European Commission published a draft for a new regulation updating and harmonizing the data protection rules that had been in place since the 1990s, making them far more stringent. This draft, which would eventually pass into law as the General Data Protection Regulation [Regulation (EU) 2016/679, GDPR], became a platform policy battleground after documents obtained and released by Edward Snowden showed that US government agencies (and its allies in the 'Five Eyes' intelligence consortium) were able to routinely access apparently encrypted data of people around the world being held by Google, Facebook, and other major American platform firms (Kalyanpur and Newman, 2019).

The GDPR, which would eventually go into force in 2018, provides a consent-oriented framework requiring firms to expressly obtain permission from users (with some exceptions, including situations in which they are able to argue that they have a core 'legitimate interest' in doing so) before collecting, storing, and transmitting personal data (Zaeem and Barber, 2020). The GDPR also went further than any existing data protection framework by legally enshrining certain data rights to users (Albrecht, 2016)—such as the right to erase information being held by platforms (Ausloos, 2020).

The most comprehensive data available on the global state of data protection laws suggests that privacy legislation has been enacted in 157 countries as of 2022, almost twice as many countries as in 2012 (Greenleaf, 2022). This figure indicates that about three-quarters of United Nations member states now have some sort of data privacy laws. Much has been written about the effect of regulations like the GDPR on the ability of users to gain power in technically inscrutable markets—allowing them a degree of rights that they can leverage to request access to, or the deletion of, personal information held by technology companies (Fuster, 2014; Ausloos, Mahieu, and Veale, 2020). Due to the GDPR, industry operating in Europe is now required to set up processes for handling these complaints and requests for access or erasure, as well as structured channels for interaction with regulators. In this way, data protection regulation can also have important administrative, process-based effects on major firms.

Under European data protection frameworks, data protection authorities can issue corrective orders against infringing practices at firms, which can then lead to fines. National-level data protection authorities have increasingly been proactive in seeking to shape the practices of firms; a key dynamic, especially given the enforcement difficulties exhibited by the Irish Data Protection Commission—which under the GDPR should serve as the lead supervisory authority for complaints involving the companies that established their European headquarters there (Li and Newman, 2022). An example of this proactive action from regulators was highlighted in reporting from 2022 that suggested that TikTok was planning to stop asking customers to consent to the tracking the company used to serve targeted advertising: the increasingly popular video-sharing platform scrapped the policy change after receiving warnings from the Italian and Irish data protection authorities that such a change would be in violation of the GDPR and that they would be ready to begin enforcement actions if the changes were made (Lomas, 2022). Because most platform business models rely on user data to continually tweak their services and obtain competitive advantages and network effects, data protection frameworks can have a substantial impact on the internal policymaking decisions being made by platform firms, especially relating to profiling, tracking, and data sharing.

3.2 Competition Law and Policy

Since the 1970s and 1980s, competition law has shown its potential as an important part of the technology policy toolkit in Europe, the United States, and beyond. It was in these decades that we witnessed the American antitrust investigation into the American Telephone and Telegraph telecommunications monopoly, and the investigations into IBM's market power. But the highest profile competition investigation directly connected to the modern digital economy was launched by the US Department of Justice into Microsoft in the late 1990s. The initial outcome was a verdict that Microsoft had violated the Sherman Act, the piece of anti-cartel legislation that historically had been used against the American oil and rail monopolists of the late nineteenth and early twentieth century (Wu, 2018). Amid much furor, the initial ruling that the Windows operating system should be owned by a separate company from Microsoft that could also compete with it was overturned on appeal, and the American executive branch would eventually land on a more limited agreement with Microsoft, which involved it pledging to implement some transparency measures and to permit third parties to more easily build software for its systems via structured technical interfaces (Fitzpatrick, 2014). Since then, there have been no major competition interventions of that scope into a leading market player in the technology industry, although the Federal Trade Commission has intervened in a number of relatively peripheral digital cases (Hoffman, 2018).

Despite this all, there is an active movement ongoing in the United States seeking to spur a revival of muscular competition law in the tech and other sectors. The general hesitance of US regulators to intervene in mergers has led to a revival of critical competition policy scholarship, and a movement sometimes termed 'neo-Brandeisean' or 'hipster' antitrust (Daly, 2017). These thinkers have argued that American competition law has erred by drifting towards a much more conservative price-based evaluative approach (involving mechanisms like the 'consumer welfare standard'), which was supposed to make competition law more objective and empirical, but significantly narrowed the legitimate grounds upon which regulators could block mergers or intervene in markets, leading to a host of anti-competitive outcomes and historic levels of market concentration in a wide range of industries (Khan, 2017; Wu, 2018).

In only a short period of five or so years, this 'backlash' to the dominant American 'Chicago School' of competition thinking has rapidly become more prominent. One of its major proponents was named Chair of the Federal Trade Commission (FTC), the main US competition regulator, by Joe Biden following his election to the presidency in 2021. Even before Lina Khan joined the FTC, against Google and Facebook were opened under Republican leadership (Federal Trade Commission, 2020). The FTC has also increased their merger scrutiny, suing to prevent Meta (Facebook's parent company), Microsoft, and other leading tech firms from making certain new acquisitions (Coldewey, 2022).

3.2.1 THE EVOLVING EUROPEAN APPROACH

In Europe, competition policy has historically been slightly more ambitious and wide-ranging in its aims for market design. The United States and the European Union diverged in the scale and scope of their interventions in two classic cases of technology-related competition policy—IBM in the 1980s, which hinged on whether or not IBM's bundling of hardware was anti-competitive, and Microsoft in the 1990s, which explored Microsoft's software bundling practices, as well as other innovations the company had deployed to try and give itself an edge over competitors (F. M. Fisher, 2000). As Gebicka and Heinemann (2014, p. 150) note, in those cases, as well as most of the other major cases relating to technology firms (such as investigations of Google and Intel that would follow), the "degrees of intervention" on behalf of European competition authorities, and the requirements for transparency and sharing information with competitors, have generally been higher in Europe.

Table 3.1 **Key Competition Policy Issue Areas and Actors.**

Competition Policy Area	Example Tech Actors	Key Third Parties	Key Issue Areas
Marketplace Design (app stores)	Google, Apple	Incumbent Hardware Firms, App Developers	Platform Fees, Mandatory App Stores
Marketplace Design (e-commerce)	Amazon	Sellers, Traditional Retail	Self-Preferencing, Ranking and Visibility, IP theft
Media and Journalism	Facebook, Google	Traditional Media Industries	Licensing, Visibility and Ranking, Copyright
Hardware and Software	Microsoft, Apple	Developers, Consumer Protection Organizations	Bundling, Compatibility, Planned obsolescence
APIs	Facebook, Twitter	Developers, Academia	Interoperability, API Access and Notice

This has long been a fast moving space, full of network effects, rapidly growing startups, and other technological and economic features that might make competition policy in digital markets especially tricky (Crémer, Montjoye, and Schweitzer, 2019). The European Commission—which handles competition policy in the European Union directly through its Directorate General on Competition, rather than through an independent regulatory agency (Just and Latzer, 2000)—chose not to intervene in the key potential competition cases that set the stage for the platform era (Graef, 2018), such as Google's acquisition of the online advertising company Doubleclick (2007), Facebook's takeover of Instagram (2012) and WhatsApp (2014), or Microsoft's purchase of LinkedIn (2016). The Commission has levied big fines against major platform companies in a number of cases, such as a 2.4 billion Euro fine against Google in the Google Shopping case (2017), but has largely refrained from major market-shaping interventions like blocking mergers or pushing for breakups.

However, in the last five years, there have been notable shifts in the European approach to competition policy in platformized markets. This trend has been at least partially driven by action from member states and a number of proactive investigations from national-level competition regulators, which have conducted multiple investigations of platform firms, and, in certain cases, levied sizable fines (Graef, 2019). For example, the French competition authority levied a 150 million Euro fine on Google in 2019, and a record 1.1 billion Euro fine on Apple in 2020, updating their theories of gatekeeping and dominance in the platform specific context while doing so (Pentzien, 2022). In Germany, these changes have been enshrined in legislation, with notable 2017 and 2021 amendments to the statutes governing the behavior of the Bundeskartellamt, Germany's main competition authority. These have impacted how market power is understood in the platform domain, and also provided German regulators with an expanded competition toolbox for digital markets, including some pre-emptive ('ex ante') intervention tools to help deal with future market abuses (Budzinski and Stöhr, 2019).

These shifts in the approach of two of the European Union's largest and most powerful countries have affected the European Commission. The 2.7 billion USD judgment against Google's self-preferencing in search and its 'Google Shopping' marketplace in 2017 was followed by further 4.3 billion and 1.7 billion USD fines levied in 2018 and 2019 for anti-competitive behavior in the online advertising and mobile operating system spaces (Coyle, 2019; Kotzeva et al., 2019). Perhaps due to its ability to issue fines and investigate firms, the Commission under the leadership of Jean-Claude Juncker maintained that its existing competition policy toolbox was fit for purpose (Cini and Czulno, 2022). However, upon taking over in December 2019, the Ursula Von der Leyen-led Commission has instead focused on introducing a new set of competition policies that would entrench the evolution from predominantly ex post measures (after the fact) towards more ex ante, proactive procedural safeguards for digital markets.

The flagship competition initiative of the Von der Leyen Commission is the Digital Markets Act [Regulation (EU) 2022/1925, DMA]. The DMA—which was proposed in the winter of 2020, signed into law in fall 2022, and will officially go into force in the spring of 2024—introduced a number of obligations for companies that operate what it calls 'gatekeeper' platforms: services with more than 45 million monthly active end users and 10,000 yearly active business users, as well as a turnover of more than 7.5 billion Euro per year or a market capitalization of 75 billion Euro in the last year (Cabral et al., 2021). When the regulation goes into effect, gatekeeper platforms can be fined if they are found to engage in a number of potentially anti-competitive behaviors that are typical in platform ecosystems.

The DMA allows European regulators to issue fines if a platform makes their own products or services more visible than those of competitors (self-preferencing), combines personal data collected during a service with another service without explicit consent, or creates technical chokepoints, such as "requir[ing] app developers to use certain services (e.g., payment systems or identity providers) in order to be listed in app stores" (European Council of Ministers, 2022, n.p.). As well, the DMA features some language about future interoperability requirements for gatekeeper platforms (Brown, 2020), which if implemented and enforced in an ambitious way, could have wide-reaching effects, especially as decentralized platform services built upon open protocols become more popular.

One additional interesting piece of policy that has largely flown under the radar is the Platform-to-Business regulation [Regulation (EU) 2019/1150, P2B], which went into force in July 2020. P2B seeks to provide some baseline rules for how major online gatekeepers interact with the commercial third parties that rely upon them (Busch, 2020): for example, it features a provision that platforms must provide business users with at least 15 days of notice when changing their terms of service, and offers some procedural safeguards regarding account deletion. If, for instance, an app developer is blocked from a major app store, the regulation mandates a mechanism for appeal, with provisions for third-party mediation structures. The regulation is emblematic of a burgeoning European approach that recognizes that the decisionmaking of major platforms can have a sizable impact on citizens and businesses using the platform, and as a result seeks to put some due process and procedural safeguards in place (Busch, 2020).

3.2.2 ADDITIONAL GLOBAL CONTEXT

It is not just the European Union that is demonstrating an appetite for developing innovative competition approaches seeking to rein in platform policies and decisionmaking. India, for example, has deployed various measures seeking to limit platform self-preferencing on large marketplaces like Amazon. According to rules instated in 2020, which were developed as part of a non-legislative process led by the Indian Ministry of Consumer Affairs, marketplace platforms face constraints on how they offer products from 'associated sellers' (PRS Legislative Research, 2024). The regulation seeks to keep a company like Amazon from operating a marketplace and also selling its own products on the marketplace, and seems intended to fight back against the Amazon Basics brand, which Amazon uses to shrewdly capture emerging product markets (Mattioli, 2020).

If we take a global snapshot of the punitive interventions made by competition regulators against major platform companies, one can quickly see that their number has been rapidly rising since 2020. Many G20 countries are now conducting competition-related inquiries across a range of issues, ranging from

Table 3.2 **Summary of fines issued against platform firms by G20 competition authorities. Historical exchange rates to USD; figures rounded.**

Jurisdiction	Date	Company	Fine (USD, millions)	Issue
EU	06-Mar-13	Microsoft	731	Software Bundling
USA	19-Jan-17	Uber	20	Driver Compensation
EU	12-Jun-17	Google	2, 700	Self-Preferencing (Google Shopping)
Australia	19-Jun-18	Apple	6	Right to Repair
EU	18-Jul-18	Google	4, 300	Operating System
EU	27-Mar-19	Google	1, 700	Advertising
USA	24-Jul-19	Facebook	5, 000	Data Protection
Canada	19-May-20	Facebook	6	Data Protection
Turkey	13-Nov-20	Google	26	Advertising; Self-Preferencing
USA	02-Feb-21	Amazon	62	Employee Wages (Logistics)
Russia	27-Apr-21	Apple	12	App Stores
Italy	13-May-21	Google	122	App Interoperability (Android Auto)
France	07-Jun-21	Google	268	Advertising
France	13-Jul-21	Google	590	Copyright
Russia	25-Aug-21	Booking.com	17.5	Market Concentration

Table 3.2 **Continued**

Jurisdiction	Date	Company	Fine (USD, millions)	Issue
South Korea	26-Aug-21	Facebook	5	Data Protection
China	01-Sep-21	Alibaba	2, 800	Market Concentration
South Korea	15-Sep-21	Google	176	App Stores
United Kingdom	20-Oct-21	Facebook	70	Merger & Acquisition
Italy	26-Nov-21	Google	11	Data Protection
Italy	26-Nov-21	Apple	11	Hardware
Italy	09-Dec-21	Amazon	1, 200	Self-Preferencing
Russia	25-Jul-22	Google	34	Market Concentration
Australia	12-Aug-22	Google	40	Data Protection (Android)
Indonesia	16-Sep-22	Google	2	App Stores
France	06-Oct-22	Apple	365	Retail and Distribution
India	21-Oct-22	Google	113	App Stores
Turkey	27-Oct-22	Facebook	19	Data Protection
Australia	07-Dec-22	Uber	14	Prices

potential data-related harms (e.g., the combination of data across services without proper legal basis or consent, for instance—think of Facebook's use of telephone numbers provided by WhatsApp users as an example) to anti-competitive practices relating to mobile operating systems, app stores, online advertising, and more. These approaches have varied in their level of scrutiny: for instance, the Japanese competition regulator appointed a new digital markets unit, conducted investigations and published various reports, but has not issued any fines (McConnell, 2022)—a commonality it shares with Brazil.

Out of all the G20 nations, Italy and France have been particularly assertive, with Italy issuing its largest ever fine of more than a billion USD in December 2021 against Amazon, alleging anti-competitive activity in their fulfillment and logistics operations (Maggiolino and Ghezzi, 2022). France has been active in taking on cases relating to online advertising (Kayali, 2021). India and South Korea have also seen some action, issuing fines in the 100 million USD range that relate to Google's Play Store and its integration in the Android ecosystem (Park, 2021; Kalra, Vengattil, and Vengattil, 2022). In an especially notable development, the United Kingdom's new digital-focused competition regulator, the Digital Markets Unit, successfully executed the first recent blockage of a relatively high-profile tech-related acquisition: their 50 million pound fine of Facebook for its takeover of Giphy, and the investigation and scrutiny than have followed, led Facebook to announce in late 2022 that it would sell off Giphy at a loss after acquiring it for 400 million USD in 2020 (Sweney, 2022).

From mergers and acquisitions review to rules around contracting relationships, fairness, and interoperability, competition policy offers a wide range of tools that regulators around the world are seeking to deploy to shape platform operations, especially as they pertain to general market conditions, contracting relationships with third parties, and other more general structural aspects of their platform power.

3.3 Labor Law

Many of the companies operating user-generated content, cloud service, streaming, or other entertainment-related or services generally employ relatively few people, especially when compared to other major service sectors. Facebook has fewer than fifty thousand employees as of 2023, and less-profitable firms oriented in services like food delivery, transportation, or last-mile service provision often have far fewer than that, even after having grown into multiple markets. The exceptions are sprawling tech companies like Microsoft and Alphabet, which are generally active in a range of tech sectors from consumer goods to enterprise software services: Microsoft's roughly two hundred and twenty thousand employees as of 2022 put it about on par with HSBC, one of the largest globally active banks.[2]

Tech work is still often assumed to largely consist of high-paying, highly skilled jobs with good benefits and stable employment. Social media or search-oriented platform firms like Facebook and Google recruit talent from all around the world, with these jobs mainly concentrated in the United States and other high-income countries. For a long time, the ability of these firms to attract the top global talent to the United States was seen to be a major source of their competitive advantage,[3] and lavish compensation packages, stock options, and all sorts of at-work benefits were standard offerings. The leading players even lobbied actively on labor issues, seeking to continually improve their access to visas and fast-tracked immigration options for their recruits (Popiel, 2018).

But not all tech work is so glamorous, especially when a platform company is involved in areas that involve tangible goods. The biggest e-commerce platforms employ huge quantities of warehouse 'pickers,' delivery drivers, and other employees conducting physical work handling, sorting, packing, and shipping products. Amazon alone hired more than a hundred thousand of such workers in 2019–2020.[4] Similarly, when it comes to technology companies that create physical products (computers, phones, or other devices), manufacturing hardware necessarily involves vast supply chains and complicated industrial processes, often with less than ideal labor conditions at the mining/resource extraction and assembly/factory links in the value chain (Notley, 2019; Crawford, 2021).

Beyond this, certain types of platforms have created a vast digitally coordinated and algorithmically managed service economy. Whether they be taxi-esque transportation services, grocery or food delivery apps, marketplaces for care work, or online labor markets for freelance tasks big and small, these platforms—sometimes called 'gig economy' or 'service delivery platforms'—are having an increasingly influential impact on the transnational dynamics of work in a globalized world (Woodcock and Graham, 2020). In Europe, for example, studies prepared for the European Commission have estimated that more than 28 million people in the European Union work through digital labor platforms, with more than 500 various work-related platforms operating in Europe (European Commission, 2021). They have quickly become controversial in many contexts—hailed on one hand as the potential facilitators of flexible, low-commitment ways for people to work, while critiqued on the other as under-regulated entities that can exert huge managerial and algorithmic control over workers without living up to their core promises (Dubal, 2017; Shibata, 2020). There has been active worker resistance in cities around the world seeking to motivate government or firm-led policy to address these key questions, and set some minimum standards relating to pay and working conditions (Bessa et al., 2022).

Work is one area that has historically been highly regulated by governments. For that reason, it is not surprising that the emergence of service-delivery platforms has led to clashes between these firms, and their ostensibly disruptive business-models, and municipal, federal, and international institutions, politicians, regulators, and courts (Koutsimpogiorgos et al., 2020). One of the main points of contestation has been over employee classification, and whether or not platform workers are 'independent contractors'—as most labor platforms claim—or employees entitled to benefits (van Doorn, 2020b). This has become a global point of debate, involving workers from Cape Town to Chengdu negotiating with platforms about their status (Bessa et al., 2022).

In Europe, there have already been more than a thousand court decisions and legal judgments grappling with the employment status of people working through platforms since these platforms emerged as major players (Heissl, 2022). A smaller number of countries have passed national legislation seeking to set rules that would create a more stable policy consensus in this area. In one notable example, after active mobilization by Spanish delivery couriers, the Spanish Ministry of Labor and Social Economy was able to enact a regulation in 2021—colloquially known as the 'Riders Law'—that sets conditions for workers to be classified as employees. The law assumes in most cases that workers are indeed employees, if they "render paid services consisting of the delivery or distribution of any consumer product or merchandise for employers who directly, indirectly or implicitly exercise the corporate powers of organisation, management and control," and establishes a set of transparency and redress mechanisms (Todoli-Signes, 2021, p. 400).

The French government, in contrast, has opted for pro-business policies. Under the guidance of Emmanuel Macron—a public fan of venture capital-backed tech firms generally, and of Uber specifically (Henley and H. Davies, 2022)—France adopted rules that were so appealing to industry that companies are still hailing them as the ideal laissez-faire regulatory outcome for platform-service firms in Europe (Wray, 2021).

Member-state policy intervention has led to different rules across the European Single Market. In an effort to create a European standard affecting the working conditions of platform-mediated workers across the European Union, the European Commission announced in late 2021 a draft text for a Platform Work Directive which sets out a number of protections for platform workers and classifies them as employees if they can make an argument that their work meets two out of the following five conditions: the platform 'effectively determines' pay levels; requires workers to wear uniforms or follow certain rules about their appearance; supervises work and verifies its quality either physically or algorithmically; enacts measures to restrict the freedom of when one works, for example through sanctioning mechanisms or not permitting workers to turn down tasks or subcontract tasks to others; and restricts the possibility to build one's own client base or work for other third parties (text from the draft Directive paraphrased from Stefano, 2022). The Directive also features provisions for improving the transparency of systems of algorithmic management and control, and for improving due process (e.g., notification, appeals possibilities) around major decisions made by labor platforms, such as employee termination or suspension (Fairwork, 2021).

The political stakes are especially high here as the continued viability of these firms' business models is potentially in play. All of these efforts to regulate how platforms govern and interact with the workers that they seek to coordinate via their services have faced significant lobbying campaigns from industry, which has mobilized aggressively to protect its business model and dilute worker protections in any new regulation (Verheecke, 2022). For instance, in California, the ride-hailing industry engaged in a multi-million dollar lobbying effort and a counter referendum, which succeeded in eventually overturning a pro-worker ballot initiative passed only a year earlier (Dubal, 2022). In other cases, firms have sought to make use of potential regulatory loopholes. In Spain, for example, some platforms are now simply using subcontractors to issue temporary contracts to workers, even though "the subcontracting company offers virtually nothing, while the platform connects the client and riders, assigns the tasks through its algorithm and ultimately sets the prices of the delivery services" (Aranguiz, 2021, n.p.).

Overall, these developments show how locally tethered platform companies and policymakers have begun to engage in a 'cat and mouse game' on multiple continents. As trade unions, workers collectives, and activists try to get policymakers to increase labor protections in the platform-mediated service delivery sector (Cant, 2019; Englert, Woodcock, and Cant, 2020), industry is responding in turn through lobbying, loopholes, or simple non-compliance to force direct confrontation with government. In most cases, however, these debates have remained separate from broader policy trends facing other types of platform firms. The business models at here are quite distinct from those in other platform sectors, and because these firms necessarily have an impact at the local level (e.g., on local taxi industries, public transit, hotels, housing, established retail businesses), shaping their governance efforts has become largely the purview of municipal governments. That all said, one clear synthesis is being drawn by workers (Alon-Beck, 2020), who increasingly are finding commonalities across platform business models and forming collectives—such as the US-based Tech Workers Coalition, which offers a big tent for everyone from logistics pickers and Uber drivers to white-collar software engineers—seeking to collapse these boundaries and mobilize for broader change in labor conditions across the sector (Tarnoff and Weigel, 2020). If that happens, the area of labor policy could send reverberations felt across other areas of the tech industry's structural power.

3.4 Content Regulation

As in the domains of competition policy and data protection law, the origin of online content regulation pre-dates the rise of today's largest platforms. This history is long, and in many cases, highly technical in ways that do not lend themselves easily to an accessible and abridged overview. Depending on the specific platform in question, the business models they rely on, and the specific national context, telecommunications policy, media or broadcast policy, and internet specific 'intermediary liability' laws are all potentially relevant, alongside wide-ranging content-specific legislation (e.g., regulatory efforts pertaining to copyright, terrorism, or child safety that span different media) and a spate of more recent platform-specific regulatory efforts.

Despite that complexity, one may argue that there are four broad policy levers that are notable for their prominence in the historical toolbox that governments around the world have turned to when seeking to regulate platform companies in the user-generated content area: liability shields, control regimes, informal negotiation, and platform-specific rules.

3.4.1 LIABILITY SHIELDS

Not long after the popularization of dial-in bulletin board services like CompuServe and America Online, a slew of legal cases were fought that would shape the landscape for future online content hosts in the United States and beyond. Some of these companies were taking measures to set rules for what their users could acceptably say, for example removing pornographic material in an effort to provide 'family friendly' or otherwise curated services. These bulletin-board providers were in effect the precursors of modern social platforms like Facebook that seek to provide a community-friendly experience for their users and their advertisers (Gillespie, 2018). However, due to the quirks of an American legal tradition grounded in the First Amendment, which in the global context can be said to have unusually wide protections for all forms of speech (Krotoszynski, 2006), by conducting this type of community content moderation and curation, these early platforms were exposing themselves to potential legal challenge. In a set of lawsuits, lower courts in the United States had begun in the early 1990s to interpret the moderation these ur-platforms were undertaking as curatorial responsibility akin to that exhibited by publishers or distributors, thus opening them to liability for the content posted by their customers (Chander, 2016).

After a number of cases where bulletin board operators were sued for defamation or other torts, two congressmen inserted a short clause into a piece of telecommunications reform regulation with the goal of creating an legal environment where companies would not be afraid to crack down on illegal or unsavory content (Kosseff, 2019a). Their amendment was so ahead of its time that, according to the detailed history provided by Kosseff (2019b), it was met with effectively no lobbyist or outside political influence, and in fact was almost totally ignored by commentators and the popular media following its adoption into law. Their language would eventually be codified as Section 230 of the Communications Act (commonly referred to in shorthand as 'CDA 230'), which provided operators of internet services with a 'safe harbor' through which they could conduct moderation without taking on legal liability (Wagner, 2016; van Hoboken and D. Keller, 2019).

This framework sought to protect internet innovators by giving companies wide latitude to deal with—or not deal with—potentially harmful online content. However, it was tilted towards providing legal protection for companies, something which was met with resistance some years later when the economic rubber met the road on the question of online copyright and intellectual property violations. The film and music industries were very concerned about losing profitability as their content spread via internet services (Soha and McDowell, 2016; Burgess and Green, 2018). After a successful bout of lobbying from Hollywood and the creative industries, online copyright in the United States would be covered instead by the more stringent Digital Millennium Copyright Act (DMCA) of 1998, which developed the idea of conditional immunity: online services providing access to copyrighted content have safe harbor, but with conditions, such as the implementation of functioning processes for receiving and enforcing complaints from copyright holders (Haggart, 2014).

The approach laid out via Section 230 and the DMCA influenced many other international approaches to regulating a broad array of online services. In 1997, the European Commission published a communication on European commerce (Julià-Barceló and Koelman, 2000), which kicked off a regulatory process that eventually resulted in the E-Commerce Directive [Directive (EU) 2000/31, ECD]. The ECD sought to harmonize European rules for 'information society services' provided by a wide range of different online intermediaries, from network operators (e.g., telecommunications companies), search engines, web hosting providers, and social networks, with the goal of reducing divergence among national standards (Baistrocchi, 2002). The Directive distinguishes between intermediaries that are 'mere conduits' and thus should have less responsibilities, and those that are more active 'hosts' and thus have more responsibilities (Kuczerawy and Ausloos, 2015). It establishes a safe harbor for intermediaries that host user-generated content from third parties as long as they do not have knowledge of the illegality of content and act to remove or restrict access to content once they obtain knowledge of that content's illegality (Angelopoulos and Smet, 2016). Article 14 of the Directive thus established the conditions for what is commonly called a 'notice-and-action' scheme, with a high bar for intermediaries to be found criminally or civilly liable for the content of third-party users using their services.

3.4.2 CONTROL REGIMES

If a country created a liability regime protecting companies from being held criminally responsible for the conduct of their users, those same protections could be taken away, or designed in such a way that they could be used as a tool for coercion. From the moment that internet-enabled technologies started being used for political expression and organizing, governments have deployed mutifaceted strategies to exert control over how their citizens could consume information online (Deibert et al., 2008, 2010)—implicating search engines, social networks, and other large user-generated content platforms. This development has usually been at its most overt in countries with mechanisms of control over the domestic media ecosystem, weaker forms of multi-party competition and elections, and high levels of government interest in shaping the types of political expression occurring in the information sphere.

Countries with strong state control over media sought to establish licensing regimes and strict liability frameworks. China led the way in this department, followed by countries like Turkey and Russia in 2006 and 2007: under these systems, corporations wishing to operate online services that country would not just need to receive a license to do so, but would also need to follow certain moderation rules and procedures (Wenguang, 2018). Another technique has been to simply take the basics of the conditional immunity approach developed under the US DMCA and the European Union's ECD but make the conditions stricter and liabilities more onerous. Laws like Iran's 2009 Computer Crimes Law or Turkey's 2013 Omnibus Bill created a procedure for government removal requests for specific pieces of content (such as posts, news articles), and the failure to comply could result in significant criminal sanctions and the possibility of services to be blocked by state-influenced or state-controlled internet service providers (Stanford World Intermediary Liability Map, 2018). In India, a formalized procedure under which the government could attempt to compel the removal of specific instances of online content was adopted in 2009 (Stanford World Intermediary Liability Map, 2017).

More than a decade ago, MacKinnon (2013) described how these legal strategies of 'networked authoritarianism' clashed directly against the US State Department's policy of 'internet freedom' that promoted the unfettered global activity of US multinationals like Facebook and Twitter. As 'color revolutions' spread across the Middle East and North Africa, some governments did their best to influence platform companies to further domestic control. Firms often resisted these efforts by refusing to set up physical offices or other presence in certain countries, sometimes declining government requests to remove content or hand over user data (York, 2021). When their legal control regimes failed to achieve the desired outcomes, some governments then reached for cruder tools, like internet shutdowns, domain-specific blocking of platform services, and physical coercion targeted against platform employees (Arun, 2018; Rydzak, 2019).

3.4.3 INFORMAL NEGOTIATION

Policymakers in Europe, both at the European level and domestically, at the member state level, have for about two decades been actively engaged in trying to steer online intermediaries to take their policy priorities into consideration. In particular, European policymakers have from the earliest days of major 'Web 2.0' platforms sought to use soft law, informal negotiation, and co-regulatory tools to get firms to develop stronger standards on issues like child protection. For example, in 2005, the European Commission convened a Safer Internet Forum with telecommunications companies and online service providers (Marsden, 2011, p. 139), and in 2008, the Commission's 'Social Networking Task Force' organized multistakeholder meetings with regulators, academic experts, child safety organizations, and a group of 17 companies active in the emerging social networking industry, including Facebook, MySpace, YouTube, Bebo, and others. This process led to the creation of the 'Safer Social Networking Principles for the EU,' described by a group of academic observers as a "major policy effort by multiple actors across industry, child welfare, educators, and governments to minimise the risks associated with social networking for children" through more "intuitive privacy settings, safety information, and other design interventions" (Livingstone, Ólafsson, and Staksrud, 2013, p. 317).

This type of hands-on pressure from European regulators remains a core part of the European Union's strategy for dealing with platform firms. For example, the Commission launched the "CEO Coalition to make the Internet a better place for kids" in 2011, a series of working group meetings that led to a set of five principles ("simple and robust reporting tools for users, age-appropriate privacy settings, wider use of content classification, wider availability and use of parental controls, and effective takedown of child sexual abuse material") signed by Apple, Facebook, Google, Microsoft, a number of EU telecoms, hardware manufacturers, and other firms (Livingstone et al., 2012). These initiatives weren't just confined to the child protection domain: in 2010, The Netherlands, the United Kingdom, Germany, Belgium, and Spain sponsored a European Commission project called 'Clean IT,' which would develop "general principles and best practices" to combating terrorist content and "other illegal uses of the internet [...] through a bottom up process where the private sector will be in the lead."[5] The Clean IT coalition, which featured significant representation from European law enforcement agencies, initially considered various hawkish proposals such as requiring all platforms to enact a real-name policy, and policies requiring that social media companies allow only real pictures of users (European Digital Rights, 2013). But these strict measures led to push-back from civil society and the eventual end of the project. Nevertheless, Clean IT would eventually morph into the 'EU Internet Forum,' a policy network bringing together EU governments with Facebook, Google, Microsoft, Twitter, and other firms to discuss how platform companies should best combat illegal hate speech and terrorist content (Fiedler, 2016).

These EU efforts serve as probably the earliest and most influential informal regulatory efforts seeking to influence how content-oriented platforms made and enforced their rules in the Global North, incentivizing them to change how they handled specific types of content that were undesirable for political reasons.[6] By getting companies to change their practices globally, this form of informal regulation—insulated from the attendant visibility and scrutiny of the European Parliament and other entities that came with the formal EU legislative process— could be transnationally impactful if firms changed their practices in multiple jurisdictions as a result (Citron and Wittes, 2017).

Informal regulation for user-generated content platforms has become slightly more institutionalized, formalized, and transparent in recent years. European policymakers in the mid-2010s began insisting on public deliverables and guidelines as an outcome of these kinds of processes: for example, after almost two years of meetings, the companies participating in the EU Internet Forum agreed to a 'Code of Conduct on Online Hate Speech,' obtained commitments from

48 REGULATING PLATFORM COMPANIES

the signatory firms to promptly remove terrorist material and other forms of potentially problematic content believed to be extremist (Coche, 2018), and committed to create industry-wide mechanisms for resource sharing and coordination (Gorwa, 2019a). Similar efforts have led to the EU Code of Practice on Disinformation (2018, revised in 2022), the Christchurch Call discussed in Chapter 6, and other emerging transnational institutions for informal policy coordination in areas like child safety.

3.4.4 PLATFORM-SPECIFIC RULES

Building upon all this, the most important recent development in platform-related content regulation involves the growing number of policy initiatives that specifically target major platform firms and try to set out procedural rules involving how they handle politically and socially problematic content. In their purest form, these are not general rules for internet service providers or other types of online intermediaries, but rather, targeted efforts to impact the rule-making and enforcement mechanisms enacted by certain user-generated content platforms. Platform-specific rules can vary in their approach, but increasingly involve a few key features, including specific reporting procedures, complaints handling requirements, and due process and transparency measures.

The German Network Enforcement Act (NetzDG) of 2017 seems to have been the world's first law to specifically proscribe how platforms moderated socially and politically harmful content. It involved a number of new rules, requiring the companies in scope to create technical infrastructures through which German citizens could make complaints on content as specifically violating the German Criminal Code. In practice, this was realized differently by different companies (Heldt, 2019; Wagner et al., 2020), but basically required firms to add an additional button to their interfaces that would allow people with German IP addresses to 'flag' content under a special NetzDG reporting process. These measures were particularly notable because they directly sought to shape harmful content moderation, something that would later be then attempted by a host of varied policy efforts, including in Singapore (Protection from Online Falsehoods and Manipulation Act, POFMA, 2019), France (Loi Avia, 2020), Austria (Communications Platforms Act, KoPl-G, 2020) and, eventually, across the European Union through the Digital Services Act.

The NetzDG was most controversial due to its complaints-handling requirements, and in particular, a codified provision that platform companies would need to respond to reports in under 24 hours or expose themselves to sanction in the case of systemic failures to handle these reports promptly.

Complaints-handling timelines were also included in related regulatory frameworks at the EU level, such as in the Terrorist Content Regulation [Regulation (EU) 2021/784], which mandates rapid timelines for the processing of complaints. According to civil society critics, these types of laws incentivize, if not formally require, platforms to significantly increase the role that automated content detection and enforcement systems play in their complaints-handling processes if they wish to meet their regulatory commitments; they make the over-removal of legitimate content more likely (D. Keller, 2019; Bloch-Wehba, 2020; Cobbe, 2021).

The NetzDG is notable for also containing the first legally mandated framework for transparency reporting on content moderation staffing, processes, and takedown decisions (Gorwa, 2021). Transparency reports, which began as voluntary measures undertaken in certain categories by companies in response to efforts led by organizations like the Global Network Initiative (Maclay, 2010), have become increasingly popular as a way for academics, regulators, and the public to get some degree of scrutiny into platform operations (Gorwa and Garton Ash, 2020; Urman and Makhortykh, 2023). Even in the United States, there have been a number of fairly high-profile transparency bills that have been introduced in Congress since Biden took office, including the Digital Services Oversight and Safety Act of 2022 and the Platform Accountability and Transparency Act of 2021, which have sought to allow for researchers to access platform data in privacy-preserving ways. In recent years, far more comprehensive transparency reports have been published by firms under voluntary measures like the European Union's Disinformation Code of Practice, and the European Union's Digital Services Act features a number of transparency, auditing, and researcher data-access requirements as well (EDMO, 2022; Husovec, 2023).

Finally, platform specific rules being proposed in countries around the world are increasingly moving away from more targeted provisions about complaints-handling systems and towards more general, systemic provisions under risk assessment or 'duty of care' frameworks. The 'duty of care' approach to 'online harms' favored by the United Kingdom underpins the UK's Online Safety Act (Woods, 2019), and has been informed policy developments in other Commonwealth countries like Canada. The DSA is the gold standard in this regard however, maintaining the baseline notice-and-action liability framework previously in force under the E-Commerce Directive, adding a number of elements that complete the evolution of the European Union's approach from 'platform liability' to 'platform responsibility' (Frosio, 2018). These include a mandatory risk assessment framework, external audits, due process rules (including the

3.5 Emerging Trends in Platform Regulation

This has been an abbreviated and high-level overview of a variety of policy interventions being taken to try and shape the behavior of technology companies across a wide range of issue areas (digital competition; platformized labor regimes; data protection and online privacy; harmful content) and jurisdictions. Such an overview is necessarily limited by the huge variety of platform business models and policy issues at play, and the sheer number of countries that one would need to cover to help map these policy debates across both platform type and national context.

Nevertheless, such a summary still allows one to make a few general observations which will be helpful for framing the discussion in this book going forward. Firstly, the core trend across all of these areas is a general increase in state involvement in digital governance and digital markets issues. Across the platform policy areas of data protection, competition policy, labor law, and content regulation, we are seeing more direct forms of rule-setting by state actors. Where the state may once have been content to set the foundational laws of the land, an increasing number of high-income democracies, led by the countries of the European Union, are finding the appetite to move beyond just informal agenda-setting and steering roles into more direct forms of governance.

As well, these forms of governance are becoming more complex, spanning a range of different actors and 'modalities': not just formal regulation, but also norms-based and market oriented approaches that are initiated by non-governmental actors (such as civil society groups, advertisers, and others). We're seeing the emergence of increasingly important informal institutional structures and forums that bring various stakeholders together to discuss issues, frame the policy agenda, and in some cases develop new processes and policies that can have a global impact (e.g., the Global Internet Forum to Counter Terrorism, the Global Alliance for Responsible Media). Lessons are being learned across domains too, with the issues faced during the GDPR's early days informing the enforcement structure for new platform regulation frameworks.

All told, national-level regulatory scrutiny of the platform economy is intensifying. While more time will be needed to assess the global impact of major new policy frameworks being pursued in the European Union and beyond, it is evident that platform regulation is becoming more nuanced, complex, and complicated for target companies to implement. This is perhaps leading to concerns of 'internet fragmentation'—if not actually at the technical standards

Table 3.3 **Overview of key content-related platform policy subfields.**

Content Policy Areas	Example Tech Actors	Key Third Parties	Key Debates	Example Regulations
Copyright Infringement	YouTube, TikTok	Rightsholders, Brands	Notice, Appeals, and Creator Recourse	EU Copyright Directive
Child Abuse Imagery	Apple, Dropbox	Child Safety Organizations, Activists	Client-Side Scanning	Kids Online Safety Act
Sexual Content	Pornhub, Tumblr	Sex Workers, NGOs	Verification, Age Controls	SOPA/PIPA
Dis- and Mis-information	WhatsApp, Telegram, Instagram	Journalists, Researchers	Content Policies, Transparency	POFMA, EU Code of Practice
Hate Speech and Incitement	Parler, Facebook, Twitter	Human Rights NGOs	Content Policies, Transparency	NetzDG, Online Harms Act
Terrorism	GIFCT, Tech Against Terrorism	CVE Organizations, Police Agencies	Live Streaming Controls, Content Policies	EU Terrorist Content Regulation

layer of internet infrastructure (Mueller, 2017), than in terms of user-experience, where regulatory fragmentation at the application layer may lead to continuing discrepancies in how people based in different parts of the world experience the platforms that they rely on. A person in Brazil might not be able to share an image with their cousin in Germany if that image is flagged and removed in Europe under the DSA; in similar ways that European users in many cases enjoy better privacy protections that people in other countries with more lax privacy rules, the DSA, DMA, and Platform Work Directive could lead Europeans to enjoy better due process standards and other protections than available in other jurisdictions, unless platforms decide to make the European rules their de facto global standard—or simply make their services unavailable in Europe entirely, as some firms unwilling to bear the costs of GDPR compliance have done.

The fear of this kind of fragmentation has led some to call for global standardization and coordination around platform policy (Fay, 2019). This cause has been taken up by established multilateral channels, like the G20 and the Organization for Security and Cooperation in Europe. However, given the global diversity across certain key factors—for instance, labor standards and labor law, or norms around the appropriate bounds of free expression—effective, impactful cooperation remains unlikely. For now, despite some potentially promising developments in the realm of international tax coordination, it is the national-level governments (and regional blocs like the European Union) leading the charge in the realm of platform regulation.

4

Explaining Government Intervention in Content Moderation

The technology companies that operate platforms services are increasingly developing and deploying sophisticated socio-technical bureaucracies for private rule-making and enforcement. Social media platforms are effectively setting important rules around the acceptable boundaries of speech, policing the digital public sphere (Kaye, 2019a). Labor platforms algorithmically micromanage the activity of their workers, setting not just the wages but also the terms and conditions for an emerging planetary labor market (Graham and Ferrari, 2022). Marketplaces for apps, goods, or services decide who can sell on their platform, suspending buyers and sellers at will (Weigel, 2023). Whether we call this private ordering, content moderation, or governance by platforms, these systems and institutions are highly political, and in recent years, have been brushing up against established areas of the state's governance of markets, labor, and speech.

The central aim of this book is to help us understand the conditions under which governments seek to intervene in these practices. If the rise of impactful and unaccountable platform governance is such a threat to state power, as increasingly posited by a host of scholars across disciplines spanning media and communication (Vaidhyanathan, 2018), public policy (Owen, 2015), and economic sociology (Lehdonvirta, 2022), why isn't every government is trying to regulate how platforms govern their users, transactions, or networks? Why do some governments attempt to intervene in platform practices of rulemaking and enforcement, while others seem to sit idly by, or develop policies but fail to implement them?

Surprisingly little research has sought to answer this question. Most work from policy scholars, legal experts, and media and communication academics has sought to explore what happens after the fact: when governments do intervene and decide to regulate technology companies, what does this regulation look like? What are the broader impacts of its enforcement on the digital economy?

The Politics of Platform Regulation: How Governments Shape Online Content Moderation. Robert Gorwa, Oxford University Press. © Oxford University Press 2024. DOI: 10.1093/oso/9780197692851.003.0004

How can this regulation be improved, not only in terms of its effectiveness, but also in terms of ensuring that it does not lead to negative consequences for users?

This work is naturally foundational, but does less to tell us about the political factors and motivations that lead governments to regulate technology companies in certain cases and not others. It also does not fully explore the implications of the various different strategies through which governments are engaging in platform regulation: in some countries governments try to use formalized legal tools, setting binding rules underpinned by the threat of big fines in the case of non-compliance. Other governments may instead choose to take a softer tact, negotiating with companies in an effort to get them to change their rules voluntarily, or negotiating co-regulatory agreements where all parties collaboratively design codes of conduct or other non-binding frameworks. How do we explain the variation in these different strategies, and why are governments able to foster policy change in some cases but not in others?

The crux of my argument is that the decision of a government to intervene and regulate a platform company in a certain way, the strategy that it will choose to do so, and the likelihood of its success are all influenced by two main factors, which I call *political will* and *the power to intervene*.

Using these factors, I conceptualize a demand-and-supply model for technology policy development in the platform realm. First, for a government to decide to break with the status quo, and contest private forms of platform power, rulemaking, or authority, the first necessary condition is that it needs to want to do so. In other words, a polity *needs to have sufficient demand to change the existing rules*. In my view, this demand is not simply static, but rather a vibrant site of political contestation: I begin the chapter by theorizing how a state actor will be positively mobilized towards change when it is motivated to do so by its constituents and important interest groups—by shifts in public opinion, by the salience of certain issues and their perceived importance on the policy agenda— and mobilized against change by lobbying or other strategies that seek to depress the enthusiasm of policymakers and/or their constituents for new rules. The decision to intervene thus is a question of political will: the extent to which these positive demands (to change) outweigh the negative demands (to not stray from the status quo, or to instead dilute the existing status quo even further).

The next step, if sufficient demand for change exists, is that policy entrepreneurs will seek to meet this demand through various strategies. Not all regulation is equal, and as a long line of scholarship in public policy and regulation studies has shown, there is a complex spectrum of potential interventions that different governments can and do use in order to try and steer corporate behavior, ranging from all sorts of 'soft law' to strict, 'command-and-control' regulation closely administered and enforced by the bureaucratic state (Black, 2001; Eberlein et al., 2014). I outline three ideal-type platform

Why Does the State Get Involved? Political Demand   55

regulation strategies as a guiding heuristic to navigate this complex landscape: *contest* (legally binding, enforceable rules), *collaborate* (non-binding, voluntarily enacted rules designed with government input, occasionally featuring binding procedural constraints), and *convince* (using existing channels to raise grievances rather than striving for new rules).

The second section of this chapter argues that variation across these three broad strategies for platform regulation is shaped by a state's *power to intervene*, a concept that has a number of constitutive factors, including a state's market power, its regulatory capacity, the domestic and transnational institutional context, and norms that shape the conduct of policymakers. If a state has sufficient power to intervene, I argue that it can access the full menu of policy options. If, for various reasons, this power is limited (for example, by norms delineating what is widely perceived to be the acceptable level of government intervention in free expression, or commitments made in trade agreements to not increase the regulatory burden on firms in certain industries) then the state is more likely to instead deploy softer, less costly, but also potentially less effective efforts to collaborate with or convince industry.

The final section of the chapter draws out the broader implications of this approach for thinking about the politics of platform regulation. Firstly, I tease out some of the key factors which make this area of policy contestation unique when compared to other industries. I then provide a few examples of how these different variables and factors may be expected to vary across political contexts and regime types, from the high-income democratic countries that are the main focus of this book to a set of important emerging platform markets in the Global Majority world. Finally, I provide a quick breakdown of the high-level takeaways of my framework, and how it might inform how we think about the decisions of other important political stakeholders—such as civil society groups, firms in other industries, and citizens—and whether or not, and how, they will choose to intervene in these political battles.

4.1 Why Does the State Get Involved? Political Demand

In more legally oriented studies of regulation and regulatory politics, the central driver of regulation is frequently conceptualized as *demand* for regulatory change from policymakers, which builds when knowledge of market failures, such as negative externalities, coordination problems, information inadequacies, or other harms arises (Baldwin, Cave, and Lodge, 2012). In other words, regulatory change requires the *preferences*, or *interests*, of policymakers to be aligned with that change. Much scholarship in political behavior has sought to examine the sources of policymaker preferences, creating models based upon assumptions of rational behavior for policymakers, such as the motivating desire to be re-elected, to build influence, and the ability to signal the achievement of their policy goals (Mayhew, 2004; Fujimura, 2016). Other approaches see preferences as more complex, and based not just on individual actor interests but also on wider social factors, such as "shifting pressure from domestic social groups," where "preferences are aggregated through political institutions" (Moravcsik, 1993, p. 481).

These preferences are not only material. While many influential policy scholars can seem like hardcore rationalists, building self-interested and economic models for explaining the political world, even rationalists increasingly allow for the notion that policy actors do not exclusively simply seek to fulfill their material interests. For example, leading regulatory scholars like K. W. Abbott and Snidal (2000) have argued for interest-based explanations of demand that also include normative factors: ideas and values that may be cultural, historical, or 'baked in' to a political system just because things have always been done that way. As actors use rules to "achieve their ends whether they are pursuing interests or values," and because "rules and institutions operate both by changing material incentives and modifying understandings, standards of behavior, and identities" (K. W. Abbott and Snidal, 2000, p. 425), actor interests, and thus the demand for regulatory change, can therefore by affected by ideas (e.g., shifting public opinion, risk perception, and other discourses), values (such as human rights), and cultural norms or roles.

In my conception, following transnational regulation scholarship, demand isn't just a static variable to be quantitatively measured: it's a battleground, an active site of contestation, with a plethora of interest groups seeking to affect the preferences of the 'demanders' for new rules when the stakes are high. By lobbying and deploying various forms of structural business power, firms can seek to dampen the demand of key decisionmakers for change. For example, industry commonly expends lobbying resources to access policymakers and expose them to their arguments (commonly termed 'inside lobbying'; see Klüver, 2013). They can provide financial contributions to re-election campaigns or directly try and get policymakers in their camp; they can also threaten to 'exit' and take investment and jobs out of the country (Mikler, 2018). In certain cases, government rulemakers can even be 'captured' by business interests, so that they either do not demand changes at all, or if they do, demand firm-friendly policies (E. Keller, 2018).

Industry also seeks to affect policymaker demand for change by appealing to their constituents ('outside lobbying'), paying for public relations campaigns and advertising, and orchestrating various efforts to become more popular with the public (Dür and Mateo, 2014; Hanegraaff, Beyers, and De Bruycker,

2016). Civil society groups and transnational advocacy networks also often affect policymaker demand through strategies that include engaging in their own policymaker-focused lobbying, advocacy, and expert consultation, as well as by building public relations campaigns and other 'grassroots' initiatives mobilizing constituents to pressure their representatives to intervene on their behalf (Tarrow, 2005; Keck and Sikkink, 2014). Platform firms, in particular, have countered by leveraging their direct access to consumers (via the devices and apps in their pockets), moving beyond classic outside lobbying techniques an effort to directly activate consumers against proposed regulations (Culpepper and Thelen, 2019).

States can also seek to affect the demand of other states for domestic regulatory change, and lobby or exert diplomatic influence in an effort to depress demand in other countries. This can occur when new regulatory changes are perceived by a powerful government as against its interest: for instance, as part of the State Department's 'Internet Freedom Agenda,' the United States government actively sought to maintain a minimal global regulatory environment for internet-related services in the mid-2000s to early 2010s as part of a broader political, economic, and foreign policy agenda (Powers and Jablonski, 2015). It can also occur if firms are able to successfully lobby their 'home' state to oppose those new foreign regulations on their behalf. For example, as Bradford (2020) describes, American chemicals and manufacturing firms galvanized the US government to lobby hard against complex EU chemicals regulation in the mid-2000s, with the United States exerting economic and diplomatic pressure not only in Brussels, but also via American embassies and consulates in individual member states as part of a broader effort to minimize costs to American firms and maintain US economic competitiveness in the area. This strategy of direct state-led intervention against state demand is not common in the platform domain, but when it happens, it can be very effective: for instance, demand for a French tax on American technology multinationals rose to a crescendo in 2019, but quickly evaporated after Donald Trump's threat that the United States would retaliate with a tariff on major French exports like wine, cheese, and luxury goods if the plan went ahead (D. Lee, 2019).

These broad, macro-level notions of demand are affected by issue-area specific dimensions, which help determine how actors in different jurisdictions may demand different forms of rules affecting the online environment more broadly and the services created and managed by platform companies more specifically. Policymakers may wish to protect their constituents from content that can be harmful to either public safety or public health (e.g., calls to violence, misinformation about vaccinations), or that harms individual rights and freedoms (e.g., hate speech, child abuse imagery), but the norms around the extent to which these different issues are understood to be of national importance vary across communities and across jurisdictions. Different stakeholders engaged in regulatory contestation over the boundaries of acceptable content online might demand more or less government and firm intervention depending on their preferences; for instance, child safety NGOs are likely to demand higher standards than firms or NGOs dedicated to protecting civil liberties and free expression. These various sources of demand will vary significantly across countries and contexts, but will combine to shape government decisionmaking as policymakers decide to eventually lean one way or another and demand change.

In sum, the *political will* of a government actor can be understood as the output of a contested political process, a sort of arena where competing actor interests battle it out, mediated by a host of complex social factors that influence actor behavior, including norms, culture, and tradition.

4.2 How Does the State Get Involved? Intervention Strategies

Having outlined the various factors that might affect a government's demand for changes to a platform governance status quo, it may be helpful to now turn to a hypothetical. Imagine that a technology company called 'X' ('the tech firm') entered medium-sized Country Y five years ago, offering a set of new services that include physical hardware (some kind of internet-enabled personal computing device), and various complementary platforms: a marketplace for developers to build applications for the hardware, a social network aimed primarily at owners of the hardware, and an advertising exchange through which third parties can target advertisements at owners of the hardware on device in a privacy-preserving fashion (using activity data collected during use, as well as location data and other metadata). After flying largely under the public radar for a number of years, a major spike in usership occurs after a global K-Pop celebrity mentions that he is a fan of the product, and the company capitalizes with a well-executed international influencer marketing campaign. The firm's products become more and more popular, especially in emerging markets, but as they become more pervasive, worrying reports begin to pop up in the global media.

The first public relations crisis follows a research report that suggests that the privacy-preserving practices of the firm are actually not as good as the company claims. Even worse, a leaked set of internal emails from a company whistleblower show that the firm appears to have been actively collaborating with shady 'fintech' companies to sell access to its users sensitive personal data so that third parties can target customers predicted to be particularly vulnerable with get-rich-quick crypto and NFT scams. Other issues with the tech firm's business practices steadily emerge: the marketplace for apps hasn't just steadily increased the fees placed on developers to extortionate levels, but a lawsuit by a group of small software enterprises alleges that the firm has been copying the source code of third-party apps (submitted to the firm by developers as part of the marketplace's mandatory community guidelines review process) to create their own alternatives that they can bundle with new hardware releases. Furthermore, the social network operated by the company has lax moderation practices, and has incorporated certain design elements that powerful intellectual property holders in the creative industries and fashion worlds argue facilitate the distribution and resale of counterfeit or otherwise copyright-infringing goods.

Over time, public attention paid to the tech firm's products grows. Academics begin to study its various platforms, its governance issues, and propose new regulatory models involving various aspects of competition policy, data protection law, and online content regulation. A transnational array of rightsholders, consumer protection groups, and certain industry competitors start agitating for regulation to rein in the tech firm's business practices. The company responds by ratcheting up its lobbying expenditures—exponentially growing its policy staff in international capitals, while also funding think-tanks, consultancies, and academic institutions around the world to produce research indicating the positive economic and social impacts of its products. Nevertheless, demand for regulation in Country Y, its biggest market, seems to be building to a level where it can no longer be tamped down by the traditional corporate influence playbook.

In a moment where there are adequately high levels of demand pressuring a government actor for change (whether this actor be a municipal, state-level, or federal government), what are the next steps? What are the options available for government intervention to regulate this company and its various platforms?

The way that governments try and meet the demand for change when demand levels are high, I argue, can be summarized as generally fitting within one of three overarching categories. First, *contest*: Country Y could look to deploy domestic regulation of various forms, using binding legal tools, penalties, and enforcement mechanisms (using the sovereign authority of the state to control access to a market and citizenry, contesting company authority by bringing public authority to bear). Second, *collaborate*: the country could seek to apply informal, nonbinding forms of regulation or co-regulation that involve working with companies in an effort that they will commit to new rules and institutional processes that improve their behavior. Finally, the state could seek to *convince*: a relatively weak strategy which does not seek to legally or institutionally 'tie the hands' of platform companies, but instead seeks to convince them (through either carrots or sticks) to make changes to their rules themselves, apply their rules in specific cases, or change their processes of enforcement. Policymakers from Country

Y could secretly meet with firm X's executives, quietly exert pressure through regulatory agencies and law enforcement to try and get the firm to intervene in certain cases, and use the platform's established complaints channels to levy their concerns around specific practices.

4.2.1 CONTESTING

An empirical analysis of the types of platform regulation being proposed by actual governments demonstrates a major substantive difference in the type of regulatory frameworks that government actors have deployed to shape platform rulemaking: whether they do so via a formal, or informal mechanisms. Do states seek to contest platform rulemaking by instituting formal legal frameworks with binding commitments (that have legal repercussions, and enforcement)? Or do they seek to negotiate changes via the public-private negotiation of voluntary commitments?

There are trade-offs between the two approaches. There is much debate and discussion among policy and regulation scholars as to the efficacy (or lack thereof) of non-binding voluntary approaches in actually achieving positive outcomes when it comes to high-stakes issue areas like labor rights or environmental protection (Malhotra, Monin, and Tomz, 2019), but it is generally assumed that state-led binding regulation, overseen by capable, well-staffed, and well-resourced regulators, is the gold standard for getting companies to follow rules that may be in the public interest but not directly beneficial for revenues and the corporate bottom line.

Firms are adversarial actors working in a political system, seeking to minimize their regulatory burden and extract the greatest amount of profit possible (Renckens, 2020); there is a common assumption that firms need to have their hands tied with robust regulation to keep them from 'defecting' and shirking from change that is being demanded. This coercive regulation exists on a spectrum, from the archetype of 'command-and-control' regulation that is the classic, highly burdensome form of regulation with significant degrees of government involvement, administration, and oversight, to the much softer, 'market-making' regulation—regulation that works more through incentives and delegates more to the private sector—that has come to prominence since the neoliberal revolution in the 1970s and 1980s (Buch-Hansen and Wigger, 2010). Either way, this type of strategy to regulate a technology company has two key characteristics: it (1) features commitments that are underpinned by punitive systems of sanction and enforcement (not just 'naming and shaming,' but fines, penalties, and other measures); and (2) the rules that are being administered are developed primarily by a public body, not by industry, although industry and other stakeholders may be expected to provide input during the policymaking process.

Here, when a government contests platform rulemaking it is in effect seeking to 'take back control' of some part of that rulemaking, pushing back against the unfettered ability of platforms to moderate content or to set other policies by re-applying a form of sovereign power. This contestation can take various institutional forms, and be promulgated at various levels of government. For example, executive branches that are able to issue executive orders (that have binding weight) can do so as a form of contestation to try and meet demand for new rules. Legislative branches that can pass laws can apply various forms of market or product regulation, such as data protection policies, competition regulation, online content and intermediary liability rules relating to copyright or harmful content, consumer safety law, cybersecurity law, and other regulations that affect the processes of platform governance. Regulators and other substate entities that have the authority to issue binding judgments can get involved too: their investigations can lead to consent decrees or decisions that come with sanctions and potential negative consequences for a failure to comply.

Contested platform regulation is expected to have the highest potential payoff in terms of being able to deliver demanded change. That said, it also comes with costs: it can be expensive for the public (requiring significant resources to implement and enforce on behalf of government) and for industry (compliance costs might prompt firms to change their behavior in a jurisdiction or even exit entirely if they are deemed too high). It also can drain political capital, especially if the government actor in question needs to form coalitions around its proposals, and if the regulation is unpopular or deemed controversial by the public.

4.2.2 COLLABORATING

While some forms of policy change are developed and implemented by government, possibly with some sort of stakeholder consultation or influence (e.g., lobbying), others are developed more closely in partnership between government and industry or other stakeholders. These types of policies are less formal in that they are not codified in law, or only partially codified in law, and run the gamut of a wide range of approaches that have been called 'regulatory governance' (Levi-Faur, 2010) or 'regulatory standards-setting' (K. W. Abbott and Snidal, 2009b). On the more formalized end of the spectrum, co-regulation has long been a tool through which domestic governments, especially in Europe, have sought to shape standards for the internet industry. Marsden (2011, p. 46) has argued that co-regulation—understood broadly as a "range of different regulatory phenomena, which have in common the fact that the regulatory regime is made up of a complex interaction of general legislation and a self-regulatory body"—has been a defining part of the internet regulation approach taken by the European Union and by EU member states since at least 2005. To minimize regulatory burdens and the cost of oversight, and to promote flexibility, governments can delegate certain compliance, oversight, and reporting functions to self-regulatory bodies that will need to be set up by industry—for example, as in the case of the German Association for Voluntary Self-Regulation of Digital Media Service Providers (*FSM*), which was created by industry to comply with co-regulatory rules established under the 2002 Interstate Treaty on the Protection of Minors (Schulz and Held, 2004).

Collaborative forms of governance are often less formalized than this, involving codes of conduct that are deliberated and agreed upon by a mix of industry, firm, and potentially civil society stakeholders, and then implemented by industry voluntarily. These types of declarations and agreements may happen domestically, like in the case of the code of conduct for online hate speech developed by the German Ministry of Justice and Consumer Protection in 2015, setting the stage for the ensuing Network Enforcement Act (see Chapter 5). It may also occur internationally, as in the case of the Christchurch Call to counter violent extremism (see Chapter 6). These collaborative initiatives may be largely negotiated by firms in partnership with governments, or they might be more properly referred to as 'multistakeholder' (Raymond and DeNardis, 2015).

There are two further elements of a collaborative strategy to obtaining change in platform regulation. Firstly, this type of policy initiative does not feature binding sanctions; firms can choose to implement it or not, and cannot be formally penalized for not doing so. That said, these initiatives can be created 'in the shadow of hierarchy' (Héritier and Lehmkuhl, 2008), and underpinned by some sort of threat of future coercion from government. Despite these dynamics, firms generally have some choice in this matter, and can disengage from the collaborative regulatory process, refuse to implement its requirements, or pretend to implement commitments. Secondly, these types of rules are not created only by government actors, but by mix of actor types, with more direct industry input than an ordinary legislative process.

There are various pros and cons to a collaborative approach. In the past few decades, these sorts of informal techniques have become more popular with policymakers in many high-income and highly industrialized countries in a range of policy areas, including in online content regulation relating to platforms (Gorwa, 2019a; Douek, 2020b). On one hand, collaborative forms of regulation seem to incur little in terms of costs for policymakers: they require fewer regulatory resources and competencies on behalf of government, both in terms of implementation (in some cases, a few meetings with industry may be enough to hash out something like a code of conduct) and enforcement (as firms will be in charge of reporting results, there usually is no regulatory body that needs to be created or tasked with expensive forms of monitoring and oversight). They also are less costly in terms of political capital; as these

How Does the State Get Involved? Intervention Strategies   63

types of collaborative governance efforts have a lower profile than new laws do, they can be expected to generate less blow-back from other stakeholders and from constituents. In an expansive study of the regulation of intellectual property rights and counterfeit goods on the internet, Tusikov (2016) argues that certain economically incentivized issue groups (such as copyright holders) have sought to use informal agreements and mechanisms to privately impose content restrictions that may be widely opposed by the public when included in legislation. It is also more difficult to oppose these efforts, as industry can hardly marshal major opposition to them via lobbying or by organizing 'consumer facing' campaigns that seek to pressure policymakers against a policy if they can be said to be voluntary participants in those efforts. Opposition parties, civil society groups, or other political actors that wish to oppose collaborative forms of policy change, especially on grounds of government overreach, are likely to be met by arguments that the potential threat (for example, to free expression) of the policy is limited due to its voluntary, non-binding nature.

Collaborative platform regulation is also not always available to all actors. Governments that have relatively low levels of international legitimacy due to frequent human rights violations or the suppression of the domestic media environment can be expected to find platforms less likely to cooperate with their collaborative initiatives. If platform companies care about their international reputation, engaging in co-regulatory efforts with certain governments could hurt their brand at home and in other human-rights minded international markets.

In this sense, collaborative platform regulation can theoretically provide an attractive strategy for changing the behavior of technology companies, especially if it arises in a context where policymakers are interested in less costly ways to at least partially meet demand for regulatory change. However, when demand for change is high, collaborative strategies may be less appealing, given their major downside: their overall lack of 'teeth' and enforcement power. The common critique of these forms of regulation, across policy issue areas, is that they are often ineffective, especially when there are strongly conflicting public and private interests on an issue (Saurwein, 2011).

This seems to be especially true in highly opaque digital policy domains, where much goes on 'under the hood' and is simply not easily accessible to even the best-staffed regulatory agencies. If a technology company says that they are complying with their commitments made under a code of conduct or voluntary agreement, how are policymakers supposed to verify this? In some domains, relating to tech manufacturing for instance, hardware-producing platform firms can agree voluntarily to improve working conditions and environmental protections in their supply chain, and it may be difficult but theoretically feasible for auditors to try and verify their claims (by visiting suppliers, factories, and doing other sorts of forensic investigation). When it comes to certain aspects of platform rulemaking and enforcement that are happening within the internet application layer, the outcomes are often far more diffuse and difficult to verify.

Collaborative regulatory approaches may also put firms in an advantageous position where, after having declared various commitments, those commitments can simply be walked back or never effectively implemented when it is convenient. A shrewd industry actor that does not wish to comply can participate in a collaborative governance effort, and the once it becomes clear that the firm will not effectively implement the demanded changes, the company has managed to buy time—delaying a policy process, perhaps decreasing public demand for change to an extent, and keeping the costs of regulatory compliance low.

4.2.3 CONVINCING

In addition to these two strategies for pursuing change in platform governance, there is a third strategy. In this third scenario, governments do not fundamentally oppose the systems of private rulemaking created by the technology companies operating in their jurisdictions, nor do they exert significant political capital or power resources to shape those systems. Policymakers are relatively content with the status quo—or, as will be discussed below—do not have sufficient power to pursue contested or collaborative forms of platform regulation.

While governments may seek to obtain certain governance outcomes vis-à-vis platforms, in this strategy, they do so within the established practices of corporate-government engagement—for example, by sending takedown requests for certain pieces of content, or requests for user data, to local firm representatives (Schwemer, 2019). Efforts to convince other governance stakeholders thus can take the form of either 'carrots' or 'sticks.' A government could seek to curry favor with a company, cultivating relationships with its executives or policy staff, trying to persuade the firm that it should make certain changes to its rules or enforcement given the importance of that country's market and userbase to the company. Nationally, a government may also exert various levers of pressure against the firm to takedown pages, groups, or individual pieces of content (Kaye, 2019b), 'jawboning' companies through the use of threats of future sanctions or punishment targeted at individual employees (Bambauer, 2015). Governments might try and convince firms—through backroom pressure, through their networks inside the companies in question—to convince them to set up local points of contact, such as 'trusted flaggers' that can serve as specialized hotlines for government complaints without enshrining those changes formally in legislation or collaboratively developed codes of practice.

This kind of state influence is a constant, ongoing, and major aspect of how governments seek to shape platform behavior (Bloch-Wehba, 2019). From the rumors that Israeli Prime Minister Benjamin Netanyahu would personally call Mark Zuckerberg when he wanted Facebook to change how it moderated content relating to the Palestinian Occupation (York, 2021) to reports that the Bharatiya Janata Party (BJP), which has ruled India since 2014, was able to cultivate a network of policy employees working at Facebook India to help it pursue its preferences (Perrigo, 2020), examples abound. As a platform governance strategy, it often is pursued alongside the previous two strategies described above. But it may also form a distinct response to a particular regulatory episode. Why is this strategy pursued by government if it is not accompanied by broader efforts to fundamentally change how technology companies rule their services?

Convincing is the lowest-cost strategy for pursuing change in platform governance available to government actors. It has little in terms of regulatory implementation costs (given the lack of concrete policy being developed, implemented, or enforced) and it often occurs in the shadows, with few public-facing elements that could result in costs to political capital domestically or blowback from trading partners internationally. It also is cheap in terms of potential economic repercussions: without binding sanctions, firm exit due to unacceptable regulatory costs is highly unlikely. It can be deployed quickly to deal with a crisis, and does not require long periods of policy negotiation. However, it is also likely to be the least effective strategy of the three discussed here. Other than generally keeping a government happy, a company has no concrete commitments to legally implement. It seems to work best in targeted cases—a powerful policymaker wishes to have a specific product, page, or piece of content removed—as measuring its effects in more systematically complex cases would be difficult for the government. It might be pursued for demand-side reasons: the levels of demand for change are relatively low, perhaps due to low issue salience or other factors. It may also be pursued for supply-side reasons, as strategy of last resort when a government is unable to successfully deploy a contested or collaborative strategy for platform regulation.

Table 4.1 **Summary: key features of three government platform regulation strategies.**

	Convince	*Collaborate*	*Contest*
Supplier of Rules	Firm	Multistakeholder	State
Type of Rules	Voluntary	Voluntary	Binding
Government Cost	Lowest	Low	High
Efficacy Potential	Low	Medium	High

4.3 When Can the State Get Involved? The Power to Intervene

Having outlined the reasons why demand for regulating technology companies may build to a certain level, and some of the platform regulation strategies that governments could deploy to meet that demand, the final step is to explore the conditions which shape the state's ability to meaningfully *supply* those changes. It evidently is not simply enough for there to be strong domestic demand for new rules within a polity: many of today's platform firms are some of the most valuable multinationals to exist, purportedly as powerful as certain countries (Khanna and Francis, 2023). Commentators frequently suggest that Big Tech can successfully resist regulatory efforts if it wishes. But smaller firms headquartered outside of a country's direct jurisdiction could also pose challenges for some countries aiming to shape said firm's behavior (Farrell, 2006). In other words, demand for changing the regulatory status quo is a necessary, but alone insufficient condition for governments to obtain change in rules that would affect platform companies; they must also have the *power to intervene* and supply those demanded changes. This is a complex area which pertains to decades of political science and public policy scholarship. Nevertheless, it is worth going into some depth to examine the three factors which I consider to be particularly important for a political actor's power to intervene: regulatory capacity, the institutional context, and norms.

4.3.1 REGULATORY CAPACITY

When can a government be said to be capable of going toe-to-toe with powerful companies? How does one conceptualize government power in the global economy, especially when it comes to rule-setting in internationally exposed markets? In international political economy, especially among scholars who are of a more rationalist and realist persuasion, the classic explanation of supply is driven by notions of state capacity and power, with market size usually deployed as a proxy (Drezner, 2008). The logic is that large and powerful economies are likely to have more regulators, resources, and expertise, and therefore, a better ability to supply new regulations that meet their preferences. Furthermore, big markets matter more than small markets for the firms that might lose access to those markets, so they are more likely to take government regulations seriously in those jurisdictions (Newman and Bach, 2004). In these power-driven theories of regulatory change, the countries with the largest economies are able to intervene in globalized markets as they wish.

Nevertheless, other, more institutionally minded scholars have sought for at least a partial rebuttal of this power-centric argument, arguing that shaping firm behavior is inherently difficult, even for the most powerful actors. Even in a 'traditional' or conventional regulatory relationship where a state actor demands and supplies new rules to bind a corporate target, the firm's managers and internal structures will at the end of the day be required to implement those rules (K. W. Abbott and Snidal, 2009a). More complex 'decentered' or 'polycentric' regulatory regimes can additionally involve a host of regulatory intermediaries, such as third parties involved in the monitoring, implementation, or enforcement, of new rules, as well as other actors (Black, 2008; K. W. Abbott, Levi-Faur, and Snidal, 2017). For this reason, designing thoughtful and effective regulation for private actors—and then being able to meaningfully enforce that regulation or sanction non-compliance—requires significant regulatory capacities (Saurwein, 2011; Bradford, 2012). Because of this distribution of roles and competencies, "the ability to define, defend, monitor, and enforce a particular rule-set" is also essential for government actors seeking to make the kinds of credible threats needed for firms to take domestic regulation seriously (Bach and Newman, 2010; Newman, 2017, pp. 82–83).

Regulatory capacity is especially important in potentially complex technology policy domains: as Saurwein (2011) puts it, regulatory capacity has a major impact on the ability of an actor to intervene decisively and set rules for the targets of regulation on a policy issue, with the availability of adequate means to adopt and enforce statutory regulation determining whether a policy actor can actually make credible commitments and threats. In the domestic context, this involves power balances and rulemaking configurations—does the rulemaking branch of government have the ability to almost unilaterally create new rules, either due to its authoritarian grip on the executive or due to a commanding electoral majority, or does it need to make difficult coalitions across parties to pass new legislation? These domestic factors all matter for an actor's power to intervene when there is demand for policy change, and while the notion of the ability to supply rules is often correlated with market power and state size, there are exceptions—smaller states with strong regulatory capacities and highly competent regulatory agencies exist as well.

4.3.2 INSTITUTIONAL CONSTRAINTS

The power to intervene is also shaped by domestic and transnational institutions and the constraints they impose upon rulemakers. Although most rationalist scholarship assumes that the status quo is malleable, and can be changed whenever demand from powerful actors is sufficiently high (Drezner, 2008), on the other hand, scholars more aligned with historical institutionalism see institutions as more durable and less malleable than rationalists (Jupille, Mattli, and Snidal, 2017). Going beyond a singular focus on power and interests, historical institutionalists emphasize the importance of regulative, normative, and even cognitive structures, noting that political life is structured not only by "formal and formal rules, monitoring and enforcement mechanisms, [but also] systems of meaning that define the context within which individuals, corporations, [...], nation-states, and other organizations operate and interact with each other" (Campbell, 2004, p. 1). Institutionally oriented scholars see institutional outcomes as reflective of hard-fought political battles and processes of political contestation, leading to their interpretation that institutions are deeply embedded into political systems: as Pierson (2000, p. 262) puts it, "the key features of political life—public policies and (especially) formal institutions— are change resistant [...]. Both are generally designed to be difficult to overturn." The corollary is that decisions made about certain institutional configurations can have potentially significant and possibly unforeseen effects on the institutional 'path' and the types of choices that are available at future political junctures (Thelen and Steinmo, 1992).

For our purposes, a number of institutional dimensions are especially important. Domestically, pre-existing institutional structures shape the configuration of regulatory agencies and government bodies that are potentially equipped to handle issues of online content that straddle media, telecommunications, and internet policy domains. There are also variations in the process of making, implementing, and enforcing policy, including the various 'veto points' "where the mobilization of opposition can thwart policy innovation" or regulatory change (Thelen and Steinmo, 1992, p. 7). Transnationally, they include broader relationships of complex interdependence characteristic of twenty-first century global politics, which include a host of economic, diplomatic, and political linkages with other states (Farrell and Newman, 2014, 2016).

These institutional interdependencies might include formal institutional agreements scoping the range of policy change available—for instance, commitments made as part of a regional bloc, such as European requirements that member state legislation comply with existing European legal frameworks, or concessions made in a trade agreement that a country will not change its (intermediary liability or other) rules (Krishnamurthy and Fjeld, 2020). Other relevant institutional characteristics from the literature include informal, individual-level relationships of influence, for example between like-minded policy officials engaged in transnational regulatory networks (Slaughter, 2004; Verdier, 2009), or state-led mechanisms of international economic coercion via threats and sanctions imposed vis-à-vis individuals, firms, or governments

(Farrell and Newman, 2019b). All of these potentially important factors may conceivably have an impact and potential constraint on a government's power to intervene in the internationally interlinked platform economy.

4.3.3 NORMATIVE LANDSCAPE

Historical institutionalist lenses lend themselves well to complex patterns of political change, including those potentially not just explained by actor agency and power during a specific period, but also more intangible, contingent factors like identity, beliefs, and norms. Systems of meaning, often summarized as 'ideas,' are especially important to historical institutionalists (Weir, 1992; Majone, 1998). Historical institutionalist scholars are interested in the political role and evolution of 'macro-level' ideational structures (like class, or capitalism), and are also especially interested in the ways in which the preferences of actors are themselves shaped by various norms or ideas (Fioretos, 2011). As Thelen and Steinmo (1992, p. 8, emphasis in the original) note, in contrast to rationalist approaches, historical institutionalists assume that "not just the *strategies* but also the *goals* actors pursue are shaped by the institutional context." In other words, norms, ideas about appropriate behavior, and pre-existing world views, themselves shaped by macro-level institutions and individual historical and cultural contexts, can be expected to influence the preferences and behavior of actors, and to shape their ability and desire to supply certain types of policy change. History, culture, and overarching value-based frameworks about how regulation should work—and what the appropriate strategies for regulating technology, the media, and communications are—vary significantly across jurisdictions and also can impact the type of platform regulation that is pursued in various contexts.

The challenge for empirical analyses in this area is that these important factors are difficult to unpack and operationalize without deep historical work and thick, single-case study analyses that could command monographs of their own. Evidently, following Thelen and other leading institutionalist scholars, norms affect the demand for change (by structuring the macro-level preferences of policymakers and their constituents) as well as its supply. On the supply side, one way to conceive of this factor is through employing some features of the concept of a 'logic of appropriateness' (March and Olsen, 2011), which has been shown to be important in regulatory politics given the oft well-defined roles and identities of certain governmental actors, especially regulators, civil servants, and judges (Eberlein and Radaelli, 2010). As actors have an understanding of what their acceptable scope of action is, in this supply-side notion of normative constraints, they may be unwilling to deliver on certain demanded forms of regulatory change, even if they may be demanded by policymakers or other powerful constituent groups. Norms can thus provide a boundary delimiting the lines of acceptable intervention, and even become embedded within difficult to change institutional structures like state constitutions.

For governmental actors, normative legitimacy is also an important conditioning factor that can in certain cases shape their ability to intervene. While much global governance scholarship has focused on the legitimacy of private actors (Zürn, 2004; Avant, Finnemore, and Sell, 2010), and research focusing on technology policy has scrutinized the prospective democratic legitimacy gaps of certain forms of industry-led voluntary governance (Haggart and Iglesias Keller, 2021), the sociological legitimacy of government actors also can be important in this domain. If a certain government is perceived by important political actors as undemocratic, with poor respect for international human rights norms and free expression, certain reputation-minded industry actors may be less willing to cooperate with them. Low-legitimacy governments seeking to shape private platform governance with contested approaches are more likely to see international firms exit, rather than comply. Low-legitimacy governments are also less likely to be able to get international firms to work with them to develop codes of conduct or other forms of collaborative approaches. As alluded to above, no reputation-minded social media platform firm wishes to face the negative media backlash that news of a collaborative regulation approach it developed in partnership with an authoritarian regime seeking to control the public sphere could bring, unless the prospective economic gains clearly make it worth it.

4.4 Explaining Government Intervention in Platform Governance

Having outlined the core components of this book's theoretical framework— political will, the power to intervene, and three platform governance strategies— it is time to put all of these elements together. Why does a government actor try and intervene in platform governance in some cases but not others? When it does seek to intervene, and contest, collaborate, or convince?

These questions can be best explored by looking at the balance of political will and the power to intervene and supply change during a specific regulatory episode. If there is insufficient or no demand for change, then I expect little to happen: actors might seek limited outcomes via persuasive strategies. In situations where a government actor has adequate levels of political demand leading it to pursue change, outcomes will depend on the level of power resources it can use to intervene, as well as its power to intervene. If both demand and supply are unconstrained, the actor should be free to pursue a strategy of its choosing, with the likelihood of certain strategies being affected by the level of demand for change, as well as the institutional characteristics and normative logics operating in the particular context.

In cases where there is demand for change, but certain limitations on the power to intervene, things get more interesting. Governments may be limited from contested approaches due to a lack of regulatory capacity, and a lack of political will required to seek to deploy costly binding rules. If a government faces significant institutional constraints that would limit its ability to develop and deploy a contested strategy (for example, a minority government and an inability to easily pass new binding rules without opposition parties, or transnational pacts like trade deals that commit it to only set certain types of regulatory change), collaborative approaches are more likely. Similarly, certain governments may face normative constraints on taking a contested approach when it comes to certain platform sectors, due to normative logics in that national context about the appropriateness of government intervention on some issues, making collaborative arrangements more likely. However, broader normative considerations might also limit the ability of certain governments to pursue collaborative regulation. For this reason, authoritarian governments may be limited to strategies designed either to convince or contest, although a lack of regulatory capacity can prevent them from successfully being able to execute their strategy and obtain the changes that they wish in platform business practices. Instead, they are the likeliest to resort to the crudest strategies of persuasion, such as internet shutdowns, domain blocking of certain services, and measures seeking to retaliate against company employees in country.

While this may seem simple, there are many moving parts here that can result in various permutations. As mentioned throughout this chapter, demand is a site of political contestation: if government rulemakers demand new rules— where demand is understood as the sum of domestic actor motivations, and the preferences of constituents mobilized by civil society groups—it can be tamped down by interest group lobbying or by influence or coercion from other governments (for instance, the 'home states' of technology companies, which may get involved when seeking to protect their national champions). Similarly, the decision to pursue certain strategies will be informed by a host of particular structural, context-dependent factors—norms, the makeup of a policymaking system, regulatory cultures—as well as more flexible, case-dependent factors like the relative distribution of power between a firm and a government. These are political relationships that are almost infinitely complex, and will require careful analysis of regulatory episodes to unpack. Nevertheless, this approach provides a first step towards a vocabulary for understanding the politics driving regulatory change in the platform economy.

4.5 Testing the Framework

This is a general purpose framework, intended to be sufficiently broad to capture a wide range of contexts. The terms outlined here are intentionally flexible, allowing them to be applied in many different contexts. Rather than building a toolbox designed just to address only the largest 'Big Tech' firms in certain contexts, I developed this model to speak to a wide array of prospective policy targets (a range of industry actors with different business models, national headquarters, and sizes). It can also apply to a wide range of governmental actors at the municipal, state, or federal level across a wide set of national contexts and political regime types.

A central argument of this book is that one must look closely at the policy actors involved in regulating technology companies, and the political relations in the specific polity that is in question. The conceptual framework presented here suggests that the interplay of a political actor's demand for new rules, and a political actor's ability to supply those rules, will come together to shape a government's decision to contest, collaborate, or convince when pursuing changes in online content moderation. This conceptual framework offers a lens through which to analyze different modes of contestation around key regulatory episodes, helping us understand why—and how—certain important policy initiatives seeking to affect the behavior of technology companies are developed.

The corollary of this model is that it introduces a number of political factors to consider for the growing and interdisciplinary literature on technology policy and platform governance. When evaluating the development of a new regulatory framework, it suggests that one should not simply look at the outcome of policies, and the apparent interests of key leaders, but also at broader institutional, political, and normative factors. For example, does a government have an adequate grip on the legislative process (e.g., holding a strong parliamentary majority, and robust-enough coalition in democratic systems, or sufficient executive decisionmaking power in hybrid or authoritarian contexts) to implement new rules and meet demand for change? Or, in cases where a government faces local or transnational institutional constraints on its ability to make rules, how do the power resources to overcome those constraints manifest themselves?

The remainder of the book will apply this model in detail through cases of policy development around the world.

4.5.1 METHODS AND CASE SELECTION

There has been little focused empirical work that looks at the development of platform regulation in detail. It is a vast and complex area, potentially spanning policy fields like telecommunications and media law, competition policy, data protection regulation, intermediary liability, industrial policy, labor relations, and even transportation and housing policy, as we saw in Chapter 3. Given the huge range of potentially relevant technology companies and variety of platform business models, as well as the vast array of national contexts and constantly growing number of conflicts between governments and platform firms that could be worth looking into, how should one come up with a research design to explore this area with some more rigor?

In qualitative political science research driven by case studies, two classic techniques involve looking at either a diverse set of cases ('most different' examples, which seek to highlight the largest amount of variation for a theoretical framework to grapple with) or a more focused set of cases, seeking to provide a narrower, less generalizable 'probability probe' for an argument (Seawright and Gerring, 2008). In this chapter, I have advanced a general argument about government actors intervening in the process of firm-led platform governance, with the intention that this argument could apply to a wide range of platform firms in different policy contexts (the regulation of platform labor, battles between accommodation platforms and certain municipal governments, competition investigations of major online marketplaces). But the framework cannot be said to have this kind of general purpose explanatory power if it cannot even be helpful in a single, more bounded platform policy domain.

For this reason, the remainder of the book will test this theory framework on cases that pertain to online content moderation and online speech governance in the context of politically 'harmful' content. New regulatory efforts have set out mandatory transparency and due process regimes for companies, creating the legal frameworks that explicitly require firms to notify users of changes to community guidelines and provide possibilities for appeal. Governments have sought to create limits on what types of rules companies are able to implement, and shaped firm trust and safety efforts in various ways. These are the spaces where we currently see the most active political battles around private rulemaking online.

In the following chapters, I explore three particularly notable cases. First, I examine Germany's 'world first' effort to govern content moderation through the development of the Network Enforcement Act (NetzDG, 2017), and the less widely known informal code of conduct that preceded it. I then turn to one of the highest profile forms of collaborative platform governance developed in recent years, the Christchurch Call to Action to Eliminate Terrorist and Violent Extremist Content Online (2019), spearheaded by New Zealand following the Christchurch shooting, in a marked contrast to the regulatory approach developed by neighboring Australia in response to the same event. Finally,

I look at the unlikely development of online content focused regulation in the United States (2021–2023), where enterprising state legislators have sought to work around gridlock at the federal level to try and pass their own sweeping rules, with potentially vast implications for online content moderation in the global context.

Part Two

CASE STUDIES

5

'What Is Illegal Offline, Should Be Illegal Online'

The Development of the German NetzDG

On the 1st of January 2018, the 'Network Enforcement Act' (*Netzwerkdurch-setzungsgesetz*, commonly called 'NetzDG' for short) officially went into effect in Germany. The law, which legally enshrined a number of new obligations for the largest platforms for user-generated content, became the first regulation in the world to directly proscribe how platforms moderated harmful material. It involved a number of new rules, establishing background standards for how firms set up their complaints handling procedures, requiring a designated contact point through which the authorities could channel specific inquiries and complaints, and for the first time, mandating a level of transparency reporting around the largest platforms' trust and safety operations. At the core of the NetzDG was an obligation that companies remove content that was "manifestly illegal" under a set of provisions in the German Criminal Code within 24 hours of it being notified. These new obligations were underpinned by an enforcement mechanism that threatened fines of up to 50 million Euros in the case of multiple, systemic violations.

The NetzDG immediately became controversial and politicized, with industry and civil society voicing their concerns about the effects on freedom of expression and the possibility that the financial sanctions would incentivize companies to over-remove reported content (Schulz, 2018; Tworek, 2019). For commentators, the law highlighted a clash between not only the German and American normative and legal standards around free expression, but also questions about the ability of individual jurisdictions to assert their authority against the global private standards being enacted by multinational platform companies (Claussen, 2018; Echikson and Knodt, 2018). For supporters of the law, the NetzDG was a big victory, forcing companies to significantly improve their complaints handling mechanisms and increase the number of people that

---

The Politics of Platform Regulation: How Governments Shape Online Content Moderation. Robert Gorwa,
Oxford University Press. © Oxford University Press 2024. DOI: 10.1093/oso/9780197692851.003.0005

they employed (either directly or through third-party contractors) as content moderators in Germany, thus demonstrating the primacy of German law over unaccountable systems of private rulemaking (He, 2020).

An underappreciated aspect of the NetzDG is that the policy process that eventually led to it actually began in 2015, through a collaborative platform regulation initiative organized by the German Ministry of Justice and Consumer Protection in partnership with Facebook. Why did this initial strategy emerge, and then why, less than two years later, did Germany instead seek to contest private platform authority and impose its sovereignty over platform companies by seeking to layer a distinct, national rules-focused implementation infrastructure on top of the existing T&S practices of firms?

5.1 The Task Force, 2015–2017

In the summer of 2015, in the midst of a major influx of refugees displaced in the Syrian conflict, Germany, economically and politically the most powerful state in the European Union, decided to break with the established EU resettlement approach. The federal government announced that they would accept asylum claims from Syrians even if their port of entry into Europe was another country (Dernbach, 2015; Hinger, 2016), a policy move that was morally laudable but politically controversial, catalyzing far-right extremist groups opposing the re-settlement of refugees in Germany (Dostal, 2015). The culmination was a series of anti-refugee rallies and physical assaults upon immigrants. The number of reported criminal offenses targeting refugee re-settlement facilities would skyrocket from about twenty in 2012 to several hundred in 2015 (Gathmann, 2015), prompting a heated national conversation on immigration, racism, and multiculturalism.

Nevertheless, in the eastern state of Saxon-Anhalt, where she had been booed and harassed by right-wing protesters, Chancellor Angela Merkel infamously quipped that despite the challenges, 'we can do it' (*wir schaffen das*)—that Germany was a strong country, had accommodated those fleeing war and persecution in large numbers before, and could do it again. But as the humanitarian crisis unfolded, so did the apparent visibility of far-right extremism and Islamophobia on many social networks. Major figures in German politics, including Merkel herself, were being targeted by online harassment and threats, and commentaries in the country's largest newspapers had begun to point the finger at the content standards on Facebook and Twitter. For example, an emblematic article published in *Der Spiegel*, the weekly news magazine with the largest such circulation in Germany, posed the question of "Why Facebook doesn't delete hate," bringing up multiple anecdotal instances of xenophobic public comments left on the Facebook pages of German news outlets and not being removed despite being flagged by users (Reinbold, 2015). The article noted that Facebook was extremely opaque about its content moderation processes—what the exact rules against racist content were, how those rules were enforced, and by whom—arguing that the company appeared to conduct moderation via a network of contractors in Dublin, India, and the United States, but apparently had no actual content moderators in Germany itself (Reinbold, 2015).

The result was that dissatisfaction with platform regulation status quo began to build among key German decisionmakers.[1] The most important of these was the Social Democratic party's (SPD) Heiko Maas, who became the Minister of Justice and Consumer Protection in a Christian Democrat (CDU) led coalition government formed after the 2013 election. Maas was a vocal critic of right-wing extremism and anti-refugee sentiment, speaking out on numerous occasions against both, and an active Twitter and Facebook user (Vasagar, 2014). In the summer of 2015, he wrote a letter to Richard Allan, Facebook's head of public policy for Europe, in which he voiced his displeasure with how the company had been handling complaints around illegal or harmful speech, including slurs directed towards refugees and immigrants. Maas noted that "Facebook users are, in particular, complaining increasingly that your company is not effectively stopping racist 'posts' and comments despite their pointing out concrete examples" (Kirschbaum, 2015). The language of Maas's letter was the public articulation of what some digitally oriented policymakers had been arguing for several years: that the status quo for how major platforms conducted content moderation had shifted away from an 'imperfect but good enough' situation and towards one where the rules were becoming wholly unacceptable (von Notz, 2015).

5.1.1 NEGOTIATING (VOLUNTARY) COMMITMENTS

On the 14th of September 2015, Maas met with Allan, and at a short press conference that followed, announced that the two had agreed to begin working on a collaborative and voluntary regulatory initiative which would address Facebook's rulemaking and enforcement, with a focus on illegal online hate speech in the German context.[2] Through this 'Task Force against Illegal Online Hate Speech,' Maas promised to engage both Facebook and civil society stakeholders in order to produce "concrete measures" for the companies to implement by the end of the year. In an interview that was published a few days later by the *Jüdische Allgemeine*, a newspaper serving the German-Jewish community, Maas delivered a simple message that would become the catch-phrase of the government's efforts to regulate social networks. As he vowed to fight against online anti-Semitism and other forms of platform-mediated hate, he stated simply his policy aim to ensure that "what is forbidden offline is also not allowed online" (Krauss, 2015).

To try and achieve this goal, Maas drew on a well-established German institutional playbook, the tradition of 'regulated self-regulation.' Through this approach, task forces and codes of conduct developed collaboratively and overseen by government had been deployed in other telecommunications and media industries, in effect providing the standard model for interventions into areas like online content on search engines (Schulz and Held, 2002; Hoffmann-Riem, 2016). The action began ten days later when the task force had its first meeting in Berlin. Following an opening by Gerd Billen, a senior civil servant in the Ministry of Justice who had been tapped by Maas to lead the task force, the meeting featured presentations from Facebook and Google and concluded with inputs from the handful of civil society organizations that attended.[3] The task force had four meetings in 2015,[4] with participants including representatives from Facebook, YouTube, and Twitter, industry associations, and four German organizations working on issues relating to child protection, racism, and far-right extremism.[5] Together, the participants in the working group began negotiating a possible set of commitments, with Ministry officials pushing for content reported in Germany to be reviewed in Germany and for broader application of German law rather than company community standards.[6]

On December 15, after the fourth meeting of the group, a five-page 'results paper' from the task force was published. This document sets out the "concrete measures" that Maas had promised by the end of the year when announcing the initiative, and in it, the companies make a number of commitments to change their complaints-handling procedures "by mid-2016." This document does not explicitly refer to itself as a code of conduct, but individuals who attended the task force's meetings repeatedly referred to a "code of conduct" as the central result of the task force.[7] The main take-away of the document is its emphasis that the companies will act against "all hate speech prohibited against German law" and "review and remove without delay upon notification."[8] To achieve that goal, the document outlines a few 'best practices' and other commitments that have varying levels of clarity and ambiguity. The three main parts of these commitments are published in an infographic that Maas shared on Twitter, which summarizes the code of conduct for the public as follows: companies (1) agree to respect German law (in other words, what is illegal offline should be illegal online), (2) agree to remove reported content in less than 24 hours, and (3) promise to improve their user-reporting tools.[9]

No formal institutional structures had been changed, but a new set of general voluntary rules had been layered on top of firm's existing commitments under EU and German law; additionally, the task force created a forum for information sharing, negotiation, and discussion between industry policy employees and government. The companies agreed to implement the terms of the code of conduct in the next six months, but this was an informal agreement: the publicly released results paper was not undersigned by the companies or specific employees.

5.2 The Network Enforcement Act, 2017–2018

5.2.1 DEMAND FOR CHANGING THE (COLLABORATIVE) STATUS QUO

On the 11th of April 2016, press releases from the German Ministry for Family Affairs and the Ministry of Justice announced that the two ministries would be working together to commission a monitoring exercise to evaluate the effects of the task force's voluntary commitments (BMFSFJ, 2016). This informal evaluation would be performed by Jungendschutz.net, an organization that was established in 1997 with funding from the Ministry of Family Affairs and serves as a 'center of competence' for the German states on child protection issues. Since 2008, Jungendschutz has been conducting research and advocacy into online child safety, with their legal mandate set out in the Interstate Treaty on the Protection of Minors (JMStV). Beyond actively searching out illegal content and reporting it to the platforms (in their 2008 annual report, for instance, they claim that they successfully were able to secure the removal of 1,400 illegal videos from YouTube), they had from 2008 onwards conducted a number of simple audit studies, in which their employees would proactively attempt to find illegal content on search engines or social networks (Glaser et al., 2008). Through a collaboration with the Ministry of Justice, Jungendschutz brought some research capacity and expertise when it came to content moderation standards, even though their thematic focus was on a different issue area (child protection, not hate speech). As Gerd Billen noted in a statement, the monitoring would be an "important component of the task force":

> The monitoring provides us with important insights into how agreements with companies work in practice, how quickly they react to reports and whether they delete the reported illegal hate content. This will enable us to better assess how the agreed measures are taking effect and what further steps are necessary (BMFSFJ, 2016, n.p., author translation).

Jungendschutz employees conducted their first formal evaluation in July 2016, a point at which the firms were supposed to have implemented the code's commitments (Jungendschutz, 2016). The results were not in line with expectations. As Maas later summarized at a public event, the figures released by Jungendschutz, based on a small sample of content takedown requests, suggested that "of the illegal content reported by users, Twitter deletes about 1%, YouTube just 10%, and Facebook about 46%" (Reuters Newswire, 2016). Shortly following the evaluation, Maas wrote again to Richard Allan and to Facebook's head lobbyist in Berlin. In the letter, obtained by a freedom of information request, Maas wrote that "the results of your efforts thus far have fallen short of what we agreed on together in the Task Force" (Beckedahl, 2016, author translation). In full awareness that the task force commitments were voluntary, and thus there were no sanctioning mechanisms or enforcement capabilities built in, he threatened action at the European level if Facebook did not step up their game—writing that he had been discussing the issue with other Justice Ministers in the European Council and that they 'shared his concerns,' suggesting that he would seek to influence his European counterparts towards pursuing harder and costlier forms of regulation at the European level. (Despite the even poorer performance displayed by Google and Twitter on those same metrics collated by Jungendshutz, it does not appear that similar letters were sent to Google or Twitter representatives.)

Demand for changing the rules was growing within the German government due to the perceived failure of the firms to take the collaborative approach seriously, as well as external, global developments that were increasing the salience of platform governance as a transnational digital policy issue. First, as Tworek (2021) and others have noted, domestic legal developments were leading lawmakers in CDU/SPD governing coalition to follow in Maas's footsteps and worry that "German law could no longer be enforced in Germany" on platforms due to jurisdictional issues:

> Amongst several cases filed, one German lawyer, Chan-jo Jun, had filed a case against Facebook for not removing online content that was illegal under German law. In 2016, a regional court in Hamburg denied the complaint on the grounds that it did not have jurisdiction to adjudicate because Facebook's European operations are headquartered in Ireland. Jun called it "outlandish" that American companies could operate in Germany without being subject to its jurisdiction.
>
> (Tworek, 2021, p. 110)

Lawmakers and their staff expressed deep frustration about the opacity of the companies (especially Facebook) and their unwillingness and/or inability to speak candidly about how they enforced their global content moderation rules in the German context.[10] When firm representatives offered testimony to parliamentary committees or at public events, they refused to provide what was perceived to be basic detail about the number of German-speaking content moderators that they employed and their specific capacities in Germany. (At the time, the firms were extremely cagey about who and how these processes functioned; as Tarleton Gillespie and others have more generally noted, this was a common global strategy to avoid scrutiny and downplay the importance of their moderation practices.) But this strategy appeared to backfire in the German context. Despite the measures being instituted voluntarily by the companies through the task force, the perception among key stakeholders in the German executive was increasingly that the firms were merely doing "whatever they could to avoid regulation totally and limit their costs," as one member of the Bundestag in the governing coalition put it.[11] As one staffer, the digital policy adviser to a member of the Bundestag on the Digital Agenda committee noted, throughout the effort by German officials to achieve their preferences via collaborative means, "Facebook in effect told German lawmakers to their faces that 'yes, the issue is complicated, but we're sorry, but we can't accept the primacy of your national criminal laws'."[12]

Domestic demand for improved platform content moderation practices was also spreading to the rest of the executive due to the exogenous shock of the election of Donald Trump to the US presidency in November 2016, following a scandal-filled and salacious campaign where social media platforms, foreign interference, and the influence of 'fake news' were all said to have played an outsized role (Karpf, 2017). Following a strong performance by the far-right Alternative for Germany (AfD) party in a number of 2016 German state elections, where the AfD, in a number of cases, appeared to take votes from both the CDU and the SPD, concern was mounting in the governing coalition that various forms of digital trickery could have an adverse effect on their electoral outcome in the German federal election that would be happening in fall 2017. As Gollatz and Jenner (2018) have documented via qualitative and quantitative media analysis, the post-US election's 'fake news' discourse quickly entered the domestic debate on platform regulation and helped to frame it as a crucial issue for the democratic integrity of Germany in the context of the upcoming election.

In March 2017, about a year and a half after initiating a collaborative platform regulation strategy, Heiko Maas publicly announced a new, contested approach. He presented a draft law designed to layer platform-specific content moderation rules for firms on top of the existing European intermediary liability regime. The law, the *Gesetz zur Verbesserung der Rechtsdurchsetzung in sozialen Netzwerken* (literally, the legislation to improve law enforcement in social networks, commonly shortened to *Netzwerkdurchsetzungsgesetz*; this translates to the 'Network Enforcement Act' in English, with the abbreviation *NetzDG* commonly used in both German and English-language writing about the regulation), was a 29-page piece of draft legislation with a number of obligations set out for the regulatory targets,[13] that would have to:

- publish quarterly reports on the handling of complaints about illegal content made by users;
- delete 'obviously illegal content' within 24 hours, and other forms of illegal content within 7 days;
- appoint a contact person to receive government queries and complaints in Germany;
- inform users about content moderation procedures through various means;
- save or archive content removed as illegal for prosecutors to use as evidence;
- search for and delete copies of illegal content that existed in other places on the platform.

The preface to the draft law outlined the estimated costs that would be an outcome of the regulation: approximately 28 million Euros in annual compliance costs for all firms, reflecting increased staffing costs and the cost of putting together the transparency reports, and an estimated 3.7 million Euros annually in terms of bureaucratic costs for the government.

5.2.2 ATTEMPTS TO TAMPER DOWN DEMAND

Immediately following the announcement, there was a strong backlash from digital civil society, as well as from global human rights organizations and from industry lobby groups seeking to suppress demand. A number of civil society organizations, including the German digital rights organization *Digitale Gesellschaft* and the global press freedom organization Reporters Without Borders, predicted that the law would have deleterious effects on freedom of expression. D64, a network of digital policy experts that is closely linked to the SPD, called the law (and specifically, a provision for the automatic deletion of matched content) "the first step in a creation of a censorship infrastructure" (Reuter, 2017c, author translation). The United Nations' Special Rapporteur for freedom of opinion and expression noted in a letter to the German executive branch that the law would incentivize the overblocking of legitimate speech by users, as it was formulated around the main metrics of 'takedowns' and 'speed,' with no real mechanism for auditing the rates of false-positives made by the companies (Kaye, 2019a). A coalition of both transnational civil society organizations as well as industry groups published an open letter against the NetzDG, eventually securing a series of high-level meetings with lawmakers in the governing coalition to try and negotiate concessions or its withdrawal (Reuter, 2017a; He, 2020).

Industry was unsurprisingly also strongly opposed to the proposal: Bitkom, a industry lobby group that counts Facebook, Twitter, and Google among its members, immediately issued a statement warning that the law would spur a "deletion orgy" as firms would be incentivised to over-remove content rather than face fines for acting too slowly (Reuter, 2017c). Other groups warned that the law, as perhaps the first in the world to regulate content moderation as done by platforms in a non-copyright and intellectual property context, and additionally one being proposed by such an internationally influential and democratically legitimate state like Germany, would serve as a model for other less-democratic governments seeking to bring social media companies under closer state control (He, 2020; Tworek, 2021). The furor was intense and as the critiques in major media outlets circulated widely, Maas had to answer the critics in a number of interviews in spring 2017 with major outlets like *Der Spiegel* and in debates with civil society (Gathmann and Knaup, 2017).

Nevertheless, lawmakers in the governing coalition were supportive of the bill, downplaying the risks and emphasizing the importance of taking a strong position in fighting against illegal content online. The bill appeared to have significant support in the CDU/CSU; their legal policy spokespersons went as far as to say that "The bill by Minister of Justice Maas is a first, small step in the right direction. But we must go much further," suggesting that other types of criminal law enforcement could be also included (Reuter, 2017c). A few voices in the coalition, as well as in the opposition, discussed concerns with the law— but it seemed as if the governing coalition had the political will to drown out these voices, especially once the policy became a key signal of their fight against online hate in the lead-up to the election.[14]

5.2.3 SUPPLY FACTORS

By this time in 2017, the NetzDG was being proposed as part of a whole-of-government strategy against both online hate and the unaccountable private decisionmaking power of the US platform companies (He, 2020). Demand for change was high enough that Maas had the blessing of the executive to propose a contested approach with binding rules. He now had the regulatory capacity to develop regulation, tasking a group of civil servants at the Ministry of Justice and Consumer Protection to draft the law, building largely upon the general framework that had been developed through the collaborative task force, including the notion that there should be a contact person to handle official complaints, that content moderation standards and complaints procedures should be transparent enough to be clear to users, and that firms should generally act on content within 24 hours of it being reported. However, there were also a number of new and quite aggressive provisions proposed in the draft, which appeared to correspond to the new levels of demand in the governing coalition for stronger standards, as well as the more confrontational stance being taken by the German government as far as private platform authority went. These provisions included an obligation for firms to delete duplicates of the content that was deemed manifestly illegal under the NetzDG across their broader platforms (in effect searching for copies of content found to be illegal that had not yet been reported), and a requirement that this deleted content would be archived for potential access by federal prosecutors seeking to bring charges against individuals.

As Maas now led this whole-of-government approach, he could be confident that Germany had the regulatory capacity required to intervene and contest private platform authority. His government had a strong majority in the Bundestag, meaning that there was little the opposition could do to contest any proposed legislation. While Germany did not have a digital ministry that could have developed more technically sophisticated rules, his civil servants, including Gerd Billen, had been engaged in dialogue with platform companies for almost two years via the task force and adjacent informal forums. Their expertise and understanding of the theory and practice of how Facebook, Twitter, and YouTube moderated the content of German users had deepened as a result of this direct engagement and capacity building efforts, at least according to the firms that participated in exchanges with government over this period.[15]

While the normative landscape shaping the ability and willingness of German policymakers to intervene in this area was of course complex, it appeared to be shifting towards a space which would allow the creation of binding rules. As a comprehensive analysis by He (2020) has documented, Maas, his Ministry, and others in the German executive were able to frame the process of the NetzDG as part of the 'Rechtsstaat,' a uniquely German conception of the rule of law that is enshrined in the country's constitution. The concept in effect is that the continued functioning of the German state is dependent on the "existence, validity, and primacy of law.... Law can take the form of legislative acts such as the NetzDG, but also, more importantly, of the German constitution, the Basic Law.... The precedence and supremacy of the basic rights enshrined in the Basic Law are crucial to the Rechtsstaat idea" (He, 2020, p. 27). As He argues, Maas was the main policy entrepreneur promoting this idea via his speeches and media appearances, and this notion eventually became the central publicly articulated rationale for the legitimacy and necessity of contesting private platform authority. The debate turned upon the problematic nature of having foreign corporate entities making unaccountable decisions about the speech and behavior of German citizens at critical political junctures; the NetzDG was positioned as the answer to that problem and a reassertion of public, democratic authority. Although normatively the NetzDG may have displayed a break from the relatively laissez-faire German tradition of online content regulation (which was generally predisposed towards collaborative, self- or co-regulatory arrangements in the few areas it had touched, such as online search engines), it was able to harness a broader interventionist norm in free expression more broadly. As Tworek (2021) has argued in a historical analysis of the NetzDG's normative roots, Germany has long had a far more interventionist conception of the appropriate scope of policy influence in public expression, going back to as far as Wiemar Germany. The combination of this relatively interventionist normative foundation, when combined with the strategy of discursive legitimization around the 'Rechtsstaat,' seemed to put Germany in a strong position to supply binding rules to contest private platform authority.

5.3 Berlin vs. Brussels: The EU Harmonization Procedure

The only hitch in the SPD and CDU plan to regulate user-generated content moderation in Germany was the broader regulatory environment of the European Union's Single Market. Under a series of measures designed to ensure a level regulatory playing field across EU-member states, the European Union has a procedure for the notification of technical regulations and of rules on products and services, including 'information society services' (e-commerce, media, and internet services). Through this process, other member states and the European Commission have a formalized mechanism to review, provide input, and in certain cases re-shape or even veto these new regulations. The procedure requires a three-month 'standstill' period, in which the member state must wait to receive comments from the Commission and other member states. The upshot is that a member state cannot simply decide to regulate an issue tomorrow, whip up a draft law, and push it through parliament immediately; it must formally notify the Commission (where the draft law is placed in a publicly available database) and wait three months for the input of the Commission and other member states. Through this notification and harmonization process, the Commission can delay or effectively veto proposed member state draft regulations if it has its own concrete plans to regulate in that area (see the Regulatory Context Appendix B for more information).

When the German Ministry of Justice and Consumer Protection notified the European Commission of the first draft of the NetzDG through the Technical Regulations Information System (TRIS) on March 27th, that notification was flagged as potentially politically sensitive, according to Commission emails obtained via freedom of information requests. In internal emails, staffers in the Directorate General (DG) for the Internal Market (GROW)—the entity in-charge of managing the TRIS notification system—began to debate the

NetzDG and what would happen next. These staffers quickly mentioned the upcoming German election, and noted that another branch of the Commission, DG Communications Networks, Content, and Technology (CNECT) was considering the option of intervening more decisively.

> The German intention to regulate the matter has been recently discussed between CNECT's Cabinet and the German authorities. During these discussions, CNECT informed the German authorities of CNECT's intention to regulate the same matter with a different approach than the one presented in the notified draft. It seems that DG CNECT and DG JUST are in contact to discuss the notified draft and have contacts with the German Ministry of Justice (which prepared the notified draft).[16]

The Commission had before the NetzDG taken the position that no legal framework for raising content moderation standards for major social media platforms was necessary. DG JUST had negotiated the Code of Conduct on Hate Speech with the major internet companies in the spring of 2016, and Vera Jourova, the EU Justice Commissioner, was publicly a major advocate for voluntary self-regulation and co-regulation in areas that would have a major impact on free expression and other fundamental rights. In an internal assessment prepared by DG CNECT and JUST which analyzed the NetzDG and contextualized it within previous Commission measures, Commission staff note that the spirit of the proposal was not totally out of line with their efforts to increase transparency for company content moderation systems and move their private law into a space that more adequately reflected European legal frameworks:

> While, unlike the [EU Hate Speech] Code of Conduct, the draft German law is a legal instrument, an analysis of its objectives against the objectives pursued in the Code of Conduct shows that the two are broadly coherent in terms of the overall objective. Both instruments aim at ensuring that notifications of illegal hate speech are assessed against the law and not only against the internal terms of service of the IT companies and that the assessment is made expeditiously. An important difference is that the scope of application of the German law goes beyond the Code of Conduct in so far that it includes also other offences, such as defamation.[17]

Nevertheless, the analysis noted that the NetzDG threatens regulatory harmonization as outlined in the Juncker Commission's Digital Single Market Strategy: "The Commission considers that national solutions at this respect can lead to unwanted legal fragmentation and have a negative effect on innovation."[18]

It was clear to officials working in the Commission that the NetzDG was on shaky legal footing. It quite evidently ran against the country of origin principle established in Article 3 of the E-Commerce Directive, which states that member states may not "restrict the freedom to provide information society services from another Member State" (Hellner, 2004, p. 9),[19] and also had issues on free expression grounds with European Human Rights law as set out under the European Convention on Human Rights and other measures. As a Commission official involved in the debates at the time discussed, "it was obvious to everyone who had been following the debates in Germany that NetzDG had major issues under European law."[20] However, the situation was just ambiguous enough that what the Commission would do was a political, and not purely legal question. As the official explained, notifying a new law triggered an informal political and legal assessment, and not a fundamental rights compliance assessment, which would only be triggered in the case of the notified proposal transposing European Law (for example, in the case of an amendment to the Telemediengesetz, the German transposition of the E-Commerce Directive). The stakes were high: as one staffer for a member of the European Parliament working on digital policy issues at the time put it, "the consensus was that early law made by a major member state could serve as a blueprint for eventual European wide legislation."[21]

In effect, the Commission had three options. It could issue a comment, a non-binding public response which would advise the German Ministry on changes that the Commission recommended. It could issue a so-called 'detailed opinion' similar to a comment, except one which mandated a reply from the German government and had the additional effect of extending the standstill period by at least a month. Finally, it could try and negotiate these issues off the record in direct negotiations with the German executive branch. Because of the timing of the German notification, a detailed opinion would extend the standstill into the Bundestag's summer vacation, and thus past the last session of parliament, effectively killing the proposal.

This made the EU TRIS process an important veto point. Many of the civil society groups active domestically in Germany wrote public comments on the law via the TRIS portal. They were joined by transnational civil society networks, as well as industry. In a meeting with DG GROW's cabinet on June 12, 2017, Facebook's lead Brussels lobbyist argued that the NetzDG violated the E-Commerce Directive and sought for the Commission to engage in "a dialogue with the German authorities to change the law."[22] A scene-setter with talking points prepared for the Commission official leading the meeting outlines DG GROW's position on the burning question that Facebook was guaranteed to ask: "Does the EC intend to object to the notified German draft?" (The talking point demurs, noting that "The commission is still assessing the compatibility of the Draft Act notified by Germany with EU Law. The deadline for reaction expires . . . on 28 June 2017.")

5.3.1 OVERCOMING THOSE CONSTRAINTS: DEALMAKING WITH THE COMMISSION

On the floor of the Bundestag in early May 2017 Maas defended his bill, arguing that it would not lead to privatized enforcement but rather simply to the better existing implementation of German criminal law. Members of the opposition noted that the list of criminal code statutes covered in the NetzDG were extremely broad and went beyond just hate speech (more than 20, including not just incitement to violence and the promotion of unconstitutional organizations, but also, controversially, defamation, and some oddities like the disparagement of the ceremonial President of the Federal Republic). These advocates argued that the definition of social networks provided in the bill was also too vague, likely encompassing many other online services that featured some user-generated content, like blogs, third-party reviewing sites, and direct messaging services like Whatsapp or Telegram.[23] Multiple MdBs in both the governing coalition and the opposition complained about the very short time period in which the law was being debated. As Netzpolitik's Markus Reuter observed, "all of the CDU/CSU speakers complained about the little time remaining until summer break" as they proposed their suggestions for changes, including a bigger role for some kind of self-regulatory body used in the media industry to adjudicate on complaints, rather than the platforms themselves (Reuter, 2017b). Similarly, MdB Petra Sitte of the Left party argued in her remarks that given the "broad alliance of organizations that had already formed against the draft law" the governing coalition should "engage in a broad discussion" and revisit the issue following the election to prepare a better proposal (Deutscher Bundestag, 2017).

Nevertheless, the opposition's attempts to tamper down demand to head off the NetzDG were ultimately unsuccessful. Domestically, the opposition did not have enough seats to prevent the law's passage and demand concessions. Civil society and firms were unable to exert enough voice against the law to capture regulators or change their preferences, likely due to a combination of the very high levels of demand among key policy entrepreneurs and the apparent failure of firms and civil society to successfully deploy public-oriented campaigns to sufficiently mobilize German platform consumers against the law. While there is a dearth of good polling data about the NetzDG, the one existing poll with a purportedly representative sample of German social media users (albeit with only a sample size of 500), conducted in early 2018, found that 67% of those polled 'strongly approved' of the policy and 20% 'somewhat approved,' with only 5% of respondents 'disapproving' of the NetzDG.[24] In an interview, an employee of one of the major platform companies suggested that one of the main reasons that their company had not mobilized more aggressively against the NetzDG (in terms of both direct lobbying in Berlin and in terms of public-oriented PR campaigns) was because internally commissioned survey and focus group research had shown the policy's relatively broad support with the German public.[25]

Additionally, the potential game-changer—the mobilization of US government pressure against Germany to reduce demand, via diplomatic pressure, backroom negotiations, or potentially the threat of retaliatory sanctions against German national champions—never materialized. This may have been due to the tension (and at times overt hostility) between the Silicon Valley giants and the newly elected Trump administration, which represented a break from the relatively close relationship with government that the firms enjoyed during the Obama years (Powers and Jablonski, 2015). It also may have simply been that the compliance costs of the NetzDG were not existential enough for the firms to see the expenditure of political capital in Washington to try and get US intervention on their behalf as necessary. In effect, the lack of US government opposition meant that the only real constraint upon Germany's ability to intervene was in Brussels.

The Commission recognized this, and on May 23, a high-level meeting about the NetzDG happened with members of the cabinet for Commissioners Ansip (DG CNECT), Jourova (DG JUST), Timmermans (Commission Vice President), and Juncker (Commission President). As an internal emailed summary of that meeting discusses, Ansip, who was in charge of maintaining the Digital Single Market, "wished to send a political letter to DE on the main concerns [CNECT] have on the draft law," but Juncker, Timmermans, and Jourova did not want to co-sign it.[26] While Ansip argued on the side of maintaining harmonization and using the notification process to get Germany to stand down, the others were hesitant due to a number of political factors. The main one articulated in interviews with officials present at these discussions was that Germany was entering an election year, and there was a perception that if the Commission stepped in and deemed the NetzDG in violation of EU law it could perhaps be perceived as a high profile domestic political defeat for Maas and the SPD, potentially affecting the electoral outcome in some way. A second issue was the culturally sensitive context of hate speech in Germany and the significant pressure coming from German policymakers, including prominent German staffers in the European Commission, that this issue should be left aside as a domestic political matter.[27] Finally, while the DGs may have wished to regulate the issue of harmful content in a different manner than Germany (and indeed, Commissioner Jourova had spearheaded the development of the EU Code of Conduct on Online Hate Speech in mid-2016), the Commission had no viable policy currently in the works that it could propose to Germany as an alternative to the NetzDG, other than the code of conduct, which followed a similar collaborative approach as the task force that was already seen as ineffectual by the German negotiating team.[28]

In a turn from regular procedure and into the realm of informal governance (Kleine, 2013), rather than issuing public comments, the Commission raised concerns through informal letters and other back-channels that would minimize domestic blowback for a German government dead-set on passing the law before the election. This back and forth negotiation, underpinned with the threat of a Commission detailed opinion (and de facto veto) successfully negotiated the last-minute softening of some of the NetzDG's provisions.

On June 27, 2016, the grand coalition introduced an amended version of the bill, "revised in consultation with the Commission in order to achieve the greatest degree of compatibility with EU law" into the Legal Affairs committee of the Bundestag.[29] (The language itself on the "greatest degree of compatibility" possible, rather than actual compatibility, is insightful.) First, the scope of the law was changed slightly, by narrowing the definition of social networks so that it excluded peer-to-peer messaging services, music services, blogs, and other platforms. Combined with a threshold of 2 million registered users in Germany, the law was thus changed so that it would at its onset only apply to Twitter, Facebook, and YouTube (TikTok would find itself in scope in 2020). Second, the list of sections of the German Criminal Code that companies would need to check flagged content against was trimmed down, removing a few statutes that had been critiqued by civil society as being redundant and not pertaining to hate speech (e.g., the statues referring to defamation of the federal President or the 'denigration of constitutional organs' like the courts). Additionally, the new version removed two of the major provisions that had been added post-task force: the provision that firms should have a 'stay down' filter by which they would algorithmically search for, and remove, duplicate content from their platforms when acting upon a confirmed violation of one of the criminal statutes specified in NetzDG, and the provision that the companies would need to archive content deleted for federal prosecutors, which critics argued was especially problematic from a data protection point of view (Reuter, 2017d). Finally, the new version added a provision which allowed voluntary industry bodies to be involved in the reporting or assessment of cases of illegal content reported by users, a prospective safeguard that had been advocated for by the CDU faction.

The Legal Affairs parliamentary committee agreed with this new version, and set a date for the second reading of the bill in the Bundestag three days later, June 30th, the last day the Bundestag was in session before the election. On the 30th of June, the NetzDG was debated for 45 minutes. The law passed easily, with the votes of the majority coalition (CDU/CSU and SPD) in favor, with the Left voting against and the Greens in abstention.

5.4 Discussion

In the days following the vote, it became clear that many lawmakers—and even some within the grand coalition—were not entirely thrilled with the law, but nevertheless maintained that, given the institutional constraints at play, it was the best that could be done to fill an important policy vacuum. In an interview with the left-wing daily *Tageszeitung*, the SPD's legal policy spokesperson Johannes Fechner argued that the NetzDG supplied imperfect rules to meet what was a crucially important demand. The government had made the best of an tricky situation, noting that the SPD wished to have added more provisions that would have better protected the freedom of expression of users:

> But if we had included a new obligation for companies in the law, we would have had to re-notify the law to the EU. We would then have had to wait another three months to find out whether there were concerns on the part of the EU Commission or other EU states. So the law could not have been passed in this legislative period.
>
> (Rath, 2017, author translation)

Fechner's comment demonstrates the institutional lock-in effects that had an often underappreciated yet outsized result on the NetzDG's final form: the European Union's notification process and the short time period in which Germany sought to contest the regulatory status quo. A detailed policy and process-oriented look at the NetzDG and its origins provides an opportunity for deeper analysis of the conditions under which governments are able to contest platform authority and standards. Interestingly, the main concessions and changes to the substance of the law were made where the veto points were: in this case, not at the domestic level, where few changes to the NetzDG were successfully negotiated by the opposition parties or by firms and civil society, but at the EU level, in negotiations with the European Commission.

This story clearly could have played out differently. Looking back, various counterfactual policy options were on the table: Maas's Ministry could have continued to work with the existing task force structure, building upon the forum and framework of the code of conduct to incorporate more stringent standards or of better industry auditing and monitoring. There were obvious ways to improve that mechanism's commitments and capabilities: for instance, the research conducted by the government to measure compliance with the collaborative code of conduct was crude and unscientific, constrained by a lack of proper access to platform data or a proper sampling strategy.[30]

Since the task force had gone into effect in late 2015, a few new collaborative efforts had been instigated at the European level, the most notable of which was the EU Code of Conduct on Online Hate Speech (Gorwa, 2019a). While the EU Code remained largely insulated from the similar German collaborative efforts that were happening around the same time, and did not feature prominently in the domestic German debate, Maas and the executive could have joined the forum created through the code of conduct, trying to bring the German efforts to a broader and collaborative pan-European strategy to raise content moderation standards for platforms. However, by this point, given the growing levels of domestic demand for more stringent rules, and the perception that industry had failed to meet its collaborative commitments, that kind of approach was not particularly attractive. Instead, Maas and others in the executive demanded change that would properly contest the status quo of private platform authority, and return foreign companies to what was perceived to be their rightful place as corporate actors bound within the democratically determined context of domestic laws and norms.

The German government was able to meet this demand and successfully supply these rules simply because it had the power to do so. It had the regulatory capacity to do so both domestically (the ability of the governing coalition to unequivocally command the Bundestag) and enough power resources to expend transnationally (including to prevent the Commission from intervening against rules which were technically against existing EU intermediary liability legislation). The result of this combination of political will and power to intervene was the successful implementation of a contested platform-regulation strategy.

6

After Christchurch

Diverging Regulatory Responses
in New Zealand and Australia

On the 15th of March, 2019, a man stepped into a car full of weaponry and drove more than 300 kilometers from the city of Dunedin, New Zealand, to the larger city of Christchurch. Around 1:30 pm, he posted a Facebook status with links to a personal manifesto that he had uploaded on multiple file-sharing websites, put on a ballistic helmet mounted with a camera designed for outdoor extreme sports, and began a Facebook live stream as he walked into the Al Noor Mosque armed with a shotgun and assault rifle (Royal Commission of Inquiry, 2020). This live stream, initially seen only by a few hundred Facebook users, was quickly reported to Facebook and taken down—but not before copies were made and re-posted on internet messaging boards. Within hours, hundreds of thousands of versions of the video (some altered with watermarks or other modifications) were being re-uploaded to Facebook, as well as to YouTube and Twitter (Sonderby, 2019).

The Christchurch attack, which took more than 50 lives, provided an immediate and powerful shock to the global policy conversation around terrorism, white supremacy, and its intersections with user-generated content platforms like Facebook and YouTube. Two weeks after the event, an op-ed with Mark Zuckerberg's name on the byline was published in the *Wall Street Journal*, calling for more government guidance on how platform companies should deal with harmful content. A week after that, Australian lawmakers introduced the Sharing of Abhorrent Violent Material Act, an amendment to the Australian criminal code that reformed the liability regime for online intermediaries, which now could be heavily fined (and have their employees imprisoned) for failing "to ensure the expeditious removal of abhorrent violent material" online (Douek, 2020a, p. 4).

The Politics of Platform Regulation: How Governments Shape Online Content Moderation. Robert Gorwa,
Oxford University Press. © Oxford University Press 2024. DOI: 10.1093/oso/9780197692851.003.0006

96 AFTER CHRISTCHURCH

At the same time as the Australians were developing their response, Prime Minister Jacinda Ardern's Labor government was trying to decide what New Zealand should do. While it considered a more security-focused, contested approach to shaping platform content standards like the Australians, New Zealand ended up instead developing a collaborative international strategy, working together with the French government to steer high-level discussions with the chief executives of the major technology companies about possible voluntary commitments. The result was the Christchurch Call, a non-binding international declaration which was announced in Paris in May 2019 and would eventually be signed by nearly fifty countries and more than a dozen leading firms. New Zealand's sustained efforts to regulate harmful content on the largest user-generated content platforms built upon existing governmental and industry networks, and would result in some creative institutional bricolage. A small and informal partnership of major platform companies called the Global Internet Forum to Counter Terrorism (GIFCT) would be, at the behest of the New Zealand and French governments, expanded, formalized, and spun into a private regulatory body with formal charitable and non-profit status.

The Christchurch tragedy presents a natural comparative case study: a single regulatory episode where two neighboring countries with close economic, social, cultural, and political ties sought to respond to the same event, with the same stated policy goal, with very different regulatory approaches. Why did the Christchurch incident in Australia and New Zealand lead to divergent governance strategies? And why was it that Aotearoa, New Zealand—where the attack happened, after all—saw the successful implementation of a collaborative platform regulation strategy rather than the more stringent, contested one pursued by its neighbor?

6.1 The Early Fight to Set the Agenda in New Zealand

In the immediate aftermath of the deadliest mass shooting event in New Zealand's recent history, policymakers in the Prime Minister's department realized that the attack had been 'designed to go viral,' and that the attacker had very cannily exploited Facebook and other user-generated content platforms in order to amplify his extremist views. This made it, quite possibly, the world's first 'internet-mediated' mass shooting, and Jacinda Ardern's government needed to quickly figure out how it could respond. The conversation turned to the question of what the appropriate policy response to the online dimension of the incident should be, and multiple government departments, from the Department of Internal Affairs (which had a 'digital safety' team working on issues that included the spread of child exploitation content) to the Ministry of Justice were involved in this discussion, noting that there were a number of potential legislative and policy gaps that had been exposed by the incident.[1]

The initial tone from the government was similar to the kind of language that had come out of Germany in the lead-up to the NetzDG. In her Ministerial statement to Parliament a few days after the shooting, Ardern emphasized two policy areas that had been revealed as insufficiently developed by the Christchurch Attack: gun control, and digital platform regulation. Ardern took a quite assertive tone, suggesting that the government might need to contest the way in which firms created and enforced their private regimes of content moderation: "We cannot simply sit back and accept that these platforms just exist and that what is said on them is not the responsibility of the place where they are published. They are the publisher, not just the postman. There cannot be a case of all profit, no responsibility."[2]

Nevertheless, Ardern's government did not have a policy entrepreneur actively demanding new rules for user-generated content platforms even before the event. Ardern and her advisers were open to getting consultation from other branches of government, and a special team in the Prime Minister's Office working on cybersecurity and digital policy sought to provide advice to a Prime Minister looking for the best path forward. The head of this team was Paul Ash, a career diplomat with experience in cybersecurity policy, who would become one of the most important individuals in the development and implementation of New Zealand's Christchurch response (Shepherd, 2019).

This window of consultation created an opportunity for other actors to try and affect the level and character of demand for new rules. Given the crisis, and the apparent unambiguity of the content involved (which already violated the content guidelines of all the major platform companies), Ash recalled in an interview that "everyone wanted this content to come down," including industry and civil society, making interests in this policy space more aligned than similar discussions that might happen on other topics like hate speech (or areas where country laws clash with platform terms of service, as in the NetzDG case).[3]

Facebook had quickly and publicly described how they were actively trying to remove every instance of the video they could find, deploying all sorts of complex technical tools to do so (Sonderby, 2019). Microsoft's President Brad Smith also got in touch with Prime Minister Ardern directly to note his willingness to cooperate and to present a variety of policy solutions. He even traveled to New Zealand immediately following the attack (Sachdeva, 2019). Although his company was not a major player in the global user-generated content business (Microsoft does not operate a social network like Google or Facebook do; and while it has a search engine, Bing, its market share is comparatively small both in New Zealand and globally), Smith would become a crucial policy entrepreneur in the post-Christchurch policy discussion.[4] Smith's conversations with the

New Zealand team planted key ideas and served as a connection point between networks of government and industry higher-ups.

6.1.1 NEGOTIATING THE OPTIONS WITH CIVIL SOCIETY

Digitally oriented civil society in New Zealand quickly set out to influence this important debate about the kinds of rules that would be demanded in the aftermath of the tragedy. As one policy staffer at a major NZ-based digital rights NGO described humorously in an interview, they had heard about "the response from Australia from the people we know there, so our first response was try and talk to our contacts in NZ governments and try and make sure that they didn't do something stupid too." It helped that Jordan Carter, InternetNZ's director, had personal connections to Prime Minister Ardern through shared time spent in the NZ Labour Party (and even had once been housemates with Ardern), and thus was able to get an important early seat at the table in a way that most digital NGOs in other countries do not.[5]

Carter explained why his organization was arguing for a collaborative, non-statutory regulatory approach in a blog post that grappled with the lack of obvious solutions to the problems exposed by Christchurch:

> Making random quick laws on our own might respond to a deep seated feeling many of us will be having that "something has to be done and NOW." The quick action on gun laws taken in New Zealand could be seen as an example on this front. Sadly, that won't work in this situation. There are no global precedents for how to deal with social media and violent extremist or terrorist content. If it was already sorted, the experience we had with Christchurch would not have happened. While it might sound painful, the right place to start is the conversation (J. Carter, 2019a, n.p.).

As firm and civil society voices sought to help influence the government's demand for rules, Ash and his team eventually provided the advice to the Prime Minister that the government would need to "look at some form of collaborative and voluntary solution, and we were going to have to work internationally, including with the major tech platforms, as a way of trying to grapple with this problem and come up with constructive solutions" (Shepherd, 2019, n.p.). While there had been a discussion of prospective domestic responses, and the possibility of pursuing a more combative, contested governance response, Ash suggested in an interview that there were two main reasons as to why the collaborative strategy was chosen. Firstly, the normative implications of pursuing more interventionist online speech policies were inherently problematic for the executive. They worried about their international and domestic reputation: as Ash put it, "our country has long been saying that a free, secure, and open internet is the goal, and we couldn't do an about face on that."[6] Secondly, the New Zealand government appeared to be pragmatic about its capacity to obtain meaningful change via a contested strategy. While it is likely that they would have had the domestic power resources to pursue a domestic contested approach,[7] the executive was concerned about the costs of potentially implementing new rules and the difficulties that the small New Zealand market would have with enforcement. As Paul Ash would later put it in a media interview describing New Zealand's strategy, "We could go down the Teddy Roosevelt line, and speak softly and carry a big stick.... It's just that we don't have a big stick" (Shepherd, 2019, n.p.). Alongside the normative costs of a contested approach, the New Zealanders worried that the contested strategy wouldn't work—that firms would simply exit (or threaten to exit, creating a high-profile domestic showdown) that would be extra costly for the Ardern government politically. For a combination of normative and capacity-related reasons, New Zealand's executive felt that they could achieve their preferences, at least satisfactorily, if sub-optimally, by working together directly with firms.

6.2 Collaborative or Contested? Developing the Australian AVM Act

Across the Tasman Sea, when news began to spread that the Christchurch shooter was an Australian citizen, the Australian government needed to decide how it would respond. On the day of the attack, as Prime Minister Morrison issued a short statement, the rest of his government had to weigh potential policy options. Unusually, Australia had already created an independent regulator in 2015 to deal specifically with issues around online safety: the eSafety Commissioner's Office, which for some years been working on issues including cyberbullying, harassment, and the online dissemination of child abuse imagery. Staffers at eSafety prepared legal advice for the Prime Minister's department, discussing the existing Australian legal frameworks and how they applied to the attack via internal email:

> Australia has a robust domestic Classification Scheme for films, computer games and certain publications. [...] Under the Online Content Scheme, the eSafety Office can take action in relation to material hosted in Australia that has been assessed against the National Classification Scheme as "prohibited" or "potential prohibited" [...]. The RC category includes offensive depictions or descriptions of children and

illegal content. However, it is important to note that what is considered prohibited/potential prohibited under Australian law may not be illegal in the jurisdiction where the content is hosted.

While the eSafety Office does not have the power under the Online Content Scheme to issue a takedown notice to Facebook, which is based in the United States, it does work cooperatively with digital platforms to request removal of material that is clearly illegal in Australia and other jurisdictions.

As officials in the Communications ministry made edits to this advice from eSafety and prepared policy recommendations and 'next steps' for the Prime Minister's office, they sketched out a number of challenges facing any policy seeking to govern how companies made content moderation decisions. First, the jurisdictional tensions: because Facebook and most other content hosts were located outside of Australia, they believed that issuing direct takedown orders would have limited effect: "Domestic regulation can only go so far in addressing this as digital platforms are global entities," the policy advice noted. Second, other targeted efforts to prevent similar types of content from spreading again would be difficult to implement: "Prohibiting live streaming is not feasible as this functionality is widely available across any number of social media, OTT [over-the-top] and telecommunication platforms."[8] The summary of the legal context also noted that the major companies (Facebook and Google) had been working rapidly in an effort to take down the shooter's video, and appeared to be doing their best to remove this content that was against their formal Community Standards as well as their commercial and political interest.

Nevertheless, the Department of the Prime Minister and Cabinet, when responding to journalists over the weekend following the attack, took a more assertive tone, starting to set the agenda for harder domestic regulation. Morrison's statement began:

There has been a sea change in the attitude of the community and governments to the regulation of the internet over the last decade. The clear view of our Government and the Australian community is that the same standards and rules that apply in the physical world should apply in the online world. The internet cannot be an ungoverned and safe space for terrorists and other criminals.

After mentioning the track record of Liberal-National's tough-on-digital-issues agenda ("The Australian Government has been at the forefront of online safety legislative reform to enshrine the principle that the online world is not a safe place for terrorists. It's why we have legislated to give law enforcement agencies [...] crime fighting tools for encrypted communication [...] established and appointed the world's first eSafety commissioner [...] and legislated the world's first kids' anti-cyberbullying regime to give the eSafety Commissioner the powers to issue take down notices and fine individuals and digital platforms"), the remarkable statement argued that more needed to be done, and that the government would "not hesitate to legislate as it has in areas such as encryption, kids' cyberbullying and the non-consensual sharing of intimate images" (Prime Minister of Australia, 2019, n.p.).

In the statement, the Prime Minister mentioned that he would be calling a meeting on the 26th of March 2019 to discuss these issues directly with representatives of the technology sector. At this meeting, various possibilities for an Australian policy response would be discussed. The statement concluded on an assertive note: "A best endeavours approach is no longer good enough. It's clear that while social media companies have cooperated with authorities to remove some of that disgusting content, more needs to be done. If they won't act, we need to."[9]

6.2.1 EARLY NEGOTIATIONS WITH FIRMS: THE BRISBANE SUMMIT

The goal of the March 26th summit, according to the official invitation, was for "Summit participants [to] work collectively to identify what can be done to prevent the streaming and reposting of extremist material, both now and into the future."[10] The briefing paper prepared before the meeting claimed that the "objective of the Summit is to get a commitment from the digital platforms and telecommunications industry that they will lift their game and do more to deal proactively and decisively with inappropriate content."[11]

Industry began circulating some of their key arguments for the meeting. In an email sent on the weekend before the Brisbane summit with firms and government, a Microsoft staffer sent a pre-publication version of a blog post written by Microsoft President Brad Smith to the official coordinating the policy response within the Department of Communications and the Arts, asking for input and advice on whether the tone of the blog was appropriate.[12] In the post, Smith acknowledged the role that platform companies had played in the dissemination of the Christchurch shooter's video and manifesto, and offered some policy solutions while making a few important agenda-influencing moves of his own. Smith offered up two concrete voluntary self-regulatory proposals. The first was to foster increased industry collaboration on terrorist content via a (then) little-known entity called GIFCT. The second proposal was the development of a shared rapid response mechanism: "the tech sector should consider creating a 'major event' protocol, in which technology companies would work from a joint virtual command centre during a major incident."[13] Australian officials liked the post so much that they discussed including it as part of the briefing pack for the summit.[14]

Via email, an inter-agency discussion of the bargaining position of the government laid out the following changes desired in the rules affecting how firms governed their platforms:

> As discussed, can each agency turn their mind to tangible outcomes and changes we would propose to platforms and ISPs. As per the discussion, we propose that these outcomes would be grouped under the following elements:
>
>> 1. Instantaneous or quicker takedown of violent and extreme material (or blocking of access); 2. Improving transparency of the actions the planforms and ISPs take in relation to violent and extreme material; 3. Holding platforms, ISPs, and individuals to account for the upload and distribution of violent and extreme material.

The Brisbane Summit was two hours long. It was attended by the key members of the cabinet (Prime Minister Scott Morrison, Minister for Communications and the Arts Mitch Fifield, Attorney General Christian Porter, and Home Affairs Minister Peter Dutton), and representatives from the three major user-generated content platforms (Google, Facebook, and Twitter), four of the major Australian internet service providers, and Communications Alliance, an industry association.

After an introduction from the Prime Minister and an overview of the structure and 'expectations' for the discussions with the Ministers, the platform companies were each allotted time to discuss their response to the Christchurch incident, the failures of their relevant self-regulatory 'rules and standards' that were highlighted by the incident, and what lessons they had learned for the future. Government then sought to get specific commitments that firms would change their policies and practices around how they moderated harmful content: the talking points for Minister of Communication Mitch Fifield summarized that he wished industry to focus their action on three areas:

> Prevention and protection—including detecting, blocking, and instantaneous and faster takedown options for violent and extreme material. Transparency—improving transparency of the actions taken by platforms and ISPs in relation to violent and extreme material. Deterrence—enhancing responsibility for the upload and distribution

of violent and extreme material by individuals, platforms and ISPs. Today we are seeking concrete actions and commitments from industry.[15]

The briefing packs circulated to the participants featured specific asks from the platform companies. There were clear similarities with the core asks of the German task force, which had been having similar conversations four years prior, including more detailed transparency reporting on how the platforms conducted their moderation, the acquisition of more moderators domestically within the country, and the streamlined takedown of illegal content.[16] A number of the industry representatives that attended the summit said that the outcome from the negotiations with government at the meeting was positive: that they would develop a collaborative code of conduct and set of best practices that would affect their content moderation policies and practices domestically.[17] The platform companies agreed to form a task force with the Ministries present to develop new informal rules voluntarily, with the additional longer-term aim of providing input into prospective future amendments to the Enhancing Online Safety Act, the regulatory framework which had created the eSafety regulator in 2015.

6.2.2 HERE COMES THE ELECTION...

The summit happened on Tuesday, March 26, 2019. It looked as if the government and the firms had agreed to pursue changes to content rules via a collaborative governance strategy. However, following the summit, email summaries of the day's discussions included a new major deliverable—not included in the original meeting agenda or briefing materials—that was being fast-tracked: a set of new platform-related criminal offenses and sanctions being developed by the Attorney General's department. The last day of Parliament before dissolution for the 2019 federal election was the following Thursday, April 4th. It appeared that Attorney General Christian Porter, in consultation with Morrison and perhaps the broader Cabinet, decided that they might be able to pursue a contested platform regulation approach instead.

It is difficult to pinpoint exactly when this strategy came into effect, but with the campaign trail looming, executive demand for binding rules suddenly increased. While the pre-Summit public communication discussed the possibility of the government stepping in if necessary, the post-Summit statements framed this intervention as a done deal. A press release put out by the Prime Minister's department on the 30th of March was emblematic of this newly assertive approach. Prime Minister Morrison offered a number of explications of the way that they would 'force' firms to do what they perceived to do the right thing: "Big social media companies have a responsibility to take every possible action to ensure their technology products are not exploited by murderous terrorists," Morrison said. "It should not just be a matter of just doing the right thing. It should be the law. And that is what my Government will be doing next week to force social media companies to get their act together" (Prime Minister of Australia, 2019, n.p.).

6.2.3 PARLIAMENTARY DEBATE AND OPPOSITION

This new bill, titled the Sharing of Abhorrent Violent Material Act (commonly abbreviated as the AVM Act) was written over the weekend and introduced into the upper house of the Australian Parliament on the 3rd of April, about two and a half weeks after the Christchurch attack. It was the last session that the Senate would sit before the election, the agenda was incredibly packed, and party politics and last-minute maneuvering and electioneering abounded.

The ordinary legislative process involves a bill being introduced, read, and passed in one of the two houses, and then read and passed in the other house in identical form.[18] Because of the way that the parliamentary sitting calendar for 2018–2019 had been drafted, however, with a shortened schedule, it happened that the Senate had its last session on April 3rd followed by a final House session on April 4th. For this reason, the Liberal/National government was unusually introducing a number of bills into the Senate on the 3rd with the aim of passing them in the House the next day.

As the leader of the Australian Green party (which at the time held nine out of the seventy-six Senate seats) stated in comments a few minutes after the session began at 9:30 am:

> The Senate's been on strike for the past few months and now we're being asked to support 30 bills, ramming them through this parliament with the support of the Labor Party. We haven't even seen some of these bills! We have not even seen the bills that will be rammed through this parliament. We're dealing here with some legislation that will fundamentally change people's lives.

Senator Di Natale outlined his critiques of three new pieces of legislation that he saw as being introduced last minute before the election with inadequate consultation and discussion: a welfare reform bill, a fossil fuel infrastructure bill, and, as he put it, "some of the most significant changes to social media online regulation that we have ever seen." He protested about the process, and the rapid pace at which legislation was being pushed through via the force of the Liberal/National coalition's executive power (which under the Westminster system, is considerable in the case of a majority government):

This bill hasn't even been introduced. It hasn't even been introduced and it's going to be rammed through. We haven't had an opportunity to see it. Of course, in the wake of Christchurch, we need to look at how we regulate social media and online content. Of course we need to do that. People shouldn't be subjected to the abhorrent material that's posted online. But you don't go about this by introducing legislation that the parliament can't even debate and scrutinise.[19]

Twelve hours later, the session was still going, and the Liberal government was trying to pass bills at a tremendous pace. The AVM Act was introduced at 9:13 pm, and two minutes later the next item on the docket was already being discussed, the bill magically having gone through both a first and third reading. The official Senate record documents the slightly comedic confusion and frustration of Senators who were unable to follow which bills were being introduced and voted on.[20] As one crossbench Senator complained to the media the following day: "It is bad enough when the government forces a vote on a Bill that members of the public haven't had a chance to respond to. But in this instance, even the Senators haven't had a chance to look at it" (Duckett, 2019, n.p.).

In the House of Representatives the next day, Attorney General Porter gave a speech outlining the core of the new policy approach, which involved the amendment of the existing Criminal Code to include a new type of content, "abhorrent violent material."[21] Two criminal offences were proposed in the amendment, relating to this new type of content. The first was "a failure to notify" the Australian federal police about abhorrent violent material circulating in Australia when there are "reasonable grounds" for believing the acts being depicted happened in the country.[22] The second offence related to companies that "fail to remove" abhorrent violent material propagating via their services "expeditiously." These offenses would apply not only to large social media companies, but also potentially to complementor firms that provide technical or other infrastructure, as well as internet service providers and telecommunications companies (Douek, 2020a). They were underpinned by significant punitive sanctions: the penalties stipulated for failure to remove could be up to 10 million Australian dollars or 10 percent of annual global turnover; as well, as Attorney General Christian Porter repeatedly emphasized, potential prison time for executives of social media companies. In the speech, the Attorney General deployed securitizing language, framing social media platforms as responsible for hate, terror, and violence, and a 'tough on platforms' stance as the only appropriate response to a crisis event like the Christchurch shooting.[23]

Multiple members of the opposition Labor party pointed out potential flaws with the hastily drafted legislation and complained about the lack of serious scrutiny that it had received, noting that the legislation had not even been circulated to members of the opposition. Although Labor's Shadow Attorney General critiqued both the process and the policy, Labor ended up supporting the bill, knowing that its lack of a House Majority meant that it was in effect powerless to stop it.[24] The party stated that it would vote for the bill with the caveat that it would amend it after the election if elected, a strategy seemingly chosen to reduce the chance that the party would be tarred as 'pro violent extremism' by the right in the upcoming campaign.

The bill was voted on and passed via the Liberal/National majority on April 4th. The Prime Minister touted the legislation as a symbolic centerpiece of the Australian government's Christchurch policy response, one that would not just provide a signal to the platform industry, but also to voters in the lead-up to an election. "It's a very strong message and we are not mucking around," Morrison told the media (Lynch, 2019).

6.3 New Zealand's Platform Diplomacy

In New Zealand, the day before the Brisbane summit featuring platforms and the Australian government, a work program for a collaborative regulation initiative called the 'Christchurch Call' was set by the Prime Minister's department, with the Ministry of Foreign Affairs as lead on implementation. Prime Minister Ardern had discussed the idea for the initiative with a number of world leaders— Theresa May, Justin Trudeau, Angela Merkel, and Emmanuel Macron—and Germany and France had pointed Ardern towards the 'Tech for Good Summit' that was being hosted in Paris in May 2019 as a possible venue for an international meeting.[25] Paul Ash, the top New Zealand civil servant on the case, traveled globally collecting feedback with his colleagues. They obtained the official partnership of the French government, which not only boosted the capacity of the comparatively small New Zealand team, but also made sense diplomatically given the Paris location. By mid-April, Ash's team had developed a draft of the call to be circulated to other stakeholders.

In late April, they traveled to California, and the draft went through its first proper negotiation with firms at meetings in the San Francisco Bay Area. The public policy heads of the major five companies, including Nick Clegg of Facebook, Kent Walker of Google, Brad Smith of Microsoft, and David Zapolski of Amazon, along with the respective company General Counsels, attended the meeting to discuss the details. From there, the draft went through multiple rounds of revision in the two weeks before it went to Paris. They received input from multiple corners, including from firms on what was technically feasible and desirable, international lawyers who gave advice on potential customary law effects of the final Call, as well as its synergy with the UN Guiding Principles on Business and Human Rights ('The Ruggie Principles'). Other governments which were being courted as potential signatories, including the United States, provided comments as well.

By early May, the text that was almost finalized. A short document, running at around 1,300 words, 2–3 pages in length,[26] it was structured in four sections: an introductory pre-amble setting the stage ('the pledge'), followed by three sections with commitments that actors agreed to implement. The first outlines the measures government signatories would publicly commit to (e.g., "strengthening the resilience and inclusiveness of our societies to enable them to resist terrorist and violent extremist ideologies"; "Ensur[ing] effective enforcement of applicable laws that prohibit the production or dissemination of terrorist and violent extremist content"). The second moves to the commitments that firms would implement ("Take transparent, specific measures seeking to prevent the upload of terrorist and violent extremist content and to prevent its dissemination on social media and similar content-sharing services").[27] The document concludes with a final section detailing joint measures for both governments and firms to follow.

An annotated version of the text obtained via a freedom of information request features a table breaking down the text almost line by line, discussing key negotiations and additions, as well as making plain the reasoning behind specific sections and particular wording. These demonstrate the care that the drafters put into crafting the document so that it would feel like a genuinely multistakeholder initiative—for example, in a significant contrast to the approach being taken by the ostensibly collaborative Australian task force, the Call begins with commitments being made by government signatories, and not firms. As the annotations note, "We want tech companies to know this is a genuinely cooperative effort—we need to recognise the role governments play in addressing the drivers of violent extremism."[28] Additionally, the annotations explain the document's mention of government-led regulatory proposals, and that government action in this policy arena might also involve:

> a full range of regulatory-type measures, from voluntary frameworks through to black letter law. This framing means that we still acknowledge the importance of domestic regulation (as countries have and will, regulate on this issue as well as alternative measures that could be designed in a collaborative way).[29]

The annotations for other parties note the Call's bounded scope ('the Call is not seeking to address all of the ills of the internet'), carefully diplomatic language about acknowledging existing work being done on similar topics through existing policy networks like the EU Internet Forum, and New Zealand's "intended approach, which is to be collaborative."[30] This was a whirlwind diplomatic process which involved managing multiple relationships, ensuring that the corporate and governmental signatories would stand by the text.

On May 15, exactly two months after the Christchurch shooting, the Christchurch Call Summit was held in Paris. The summit included heads of government from "New Zealand, France, Jordan, Senegal, Norway, Canada, the United Kingdom, and the Vice President of Indonesia," as well as the President of the European Commission (J. Carter, 2019b). The Chief Executives of Facebook, Google, and Twitter also attended, and representatives from Microsoft, Amazon, and Wikipedia. At the end of the meeting, the call was signed by world leaders and platform company executives. Countries supporting the Call on 15 May were New Zealand, France, Australia, Canada, Germany, Indonesia, India, Ireland, Italy, Japan, Jordan, the Netherlands, Norway, Senegal, Spain, Sweden, and the United Kingdom. The European Commission also was a signatory.[31]

6.3.1 IMPLEMENTING THE CHRISTCHURCH RESPONSES

Unlike many of the general non-binding international declarations made through forums like the G20, the New Zealand government was committed to ensuring that the collaborative governance approach of the Christchurch Call would actually lead to changes in firm policies and practices. In a post-Paris debrief report, New Zealand Ministry of Foreign Affairs and Trade staffers summarized the four outcome areas that had been identified during the negotiation of the call text as next steps:

> Following the Paris meeting, [redacted], four priority areas for action were identified: reform of an existing industry body (the Global Internet Forum to Counter Terrorism) to be more inclusive and effective, and take forward Call-related work; developing a shared crisis response protocol to enable countries and companies to work together better in future attacks; better understanding where there are gaps in the research on terrorist and violent extremist content online; and better understanding how companies' algorithms can drive users to more extreme content, and identifying intervention points.[32]

The document further notes that at the conclusion of the Christchurch summit, Prime Minster Ardern and French President Macron "undertook to regroup with Call supporters on the margins of UNGA [UN General Assembly] Leaders Week to assess progress against the call."[33] It was time to start the implementation process, and for New Zealand and France to assess whether the Call commitments were indeed being voluntarily and satisfactorily met. While firms made individual policy changes, the main institutional channel through which the implementation of the Call's general proscriptions would happen, however, was the GIFCT. Here, New Zealand's collaborative efforts linked up transnationally with the previous collaborative governance strategy that had been pursued in Europe by the European Commission.

The roots of the GIFCT go back to some of the earliest policy conversations in Europe about the problem of terrorist content on emerging user-generated content platforms. As briefly mentioned in Chapter 3, after preparatory meetings held in 2014 and 2015, the European Commission officially announced the creation of the EU Internet Forum, which brought together EU officials with representatives from Google, Facebook, Twitter, and Microsoft (Gorwa, 2019a). After a process of negotiation, the members of the Internet Forum announced the EU Code of Conduct on Online Hate Speech, committing the firms to a wide-ranging set of principles, including the takedown of hateful speech within 24 hours under platform terms of service and the intensification of "cooperation between themselves and other platforms and social media companies to enhance best practice sharing" (European Commission, 2016, p. 3). To comply with that commitment, the four firms announced the creation of the GIFCT in 2017 to coordinate the use and improvement of automated systems to remove extremist images, videos, and text (Microsoft Corporate, 2017). After being founded, the organization was initially highly secretive, and other than noting that it had a board made of "senior representatives from the four founding companies" it revealed little about its operations (Gorwa, Binns, and Katzenbach, 2020, p. 8).

At the core of the GIFCT is a technical infrastructure called a hash-sharing database (Llansó, 2016; Huszti-Orban, 2017). These are systems for automatically matching content, which typically involve 'hashing,'—i.e., the process of transforming a known example of a piece of content into a 'hash,' a string of data meant to uniquely identify the underlying content. Hashes are useful because they are easy to compute, and typically smaller in size than the underlying content, so it is easy to compare any hash against a large table of existing hashes to see if it matches any of them.

Through the GIFCT database, the core firms (as well as a subsidiary group of about ten different companies that have also joined the GIFCT) can upload and share hashes of content that they consider to be prohibited extremist material, allowing the other firms to also automatically block that content if they choose. This shared database was the core 'product' of GIFCT, but before Christchurch, the organization also served as a policy network, with a closed annual meeting in San Francisco that brought together firm representatives with key counter-terrorism and national security officials from the European Union, United States, and the Five Eyes countries.[34]

The pre-existing GIFCT structure caught on as a central institutional channel through which industry could implement the commitments made by the call. As one firm representative put it in an interview, "The Christchurch Call requires people to work together. And you need to have a way to do that (and build structures to do that). But rather than create something new, its easier to build up something you already got."[35]

The New Zealand team continued to drive towards concrete deliverables that they could report after Paris Summit. On one hand, they were continuing their engagement with 'foundational supporters' (countries that supported the Call on 15 May), and working with France to deliver a 'second wave' of new country supporters, to be announced and profiled in late September 2019 at the UN Meeting.[36] These included "Denmark, Mexico, Sri Lanka and South Korea, as well as UNESCO and the Council of Europe—bringing the total numbers to 48 countries and three international organisations" (McCulloch, 2019). On the other hand, the New Zealand government kept the pressure on industry, negotiating the details of specific organizational changes to GIFCT that would have an impact on its core functions, policies, and legitimacy.

A Christchurch Call 'Leaders Dialogue' event was held on September 23 at the UN General Assembly, hosted by New Zealand, France, and Jordan (which had been long engaging in policy conversations relevant to terrorism through its Aqaba Process meetings). Government leaders (including Prime Minister Ardern) as well as corporate representatives (including Twitter CEO Jack Dorsey) delivered speeches, announcing three major updates: the future restructuring of GIFCT, so that it would include an 'independent advisory committee,' and would have permanent staff and a formalized institutional structure; the creation of a crisis response protocol that would be tested through a simulation event held in New Zealand in December 2019; and the broadening of the Call's membership through both a new wave of government signatories as well as a formalized 'Christchurch Call advisory network' of civil society groups.[37]

In her speech to the UN General Assembly the next day, Ardern was optimistic about these developments:

> Yesterday, I met with Call supporters to check on our collective progress. We announced that a key tech industry institution will be reshaped to give effect to those commitments—and we launched a crisis response protocol to respond to such events in the future. Neither New Zealand nor any other country could make these changes on their own. The tech companies couldn't either. We are succeeding because we are working together, and for that unprecedented and powerful act of unity New Zealand says thank you.[38]

As New Zealand's Paul Ash put it, the work did not stop there. Their team continued informally monitoring and pressuring firms to realize their commitments. This work was often time consuming, slow, and burdened by the day-to-day difficulties of creating a new organization—getting official non-profit status, drafting an official governance charter, building up staff. Nevertheless, in June 2020, the revamped post-Christchurch Call GIFCT announced an independent advisory committee, with representatives from seven governments, the European Union, the UN Counter Terrorism Executive Directorate, and twelve civil society organizations.[39] In 2020–2021 the organization published its first transparency report, turned its closed annual summit into a 'multistakeholder forum,' and started inviting researchers and civil society groups into working groups developing specific aspects of the GIFCT's work.[40] It now is arguably one of the most important players in the global content governance space.

6.4 Discussion

How do we explain the differences in the New Zealand and Australian government's approaches? Through the speedily developed AVM Act, the rules governing user-generated content platforms in Australia were changed quite significantly in just over two weeks, through a securitized, contested regulatory approach that sought to layer new binding commitments and criminal sanctions on top of what platforms were already doing. In New Zealand, the government instead opted to work collaboratively. Interestingly, by helping shape an important new global institution in GIFCT, it may even have achieved much more substantive regulatory change than the Australians did.

In Australia, the demand for the regulatory status quo to change became interlinked with the Liberal/National coalition government's pre-election strategy. Both the Prime Minister and the Attorney General, immediately after the Brisbane meeting on March 26th (which also signaled the exploration of possible collaborative options with industry) began to deploy securitizing rhetoric, framing their strategy as an ambitious 'world first' effort to stand up to these powerful foreign multinationals. This combination of political will and rulemaking power, with Liberal/National control of both houses of Parliament, made it possible for them to work the legislative system to the extent that the bills could be so rapidly introduced, voted upon, and advanced. They were helped in this effort by a lack of domestic institutional features that would have made this more difficult, such as legislative choke points for the opposition to 'filibuster' or stall these policies.

What about lobbying from other actors? Australia is not a world power in terms of economic might or market size in the way that the United States or the

European Union is, and one would expect major disadvantageous changes to the platform liability regime in the country—changes underpinned with potential fines up to 10 percent of global turnover or employee imprisonment—to be strongly lobbied and fought against by industry. But firms seem to have been caught flat-footed by the extraordinarily quick turn around, and were not able to significantly mobilize policymaker-facing or public-facing campaigns in time (Cameron, 2019). The United States also did not intervene, despite concerns that the bill might problematize US-Australian trading and security relationships, including through a bilateral free trade agreement that arguably could have come into play (see the Regulatory Context Appendix B). If the United States had voiced some opposition, or if American-headquartered firms had managed to meaningfully mobilize Washington's support, the AVM Act could have been scrapped.

In New Zealand, the situation was very different, despite the initial allusions to a contested response. Firstly, the electoral context was different: it was not an election year, and the government did not feel the same need to 'do something big immediately.'[41] As well—and crucially—civil society leaders and firms managed to quickly shape the policy agenda, and New Zealand policymakers were sold on the logic of a more human-rights, 'free and open internet,' and properly collaborative solution. They had the international legitimacy to bring firms meaningfully to the table to negotiate a collaborative regulatory project. Capacity that they may have lacked organizationally to supply those rules (given the complex multi-actor feat of public-private international diplomacy it eventually became) was gained through a strategic partnership with the well-resourced French.

Although one might simply argue that the divergence between these two Christchurch responses can be easily explained by national culture and political identity—Australia, after all, is very different from its smaller neighbor in many key ways, especially in terms of its regulatory tradition; it also had a more interventionist, security-oriented right-wing government in power compared to New Zealand's ostensibly more cooperation-oriented left-wing one. But related policy developments in Aotearoa show that this should not be taken as a given: in the neighboring policy domain of web filtering (which can be done by local internet service providers, and thus demands less cooperation from platforms) a much more stringent and controversial policy approach was introduced by the same Labour government in New Zealand in 2020 (George, 2020). We should not discard the possibility of the government, under slightly different circumstances, pursuing an approach much more similar to the AVM Act—in effect, following through on the types of policy change that Ardern initially suggested after the attack.

The jury remains out on the long-term effects of the Christchurch Call as a governance instrument and institution. As Thompson (2019, p. 99) has put it, the Christchurch Call could have a major impact by representing "a very initial step toward the formation of a multilateral regulatory framework for controlling online terrorist and extremist content, along with other practices of social media and online intermediary operators." It will be fascinating to follow the effects of the Call, and the GIFCT, as well as the role that New Zealand maintains as the orchestrator of a transnational initiative that now features many larger and potentially more powerful state actors. Scholarship on public-private transnational institutions has noted that "informal governance structures may also be a source of power in their own right and may even empower otherwise weak players, such as small states and NGOs" (Westerwinter, 2021, p. 14). Will this be the case for New Zealand, or will bigger players step in to take over the institutional structures that the New Zealanders initially negotiated to better suit their own aims and goals? While collaborative platform governance has to date largely been the purview of powerful states and the European Commission, events like Christchurch have increased both the interest and legitimacy of non-European and small states in transnational efforts to shape platform authority, and certainly provide an important space to watch for the future of collaborative platform regulation.

7

From Coast to Coast

State-Level Platform Regulation in the United States

The 9th of September 2021 was a hot fall day in Austin, Texas. A group of legislators met at the Texas State Capitol building, where following the assent of Governor Greg Abbott, Texas House Bill 20 (HB20)—"Relating to censorship of or certain other interference with digital expression, including expression on social media platforms or through electronic mail messages"—was signed into law. The two main sponsors of the bill posed for a photo with the Governor, shared later that day alongside a press release with an extended quote from Abbott:

> We will always defend the freedom of speech in Texas, which is why I am proud to sign House Bill 20 into law to protect first amendment rights in the Lone Star State. Social media websites have become our modern-day public square. They are a place for healthy public debate where information should be able to flow freely—but there is a dangerous movement by social media companies to silence conservative viewpoints and ideas. That is wrong, and we will not allow it in Texas.
> (Office of the Texas Governor, 2021b, n.p.)

The Texas bill was the highest-profile salvo in more than a year of action from state-level law makers in the United States who were seemingly dissatisfied with the content moderation status quo. Republican legislators in Kentucky, Oklahoma, Arizona, North Dakota, and numerous other states also sought to introduce user-generated content-related platform regulation (Brennen and Perault, 2022b). In Florida, Republican Governor and presidential hopeful Ron DeSantis signed into law Senate Bill 7072, which he initially presented as part of sweeping "transparency in technology reforms" (Masnick, 2021b). Both the Texas and Florida laws sought to place limits on how firms could enforce their rules, trying to prevent platforms from 'deplatforming' or 'shadow banning'

The Politics of Platform Regulation: How Governments Shape Online Content Moderation. Robert Gorwa,
Oxford University Press. © Oxford University Press 2024. DOI: 10.1093/oso/9780197692851.003.0007

political candidates and other users. They also created the first US legal frameworks mandating transparency reporting and public disclosures around changes to community guidelines, among other further reaching requirements. Blaise Ingoglia, the Florida legislator serving as the Chair of the state house's Commerce Committee, who introduced SB 7072 at the behest of the Governor, summarized his party's policy efforts in no unclear terms: "Big tech must be held accountable. Big tech cannot be left unchecked" (Klas, 2021, n.p.).

A year after the Texas bill was signed, another mandatory content moderation transparency framework was entered into law in the Democratic party stronghold of California. That bill, AB 587, required "social media companies to publicly post their policies regarding hate speech, disinformation, harassment and extremism on their platforms, and report data on their enforcement of the policies" (State of California, 2022b, n.p.). A week later, Governor Gavin Newsom signed an even more wide-ranging bill, the 'Age-Appropriate Design Code Act' (AB 2273), legislation modeled upon a co-regulatory approach that had been developed in the United Kingdom with significant input from child safety interest groups. Buffy Wicks, the Assembly member who co-sponsored the bill, noted that small tweaks made by industry to their content moderation practices would not be enough to satisfy the legislation: "As the mom of two young girls, I am personally motivated to ensure that Silicon Valley's most powerful companies redesign their products in children's best interest." She continued: "Today, California is leading the way in making the digital world safe for American children, becoming the first state in the nation to require tech companies to install guardrails on their apps and websites for users under 18. The Design Code is a game changer, and a major step forward in creating a global standard for the protection of youth online" (State of California, 2022a, n.p.).

Skeptical international observers have long assumed that the United States would not or could not ever regulate its sizable domestic platform sector, for reasons ranging from political dysfunction, legislative gridlock, and symbiotic platform-government interlinkages. So why are lawmakers in the United States now pushing for some of the most stringent limits on how platforms develop practices and procedures for governing conduct on their services—as Wicks put it, for new global standards and rules? And why has action from the US states, rather than the federal government, played such a central role in the United States' ongoing platform regulation efforts?

7.1 Two Waves of 'Techlash'

Many scholars and policymakers have long argued that the international proliferation of the American tech industry has been not only an economic but also a geopolitical boon for the United States (see the overview provided in Rolf and Schindler, 2023). During the Obama administration in particular, Hilary Clinton's State Department actively promoted an 'internet freedom' and 'twenty-first century statecraft' agenda that sought to increase global access to not just internet connectivity, but also to the search engines, social networks, and other services developed by major American platform firms (Ross, 2011). As Powers and Jablonski (2015) note, companies like Facebook, Twitter, and Google were often closely involved in the development of these policies, as well as a major beneficiary of their promotion. High profile policy advisers argued for the 'liberating' potential of blogging, the Web, and various platform services that could give people around the world "equal access to information and opportunity to leverage the potential of individuals and the power of markets" (Diamond, 2010, p. 77). From 2008 onward, platform companies were not only likely to be portrayed in American policy circles as leading drivers of economic growth and innovation, but also as firms creating democratizing tools that could work hand in hand with American foreign policy interests in the Middle East and beyond.

The US government's direct material, legal, and institutional support of Silicon Valley firms throughout the twentieth century has been well documented by historians (O'Mara, 2020), and these interlinkages persisted into the platform era of the early 2000s. Although the Obama administration became especially famous for its strong Bay Area ties—materializing in a sort of revolving door between the White House and major platform firms (Dayen, 2016)—historically, Democratic politicians have not been the only proponents of the American tech sector. George W. Bush's first term began in 2001, before the user-generated 'Web 2.0' platform era really took off, and his 'Information Technology Advisory Council' was focused on large software and hardware firms, involving executives from Dell, Intel, Oracle, Sun Microsystems, and Cisco (CNET, 2002). His administration was never actively focused on substantive internet-related policy issues: in 2004, Bush's 'Technology Agenda' focused mainly on research and development in energy and healthcare, although it's final point mentioned the need to expand broadband access in the country (White House, 2004). Nevertheless, under Republican leadership, the emerging platform firms of the Bay Area generally benefited from a laissez-faire domestic regulatory environment, as well as research funding and grants, trade policies, and other more direct benefits—despite the occasional national security-related confrontation (Computer Business Review, 2006; Jardin, 2006).

A turning point in what had previously been a relatively symbiotic set of platform-government relations was the ascension of Donald Trump to the presidency in 2016. Trump was a uniquely savvy political communicator who strongly relied on services like Twitter to galvanize his base and bypass traditional media outlets (Wells et al., 2020). His team appears to have cannily used digital advertising tools built by firms during his campaign (Kreiss and Mcgregor, 2019), and he was personally an active Twitter user with tens of thousands of tweets and millions of followers. Despite—or perhaps because of—this direct material interest in platform policies and governance practices, after entering into power, the Trump administration demonstrated a deeply mercurial stance towards the tech sector and the platform services they offered. This culminated in significant pro-platform efforts: for example, Trump's government went to lengths to protect the United States' pre-Trump hands-off regulatory model for internet services as the ideal global regulatory status quo, embedding platform-friendly intermediary liability rules into trade agreements like the United States-Mexico-Canada agreement that was the renegotiation of NAFTA (Krishnamurthy and Fjeld, 2020). In another notable development, Trump came quickly to the defense of the US tech sector in the international arena, threatening retaliatory tariffs on French luxury imports when Emmanuel Macron argued for a digital services tax in Europe (D. Lee, 2019).

Over the course of his presidency, however, Trump did at times take a strong anti-platform position as well. Trump clearly became frustrated as industry introduced friction into his ability to reach his online audience. During his re-election campaign, in May 2020, Twitter added a label to one of Trump's tweets, which alleged that fraudulent voting was taking place via mail-in ballot. Users clicking on the link were led to a page that stated "Trump makes unsubstantiated claim that mail-in ballots will lead to voter fraud," with additional sources and commentary refuting Trump's false claim (Edelman, 2020, n.p.). Outraged, Trump shot back with an executive order—a notable means through which he sought to shape the American policy agenda on a range of issues (Driesen, 2018)—that directed the National Telecommunications and Information Administration, an executive agency part of the Commerce Department, to try and intervene. By filing a petition for rulemaking with the Federal Communications Commission (FCC, the US telecom regulator), Trump hoped that his executive could now attack the legal foundations of intermediary liability (explored in Chapter 3) which firms like Twitter relied upon to make rules and set community guidelines around acceptable conduct on their services.

The order, 'On Preventing Online Censorship' was largely symbolic in its impact. However, it lives on as an extraordinary document marking a shift in the American Right's rhetoric on online platforms. It portrays platform firms as damaging to free expression, rather than facilitating wider access to it in the global context; it argues that conservative voices are facing undue discrimination under the content and conduct policies of the tech sector; it bashes the tech sector as being unduly beholden to China and other American adversaries; and it begins to articulate the seeds of an argument that would become influential in conservative re-interpretations of US intermediary liability law—that platform firms facilitating access to third-party user-generated content were 'common carriers,' 'public squares,' or 'content creators' that should have regulatory responsibilities different than those under the legal status quo:

> In a country that has long cherished the freedom of expression, we cannot allow a limited number of online platforms to hand pick the speech that Americans may access and convey on the internet. This practice is fundamentally un-American and anti-democratic. When large, powerful social media companies censor opinions with which they disagree, they exercise a dangerous power. They cease functioning as passive bulletin boards, and ought to be viewed and treated as content creators.
> (Executive Office of the President, 2020, p. 34079)

7.1.1 DISSATISFACTION WITH THE STATUS QUO ON THE RIGHT

The Trump-Twitter spat and executive order foreshadowed the showdown that would come in January 2021. On Wednesday, January 6th, as American lawmakers met on the Hill to certify the results of Joe Biden's victory in the presidential elections, Trump gave a speech in Washington, DC, in which he encouraged supporters to march to the Capitol. "We will never give up, we will never concede . . . you don't concede when there's theft involved," Trump told the crowd (BBC Newsdesk, 2021, n.p.). Trump supporters protesting the electoral outcome overwhelmed the security cordon at the Capitol, breaking into the offices of elected representatives and even entering the Senate chambers just as lawmakers were evacuated. Trump watched from the sidelines, offering running commentary via Twitter. In the early evening, as National Guard reinforcements arrived and began securing the building, Trump posted a video to Facebook and Twitter in which he argued that the riot was a natural result of a fraudulent election result. Over the following 60 minutes, Facebook placed warning labels on the video before deciding eventually to simply remove it (Kelly, 2021). Around the same time, Twitter also removed the video and suspended Trump's account (Fink, 2022).

The 'deplatforming' of someone who for a few more weeks would remain the sitting President caused massive outrage on the American right. On Monday morning, an open letter titled 'Tech Companies Pose Existential Threat, Must Be Broken Up' was published by the Media Research Center, an influential conservative non-profit organization that had for more than 40 years sought to undermine public trust in what it perceived to be a left-dominated American media establishment (Alberta, 2018). The letter featured more than 30 signatories, including the heads of some of the most powerful organizations on the American right past and present—groups like Citizens United (which famously won a Supreme Court victory in 2010 which removed many strictures preventing corporations and other organizations from making political donations), ACT for America (a noted anti-Muslim advocacy organization considered to be a hate group by observers like the Southern Poverty Law Center), and the Eagle Forum (an organization founded by Phyllis Schlafly in the 1970s to oppose efforts to legally enshrine gender equality in the US Constitution). Below an image depicting the major US-headquartered platform firms, edited so their company logos had the blue 'D' of the Democratic party superimposed over them, the letter grumbled:

> Freedom has never been threatened like this before. We live our lives online, especially now, during the pandemic. The entire conservative movement will be canceled by the left and their thugs if we let them. They will turn the screws on conservatives if we don't defend our rights. It is time to stand up and demand the breakup of these big tech monopolies. (Newsbusters Staff, 2021, n.p.)

7.1.2 SIGNS OF DISCONTENT ON THE LEFT

Unfortunately for the American right, having lost the 2020 election they no longer had control over the policymaking levers they would need to break up platform companies or enact meaningful policy reform at the federal level. Nevertheless, the salience of platform-related issues had also increased in the Democratic party. Where Republicans had become increasingly incensed by apparently unjustified forms of private censorship perpetrated by a 'leftist' Silicon Valley establishment with ideological and personal ties to the Democratic party apparatus, many major Democrats were now holding effectively the opposite concern: that platform firms were actually *insufficiently stringent* in their rules and standards and, especially in the lead-up to Trump's 2016 election, did not adequately engage in processes of platform governance that could prevent the spread of electoral disinformation, incitement to hate and violence, and foreign interference operations from countries like Russia (Fiske, 2022). Amid widespread consternation as to how a clearly unqualified faux-businessman and two-bit celebrity could, without any political experience or even longstanding ties to the Republican party apparatus, win the 2016 election, high-profile Democrats, including Hilary Clinton, argued that platform services should shoulder some of the blame for their electoral defeat (Dovere, 2020).

After winning back the House in the midterms, House Democrats investigated Trump's Russia ties and looked at the potential influence that the infamous UK political consultancy Cambridge Analytica may have had on the US election through their use of targeted Facebook advertising (Lapowsky, 2019). (The senior Republican on the House Judiciary Committee, which was leading the investigation, called it a "fishing expidition").[1] From 2018 to 2020, Zuckerberg, Dorsey, Bezos, Cook, Pichai, and other major firm executives all testified before various House and Senate Committees on a wide range of issues ranging from competition policy to free expression (Allyn, Bond, and Selyukh, 2020; Hendel, 2020). Public opinion, at least according to polling, was beginning to shift through the Trump years, with surveyed Americans steadily more likely to report unfavorable attitudes to specific tech firms and the tech sector more broadly, and report that they believed that large technology companies wielded too much power in the American political context (Schaffner, 2022).

In 2019, Elizabeth Warren placed tech policy at the heart of her campaign to be the Democrats' 2020 presidential nominee. She argued that "the government must break up monopolies and promote competitive markets," making her the first major party candidate to argue clearly and consistently for not just stronger regulation but also competition policy interventions against Amazon, Facebook, and Google (Warren, 2019, n.p.). Warren's position was influenced by that of the Open Markets Institute, an influential DC think-tank that articulated a progressive vision for antitrust policy reform. The Open Market Institute, and other 'neo-Brandesian' academics and competition policy experts, argued that corporate concentration had reached excessively high levels in a number of sectors from travel to tech, and advocated for both the economic and political benefits of vibrant competition underpinned by robust antitrust enforcement. The notion that platform firms were unquestionably innovative drivers of economic growth was increasingly being challenged from progressive corners.

The image of Silicon Valley firms as being socially aligned with an equitable, forward-looking vision of tech-enabled justice and progress was also slowly being tarnished in Democratic party circles. A rising constellation of relatively young civil liberties organizations, in concert with some more established media policy NGOs, seized on the evidence that services like Facebook could be used to target discriminatory advertisements for housing, employment, credit, and other services, and began to probe the potentially adverse social and political impacts of a range of platform services. These organizations, which included groups like Color of Change, MediaJustice, Muslim Advocates, and the National Hispanic Media Coalition, began loudly pushing for platform firms to change their practices in various ways, and argued for civil rights audits that would explore the extent to which firms like Facebook indeed adequately took efforts to safeguard minoritized groups that were impacted by platform services (Dvoskin, 2022). This platform-critical civil rights movement grew throughout the Trump years and intersected with other burgeoning strands of tech reform thinking in US progressive circles.

In interviews conducted with media outlets during his campaign, Biden argued that major tech policy reform to address content moderation issues would be needed "immediately" (Kelly, 2020). And after winning the election, his appointments demonstrated that these increasingly platform-critical ideas were becoming mainstream within the Democratic party establishment. For instance, a key member of the Open Markets Institute, Lina Khan, became Biden's nominee for the position of Chair of the Federal Trade Commission (FTC, the main US competition and consumer protection authority). The new administration also welcomed a range of high-profile critical tech policy academics into various advisory positions, from the legal scholars Tim Wu and Alvaro Bedoya to the sociotechnical researchers Meredith Whittaker, Alondra Nelson, and Sarah Myers West. The Biden administration was staffing up— it looked like the winds of change were blowing (Clark, 2021; Kang, 2021; Subbaraman, 2021).

7.2 Attempts at Federal-Level Platform Regulation

In this changing political context, where the salience of platform-related policy issues generally—as well of online content-related questions more specifically— was rising, there appeared to be a growing amount of political demand in both the Republican and Democratic parties to change the regulatory status quo after the US Capitol riots. In the US institutional context, there are three main mechanisms through which an administration can supply the types of policy changes that it wishes to implement: by executive order; through intervention from regulatory agencies; or through new legislation, promulgated at the federal level via Congress. Additionally, as will be discussed briefly to conclude this section, the courts can play an important role in re-interpreting existing law.

7.2.1 EXECUTIVE ORDERS AND OTHER EXECUTIVE POWERS

In the American political system, power is distributed across the national and state levels, and separated across multiple legislative institutions with elected officials. Although Presidents have significant executive authority when it comes to matters of foreign policy, to pass legislation they need to rely on the work of elective representatives in the Senate and Congress. One tool that the White House can deploy on its own to steer policy is the executive order, a sort of binding memorandum that provides policy guidance and direction to government agencies (Mayer, 2002). These can be a powerful way to direct government branches, and can give the presidency significant 'unilateralist' influence on some facets of domestic affairs. Tragic examples include Trump's order directing Immigration and Customs Enforcement officials to prevent people from Muslim-majority countries from entering the United States, or his orders seeking to undermine the provision of public health care under the Obama-era Affordable Care Act.

American executive power is constrained by various political and institutional forces, however. These include the influence of inter-agency bureaucratic politics, the preferences of existing civil servants, and potentially even direct resistance from administrative branches of the government (Rudalevige, 2021). Additionally, a growing body of research shows how Congress—through tools like the Senate and House appropriations process, can also constrain the actions of regulatory agencies, even when they are directed in different ways by the executive (Bolton, 2022). In the realm of platform regulation and technology policy, however, executive power is limited by the fact that this policy area directly involves shaping the preferences and practices of corporate third-party actors. Promulgating binding rules that would change the platform regulation status quo cannot be done through executive power alone.

7.2.2 REGULATOR-DRIVEN CHANGE

The US government has executive agencies (which are directly part of the executive branch) as well as independent regulatory agencies formally outside of presidential influence. A classic American model of regulatory agency involves a college of commissioners leading a group of civil servants to act in a certain area, with a number of institutional features designed to maintain the organization's independence, such as bipartisanship, and fixed-term appointments scheduled as not to coincide with major elections (Custos, 2006). These regulatory agencies, such as the Securities and Exchange Commission, or the National Labor Relations Board, have been given various powers of rulemaking and adjudication under the 1946 Administrative Procedures Act. From measures designed to promote environmental protection or labor rights to the rules that govern the conduct of banks and the financial sector, many, if not most of the concrete rules shaping American political and public life have been developed through the "legislative delegation of regulatory authority to agencies," which can issue impactful policy guidance and also binding rules governing firm behavior (S. W. Yackee, 2019, p. 39).

The American government does not have a regulatory agency with clear jurisdiction over twenty-first-century digital services and digital markets, however. The FCC was created in 1934 and currently regulates 'legacy' communications technologies: radio and television broadcasting, and communication via telegraph, telephone, or satellite. As of now, it has no direct mandate over platformized services. Instead, much has fallen to the FTC, which has a wide remit across consumer protection and competition policy issues. Despite its relatively limited size and resources, it has in recent decades valiantly attempted to become the country's de facto privacy regulator (Hoofnagle, 2016), and has been delegated some competencies relating to the protection of minors online. The FTC generally has a remit that touches issues relating to deceptive advertising, problematic marketing, and product safety, but doesn't have clear jurisdiction over most issues relating to online content.[2]

With no easy path to legislation that could reform content moderation, Trump's executive order sought to craftily create quick-hitting regulator-led change over the intermediary liability status quo in the United States. His administration's controversial executive order made an argument that the FCC could intervene in matters relating to the intermediary liability provisions ('Section 230') that offered legal protection to platform services like Twitter, as those provisions were technically part of a 1990s amendment to the 1934 Communications Act that has historically been part of the agency's jurisdiction (Reid, 2020). This effort was legally ambiguous and stalled by legal challenges from civil society organizations; it was ultimately overturned once Biden entered office (Center for Democracy and Technology, 2021).

During the Trump administration, under the leadership of Republican Chair Joe Simons, the FTC began building some more capacity relating to tech policy issues. In 2019, the agency announced the creation of a 'technology task force' that would specifically be looking at the competition policy dimensions of digital and platformed markets (Federal Trade Commission, 2019). At the end of 2020, the FTC's Bureau of Competition announced a lawsuit against Facebook "seeking a permanent injunction in federal court that could, among other things: require divestitures of assets, including Instagram and WhatsApp; prohibit Facebook from imposing anticompetitive conditions on software developers; and require Facebook to seek prior notice and approval for future mergers and acquisitions" (Federal Trade Commission, 2020, n.p.). After Biden entered office, he further empowered the FTC to continue competition and consumer protection-related matters in the platform space, bringing on Lina Khan with a clear remit to go after anti-competitive behavior in the digital economy. Chair Khan has continued to increase the competencies of the FTC on these critical issues, for example by hiring more in-house technologists.[3]

The FTC generally faces issues relating to resourcing and capacity. The agency has a little over one thousand employees, split between the divisions of Consumer Protection and the Bureau of Competition. This puts it outside the top 75 US government agencies by size, and as of 2021 the FTC has the 85th largest payroll of all government agencies; it is dwarfed not just by the SEC and other financial regulatory agencies in the United States, but also is smaller than esoteric organizations like the Agricultural Marketing Service (4,600 employees), the Federal Deposit Insurance Corporation (5,800 employees), or the US Agency for Global Media (which oversees Voice of America and other international

124   FROM COAST TO COAST

'public diplomacy' efforts with its 1,500 employees).[4] This becomes a problem when pursuing legal cases, which are extremely costly and time-consuming, especially when going up against well-resourced platform firms. The organization has a huge mandate, but limited institutional and regulatory capacity to execute it—something that is not helped by recurring attacks by Republican lawmakers on the FTC specifically and the powers of the administrative state in the United States in general.

The FTC can, however, initiate notice-and-comment rulemakings without directly being instructed to do so by congress. In 2022, the FTC initiated a request for comment around a proposed rulemaking relating to commercial surveillance, for instance (Federal Trade Commission, 2022). These can be less costly for the agency than lawsuits, and provide a channel through which it can seek to obtain penalties from firms down the line if they do not comply with new rules. Realizing them does involve a time-consuming multi-year process with many opportunities for public comment, pushback, and delays from opponents inside and out of industry, however (Hoofnagle, 2016).

Overall, although the FTC can tackle competition and privacy-related harms, other policy issues relating to content moderation processes and the substance of online content regulation are not in their traditional wheelhouse. So far, the agency has been largely focused on deceptive advertising, competition, privacy, and other more general platform policy concerns, although it could feasibly in the long term move more into the platform governance domain (tackling, for instance, misleading claims being made around content removal systems and community guidelines) if it was given a mandate and resources to do so.

7.2.3 LEGISLATION

Institutional power is divided at the federal level in the United States, and "changes in the legislative or regulatory status quo require the consensus of multiple institutional actors, including the President, the Senate, the House of Representatives, and even government agencies themselves" (J. W. Yackee and S. W. Yackee, 2009, p. 129). However, in recent decades, policymakers in the United States have had to grapple with the reality of 'divided government' (Mayhew, 2005), which has made successful policy change increasingly difficult at the federal level. In scenarios where a party wins a majority of the popular vote in national elections, the structure of the American electoral college can deliver narrow victories, or even losses, in terms of seat counts in the legislature. Parties that capture the presidency are not guaranteed to have control of both chambers of congress, and slim majorities, combined with growing levels of party polarization as well as esoteric institutional features like the Senate Filibuster, have led to substantial legislative gridlock that makes passing ambitious policy difficult for incoming administrations (Binder, 1999).

The issue is partially one of veto points. Although the House of Representatives can pass legislation by simple majority, the Senate has institutionalized rules for parliamentary obstruction that mean that "at least a three-fifths majority is necessary, in practice, to pass major legislation today, because the chamber's rules specify that 60 votes are required to force a vote on proposals" (Wawro and Schickler, 2007, p. 2). Other than a brief window in 2009–2010, since 1979 no party has held a filibuster-proof Senate supermajority that would allow it to pass legislation at will. With a two-party system that doesn't feature minor parties that could form coalitional blocks and support legislation (as in many European countries, for instance), or strong majority rule for the electoral victor (as under the Westminster system), an incoming US administration holds substantially less legislative rulemaking power than governments in most other countries.

The result of this gridlock has been a growing focus on policy workarounds, as lawmakers have still sought, despite the plethora of institutional constraints, to pursue their agendas. One of these developments involves the special procedures around the US federal budget, which, to keep government still somewhat running, is exempt from the 60-seat Senate filibuster (Jacobi and VanDam, 2013). The Biden administration's 2022 budget, for example, was able to use this 'reconciliation' process to include various tax incentives to promote investments in clean energy, and to further the Democrat's healthcare agenda (seeking to lower prescription drug prices, for instance). Because of the special budgetary process, negotiations around the Inflation Reduction Act happened inside the Democratic party, and after consensus was reached, the bill was able to pass the 117th Congress via the Democrat's House majority and slim one-seat Senate majority (Greve, 2022).

Another major development of the last few decades in American politics has been the Omnibus bill—often massive pieces of legislation that touch on various disparate policy areas packaged them all together into one law. Omnibus bills can get special treatment, shifting the regular institutional rules of the road to help increase the likelihood of their passage, while also offering a single vessel into which policymakers can pour their political capital in bipartisan negotiations. As one historical analysis of omnibus policymaking in Congress notes:

> they alter the time-honored legislative process. Omnibus packages are often fast-tracked through committees with less consideration than typical bills. Once assembled by leaders, omnibus packages are treated as one piece of legislation, seriously restricting the choices available to members on the floor. Members must 'take-it-or-leave-it'

and are seldom aware of the details contained in omnibus bills [...]. The omnibus tactic is powerful because it enables leaders to focus attention away from controversial items to other issues that enjoy widespread support. The bigger bill has its own locus (or multiple loci) of attention and is more likely to have the broad support needed for passage.

(Krutz, 2001, pp. 210–211)

This is to all say that, generally, passing legislation federally in the United States is difficult and involves many potential veto points and veto players. After the midterm elections, which happen halfway through a presidential term and gave the Republicans back control over the House in the 118th Congressional session that began in 2023, ruling Democrats were faced with an uphill battle. To pass a bill without using the budget reconciliation procedure or omnibus trickery, policy entrepreneurs need to get support from key figures at multiple layers of the legislative process: the chairs of the Committees in the House and Senate that have jurisdiction over a matter, support from Democrats and Republicans in both chambers, and the Senate and House leadership from both parties.[5]

Because of the Senate filibuster's ability to choke off legislation even when one party has a slim majority in both houses (as Biden did from 2021–2022), binding legislative approaches need to garner at least some support from the other party to have a chance at passing. Since the start of the Biden administration, very few of the many content moderation-related bills that have been introduced as drafts into Senate and House Committees (Anand et al., 2021) have been sufficiently bipartisan to have a chance. The challenge is that Republican members of Congress seem to support platform regulation bills that would make it *more difficult* for firms to set and enforce their rules, with an eye towards preserving 'more free speech' and reducing 'censorship,' especially of conservative voices, focusing on concepts like 'viewpoint neutrality' (Feiner, 2021). Democrats instead are looking for more transparency and *stronger* guidelines around how firms set and enforce their rules on issues like hate speech, disinformation, and harassment (Kelly, 2021).

These differences have led to policy stasis. Interviewees in industry, civil society, and policymaking circles all speculated that bipartisan consensus going forward will only be found on the few spaces where common ground between the two parties exists. The best examples are child safety, sex trafficking, anti-terrorism, national security issues, and other ostensibly apolitical content moderation challenges. This coalition between centrist Democrats and the Republicans was evident in the successful passage of the Allow States and Victims to Fight Online Sex Trafficking Act and Stop Enabling Sex Traffickers

Act (FOSTA/SESTA), an amendment to Section 230 that entered into force under Trump in 2018—despite the resistance of many civil society organizations, sex workers, and other socially marginalized groups (Goldman, 2018; Mia, 2020). While no similar bills have yet to galvanize enough support in Congress as this book goes to press, there have been a number of recent efforts to take a similar bipartisan policy path in the 118th Congress, such as the Kids Online Safety Act (KOSA), which was introduced by Senator Richard Blumenthal (D-CT) and Senator Marsha Blackburn (R-TN) in 2022 (Bernard, 2022). This kind of more narrowly bounded, topic-specific form of platform regulation could feasibly pass through the federal legislature if the circumstances were right.

One major piece of legislation relating generally to tech policy that did pass during the first half of Biden's term was the CHIPS For America Act, a stimulus package that intends to promote investment in critical tech supply chains (e.g., semiconductor manufacturing) and also re-shore outsourced chip manufacturing facilities back to the United States. Through a combination of industrial stimulus for businesses and securitized rhetoric around competition with China, the Biden administration's bill was able to get enough Republican support to pass (Partridge, 2022). According to one House policy staffer observing the process closely, the bill perfectly demonstrated the institutional formula needed for tech-related policy change at the federal level: "leadership from the executive branch coupled with leadership from the leaders of both parties in both chambers" (Hendrix and Lenhart, 2023, n.p.).

7.2.4 THE COURTS

A final, and extremely important, channel through which policy change can happen at the federal level is through the American judicial system. The Supreme Court, as well as the lower circuit and district courts, can play a substantial role in interpreting and re-interpreting matters of regulation and policy. From access to abortions and other essential forms of healthcare to the question of school segregation, the Supreme Court has consistently made decisions about some of the most impactful social and political issues of the day. For this reason, as the political scientist Robert Dahl once noted, it is not just a legal institution, but rather "a political institution, an institution, that is to say, for arriving at decisions on controversial questions of national policy" (Dahl, 1957, p.279).

The courts do not make their decisions in a vacuum. There has been active debate in US politics scholarship as to the exact political function of the courts, and the degree of independence they really have from the broader context within which they are embedded. Are judges acting unilaterally based upon their reading of the law, and their political and ideological priors (Segal et al.,

1995), or are they "appealing to norms implicitly held by other influential policy makers" through their decisions (Casper, 1976, p. 60)? How do the different policymaking forums in US politics overlap and influence each other not only in terms of decisionmaking but also when it comes to agenda-setting, framing, and other policy dynamics (J. Barnes, 2007)?

While the answers to these questions may be complicated, it is clear that the Supreme Court, in particular, has a number of institutional quirks which have made it a political battleground. Judges have lifetime appointments, and their power makes their selection process a key site of contestation. Lower court judges can also become politically important in the long term. Trump's judicial appointments at all levels came from the ranks of the Federalist Society—an organization founded during the Reagan years "in order to advance conservative ideas in the legal academy and ultimately in the [American] legal system as a whole" (Baum and Devins, 2017, n.p.). During his term, Trump was able to appoint conservative judges up and down the American legal stack: three Supreme court judges, more than fifty Circuit Court of Appeals judges, and more than a hundred and fifty District Court judges (Nemacheck, 2021). These appointments promise to have a lasting legacy on the American policy apparatus.

Overall, the judiciary is an key locus for policy ferment in the US political system. While it cannot be directly delegated to make policy by an administration, Presidents can shift the system in the medium to long term through their appointment strategies. Tilting the makeup of the courts over time also then opens up the door to strategic action from other actors interested in changing the status quo (state Attorneys General, interest groups, lobbying actors, and more), allowing them to launch tactical legal and even legislative interventions that they hope can provide an opportunity for the courts to rule and potentially reverse existing precedent on tech policy and beyond.

7.3 The States Join the Fray

If Congress is characterized by legislative gridlock, the same cannot be said for the American state legislatures. In the 50 states, 40 states have, as of early 2024, 'trifecta' governments, where both chambers of the state legislature as well as the Governor all belong to the same party. This provides them with far more institutional capacity to pass new laws—even if those laws are opposed by the other major party, by industry and civil society, or even if those laws may be effectively deemed to be unconstitutional over-extensions of state authority.

Since 2021, a huge number of platform regulation bills have been introduced in numerous state legislatures across the domains of competition policy, data protection, and content regulation (Brennen and Perault, 2022a). This veritable influx of state-level platform regulation activity has led to a few hundred varying policy efforts (some of which involve efforts to introduce the same model bill in multiple legislatures) that have made even the simple act of tracking and mapping all of this activity difficult. As of early 2023, more than two-thirds of all state legislatures had introduced bills seeking to shape how user-generated content platforms conducted their content moderation (Masnick, 2022b). In 2021, Florida and Texas actually passed content moderation-relevant legislation into law. In 2022, New York, and California followed suit. Looking at the 2021 bills in particular demonstrates the distinctly American contours of platform regulation.

7.3.1 FLORIDA

A little less than a month after the Capitol riots, Florida Governor Ron DeSantis held a press conference with a few allies in the state government—Florida's Lieutenant Governor Jeanette Nuñez, House Speaker Chris Sprowls, Senate President Wilton Simpson, Senator Danny Burgess, and House Commerce Committee Chair Blaise Ingoglia—to announce a new piece of planned legislation, the 'Transparency in Technology Act' (Office of Governor Ron DeSantis, 2021b). In January, after President Trump had his accounts removed from Facebook and Twitter, DeSantis had suggested that legislative intervention would be required to prevent firms from 'deplatforming' and censoring Republican political candidates like Trump in the future (Klas, 2021). According to local reporting, the Florida Governor then "made the tech-targeting measure one of his top 2021 legislative priorities, accusing tech companies of having a liberal bias and censoring speech by Republicans" (Juste, 2022, n.p.).

This policy strategy was on full display when, in February, DeSantis gave a speech at the Conservative Political Action Conference (CPAC), an annual event that touts itself as the "largest and most influential gathering of conservatives in the world."[6] Opening his remarks by patting himself on the back for not following public health advice during the early stages of the pandemic, noting that he was able to maintain Florida as "an oasis of freedom" amid pressure to initiate Covid lockdown measures, DeSantis moved directly to his vision of reforming tech policy:

> This year Florida's leading on banning all forms of ballot harvesting and banning third party political groups like those funded by billionaire Mark Zuckerberg from interfering in the administration of our elections. Bottom line is this ... in Florida, your vote counts and we will continue to have a process that is transparent and that inspires confidence. Florida's also leading in protecting our people from political

censorship and in holding big tech accountable. When our legislature convenes next month, it will pass and I will sign the most ambitious reforms yet proposed for combating political censorship and deplatforming, for preventing big tech from interfering in our elections, and for safeguarding the privacy of your personal data. In Florida, we are not going to let the terms of the debate in our country be set by oligarchs in Silicon Valley.

(DeSantis, 2021, n.p.)

The gambit, delivered to the massive CPAC audience, was perfectly timed. DeSantis appeared to be the first major political figure in the United States that wasn't just talking about Trump's deplatforming, but also actually offering some kind of legislative 'solution.' The Republicans held strong control over the state legislature, and unlike federal-level politicians, DeSantis had far better odds of getting his chosen bills over the finish line. As a local conservative blogger put it, the anti-tech proposals not only helped DeSantis "bank political capital and [...] put him on a winning trajectory for his 2022 [gubernatorial] reelection campaign," but also played a key role in building noise around him as a potential 2024 Republican presidential nominee (Manjarres, 2021, n.p.).

State legislatures, unlike Congress, are largely staffed by part-time elected members. This means that lawmakers are generally not professional politicians, but rather ordinary individuals that serve in the State House or Senate while on short breaks from their full-time occupation. In Florida, the legislature normally meets for two months of the year; House representatives are elected for four-year terms and State Senators for two-year terms.

The 2021 session began on March 2nd. In the first week, Representative Ingoglia filed the bill promised by DeSantis, HB 7013 on 'Technology Transparency.' The legislation proposed a number of requirements, including that platforms hosting user-generated content "Inform each user about any changes to its user rules, terms, and agreements before implementing the changes and not make changes more than once every 30 days," and that platforms no longer remove accounts or engage in the "deplatforming" of "candidates for political office."

Tech policy experts around the United States quickly pointed out the many issues with the proposal. First, while the provision to keep users updated of community guidelines seemed to follow the logic of international policy efforts like the European Platform-to-Business Regulation, which requires app stores and other marketplaces to keep their third-party business clients (e.g., developers) updated of major changes to their ranking systems or rules, the seeming implication that firms could not update their internal moderation guidelines more than once a month would mean that they would be unable to quickly respond to any emerging issues as they arose—for example, in a crisis or other situation where new types of problematic content emerged (Warzel, 2022). Second, as one commentator put it blithely, if the "bill would bar any moderation (or removal) of any political candidate," it "would just mean that any troll who wants to be a total asshole online would register to run for office" (Masnick, 2021a, n.p.).

More importantly, as numerous legal scholars pointed out, the bill seemed evidently unconstitutional on multiple grounds. By prohibiting firms from removing certain types of content, it could be read as compelling private firms to host speech that they might not want to, in violation of the First Amendment's free speech provisions (D. Keller, 2022). Additionally, the bill posed the question of state versus federal jurisdiction of internet and telecommunications-related issues (J. L. Goldsmith and Volokh, 2023), with critics arguing that it provided an undue burden on interstate commerce and fell afoul of the Constitution's 'Dormant Commerce Clause' (Rasheed, 2022). The argument here was that regulating internet services was in federal, not state jurisdiction, and furthermore, the Florida bill was in violation of the liability framework that had already been set up in the 1990s at the federal level.

These issues came up during HB 7013's first hearing, where Representative Ingoglia fielded questions from the other House Appropriation committee members. One Republican representative, Randy Fine, noted that he himself had been subject to horrible anti-Semitic content on Twitter, and that because the bar to putting your name on the ballot on state elections was so low (as "it's only a two-page form, that doesn't even require official notarization") he worried that all sorts of "Nazis, crazy people, child predators" would make use of the law so that they "won't be able to be removed or even downranked" from major platform services.[7] The Democratic Representative Joe Geller called out a number of other problems. After arguing that the private right of legal action embedded in the bill would likely create a deluge "of spurious lawsuits" harassing industry, he ended his remarks with a plea for fiscal conservatism:

> Members . . . we're going to pass something which we have strong reason to think is unconstitutional . . . we're going to spend tens, if not hundreds of thousands of dollars trying to defend another unconstitutional bill that we've passed. Ultimately, we're going to lose [in court] and the people that are going to really lose are . . . the taxpayers.[8]

Nevertheless, there were some voices on the right that actually argued that the bill did not go far enough. Laura Loomer, a far-right Islamophobic blogger and activist that had previously had her accounts removed by a slew of platform services, testified at the Committee hearing with an argument to make the bill even more stringent: increasing the fines, expanding the scope so it applied to a wider range of digital services (including ride-sharing services, delivery services, and ISPs), and mandating the retroactive reinstatement of previously 'deplatformed' accounts like hers. Some local commentators latched on to her arguments to note that "major concerns regarding the bill's effectiveness were raised by some leading Conservative influencers and thought leaders on cancel culture" (Manjarres, 2021, n.p.).

Despite its critics right and left, the bill retained its support in the DeSantis camp, as well as among key interest groups rallying behind the bill, such as the Heartland Institute, a conservative think-tank with roots in climate change denialism that had recently taken a hard-line position against American technology firms.[9] After going through the Appropriations Committee, and some apparent delays in the House Judiciary Committee, on April 1st a set of companion bills were filed in the Senate.

The first, SB 7072, was effectively the same as HB 7013. The second, SB 7074, created a public records exemption for bill SB 7072, allowing the Attorney General of Florida, as well as law enforcement agencies in the state, to mount investigations into platform firms without those needing to be subject to Florida's open government 'sunshine' and transparency laws.[10] As the Senate and House bills continued to work its way through the legislature, there was outcry from platform firms, technology industry associations, as well as many digitally oriented civil society groups (Klas, 2021, n.p.). The lead representative of pro-industry lobby and advocacy group NetChoice summarized the law's problems in a letter to Floridan legislators: the "First Amendment makes clear that government may not regulate the speech of private individuals or businesses" (Szabo, 2021, p. 1). Noting that alongside its violation of the US Constitution's First Amendment (dealing with government constraints on free speech), the deleterious impact it would have on the ability of user-generated content platforms to police spam, and the way it would expose firms to a host of problematic and potentially spurious lawsuits, NetChoice made a few arguments tailored to a Republican perspective: "Imagine if the government required a church to allow user-created comments or third-party advertisements promoting abortion on its social media page. Just as that would violate the First Amendment, so too does SB 7072 since it would similarly force social media platforms to host content they otherwise would not allow" (Szabo, 2021, p. 1).

The Republicans held a supermajority of more than two-thirds in both the Senate and House, meaning that they could effectively pass bills—no matter how problematic or poorly crafted—at will, as long as they could ensure that the members voted with the Speaker and party leadership. Democrat representatives were in the backseat, largely confined to serving as irritants asking tough questions during committees and on the floor during bill hearings. However, on HB

7013/SB 7072, they got crafty: one lawmaker, after hearing about the bill and the issues it could pose for the tech sector in the state, called up contacts at Disney, one of the largest firms in Florida and the biggest employer in the Orlando metro area. The broad definition of platforms in the bill potentially included video-streaming services like Disney Plus, or any other video-streaming service that included user-generated ratings or comments.[11]

Although the DeSantis administration seemed to have no issues ignoring the complaints about the legislation from the 'left-wing' Silicon Valley platforms, Disney, as well as Comcast (which owns and operates Universal Studio Theme Parks through a subsidiary), were important locally headquartered media and technology companies that therefore held more political sway. On April 29, just after the bill had received its third reading and was ready for formal assent, a final amendment was introduced by Senator Ray Rodrigues. The platform services in scope were now defined as:

> [Having] at least 100 million monthly individual platform participants globally. The term does not include any information service, system, Internet search engine, or access software provider operated by a company that owns and operates a theme park or entertainment complex as defined in 509.013, F.S.[12]

Disney and Comcast lobbyists had gotten an explicit exemption from the law—but Republican lawmakers had not substantially changed the definition of 'platform' in the bill, but rather, crudely tacked on a 'theme park' exception.[13]

On Monday, the 24th of May, DeSantis stood at a podium emblazoned with 'Stop Big Tech Censorship' in red and white capital letters and signed the bill into law, crowing in the accompanying press conference: "This session, we took action to ensure that 'We the People'—real Floridians across the Sunshine State—are guaranteed protection against the Silicon Valley elites [...]. Many in our state have experienced censorship and other tyrannical behavior firsthand in Cuba and Venezuela. If Big Tech censors enforce rules inconsistently, to discriminate in favor of the dominant Silicon Valley ideology, they will now be held accountable" (Office of Governor Ron DeSantis, 2021a, n.p.).

By Thursday that same week, the industry group NetChoice, along with another large trade association, the Computer and Communications Industry Association (CCIA), had filed a lawsuit against the state, seeking to invalidate the law (NetChoice, n.d.). On June 30, the District Court for the Northern District of Florida granted NetChoice and CCIA an injunction which prevented the bill from entering into force the following day, with the court agreeing with the industry argument that the legislation violated the First Amendment,

134 FROM COAST TO COAST

contradicted established federal communications law statutes, and additionally was problematic as viewpoint-based discrimination intended to target specific firms based on their perceived political ideology.[14] The action wasn't over, however: the Florida Attorney General appealed the District Court decision to a higher court, the 11th Circuit.

7.3.2 TEXAS

Lawmakers in other states were also seeking to intervene in similar ways to Florida. In parallel to the introduction of DeSantis's much-heralded bill in March, there had quietly been a bill put forth in the Texas legislature with similar goals.

The Texas legislature also meets extremely infrequently, and is supposed to be in session for about four months every two years. While some observers might call it 'limited government in practice,' this creates a compressed, highly intense session where a huge amount of legislation is proposed but only a minority actually finds the floor time to be debated and potentially passed.[15] Before the session, the caucuses meet and develop an agenda, which generally reflects not just the Governor's priorities but also those of the party leaders in the legislature—something that is steered in particular by the Lt. Governor, who oversees the work of the Senate, and the House Speaker, who does the same for the House. As these different actors hash out their legislative priorities, according to norm certain bills are assigned low numbers (e.g., between 1 and 20) to informally mark them as 'must pass' priority bills for members.

Senate Bill 12, "relating to the censorship of users' expressions by an interactive computer service" was introduced in early March 2021 by Senator Bryan Hughes, a state representative known for trying to pass legislation on the most hot-button issues for Republicans on the extreme right. (In the 87th session of 2021, that involved legislation seeking to make abortion illegal in Texas once the Supreme Court's Dobbs decision went effect, as well as this 'deplatforming' related legislation; in the 88th session, which began in spring 2023, Hughes introduced bills trying to outlaw the teaching of critical race theory in Texas universities and limit access to gender-affirming healthcare for trans youth.) A short two-page bill, SB 12 sought to limit firms operating in Texas from conducting 'viewpoint'-based discrimination when moderating content, as long as that content was not illegal: the bill stated that "An interactive computer service may not censor a user, a user's expression, or a user's ability to receive the expression of another person based on: (1) the viewpoint of the user or another person; [or] (2) the viewpoint represented in the user's expression or another person's expression." Clearly designed to try and prevent firms from moderating the content of Trump and other leading conservative figures, academics were quick to point out that due to this very general definition, and the wide range of speech that remained legal in the United States under the First Amendment, a huge amount of socially and politically problematic speech—from beheading videos to the glorification of Nazis to pro-anorexia content—would no longer be able to be moderated by platform firms due to this 'must carry' obligation (Warzel, 2022).

SB 12 did not sail through the legislature as smoothly as SB 7072 did in Florida, however, even though Texas also has a Republican trifecta, with Republican control of both the House and Senate as well as the Governor's office. After its introduction, the bill was promptly referred to the State Affairs Committee, chaired by Senator Hughes, and a public hearing was scheduled for March 8th. Any individual can show up to this hearing and get a chance to speak, and two unaffiliated members of the public offered support for the bill with only three registered opponents: representatives from NetChoice, the Internet Association, and TechNet, an industry organization with special expertise in state-level tech policy (and a regional presence in Texas).

These organizations receive dues from their member organizations, which generally run the gamut from assorted platform firms with various business models to more established 'legacy' technology (software, hardware, telecommunication, service provision) companies largely pursuing non-platform business models. Industry associations help these firms monitor policy developments at the fragmented and fast-moving state legislature level (by hosting frequent meetings that policy and legal staff at member companies can join to be updated on the latest developments, for instance) and in recent years have been delegated expansive lobbying and advocacy functions in a wide range of policy negotiations by industry. These organizations also can help firms present a united industry front when facing prospective policy change (even when actual preferences relating the legislation might be heterogeneous across different firms and firm types), and have the additional benefit of helping the largest firms maintain a lower public profile, given the press coverage that often accompanies direct forms of platform opposition to a policy via a legal challenge, public statement, or inside lobbying. As one industry association representative working on the Texas bills described, their organizations are constantly working behind the scenes, "meeting with lawmakers, providing concrete feedback on policies, working votes, and massaging legislation" on behalf of the tech sector.[16]

These industry groups sought to introduce friction into SB 12's passage, in particular by amplifying potential cleavages in the Republican caucus—between the slightly more centrist tendencies of House leader Phelan and the more extremist agenda of Senate leader Patrick (Garrett, 2023)—and in the American conservative movement more generally. For example, documents submitted

136 FROM COAST TO COAST

to the Committees conducting hearings on content moderation policies by TechNet featured a discussion of 'what conservatives are saying about content moderation,' featuring quotes about the problems of content-based technology policy from think-tanks on the right, Texas Republicans opposing similar bills, and even some classic remarks made by Ronald Reagan.[17]

The briefing package also highlighted a number of insights from the American Legislative Exchange Council (ALEC), a highly influential policy network that provides state legislators across the United States—many of whom are only part-time politicians and operate without significant resources or policy staff—with access to a vast archive of pre-written model bills across a range of topics relevant to the conservative movement, as well as advice from policy experts on various topics (Hertel-Fernandez, 2019). ALEC is now widely recognized as one of the key actors in the American right's highly effective strategy of policy mobilization at the state and local levels in the past decades, and has been instrumental in fomenting a pro-business, de-regulatory agenda of tax cuts, public service privatization, and lower environmental, health, and labor standards through state legislatures across the country (Hertel-Fernandez, 2019). However, its agenda has occasionally come into tension with the recent Republican 'culture wars,' including around Big Tech: as the Utah lawmaker elected as ALEC's President in 2021 put it, "how do you want to regulate someone if you don't believe in regulation?" (McKellar, 2021, n.p.).

Instead, the longstanding ALEC consensus has been non-interventionist and pro-industry, with its multistakeholder policy development task force on communications and technology (composed of company representatives as well as legislators and policy advisors) having historically taken a strong stance against virtually all kinds of government-led tech regulation. Industry groups sought to leverage ALEC's networks and reputation among conservative state lawmakers, circulating widely a 2018 declaration from the group that seemed to envision exactly the kinds of regulatory intervention that Texas and Florida were pursuing. The declaration notes that "even if online platforms were to exhibit political bias in content display or moderation, the First Amendment protects this exercise of editorial discretion from government intervention" (ALEC, 2018, n.p.).

SB 12 was one of Lt. Governor Dan Patrick's 30 top bills for 2021 (Patrick, 2021), but it wasn't initially one of Governor Greg Abbott's stated priorities. In his 'State of the State' address on February 1st, Abbott did not mention content moderation or platform policy, focusing instead on issues that included pandemic recovery, broadband access, buttressing police budgets, tightening bail conditions, and outlawing abortion. But a month later he voiced his support for SB 12 in a press conference, saying that he would actively work with Senator Hughes to ensure that the bill became law (Keene, 2021). After the hearing on SB 12 in the Senate State Affairs committee on March 8th, Senator Hughes made a number of changes to the bill, which was re-introduced via a vote of the State Affairs Committee as 'the new committee version' on March 22nd, 2021. This bill updated some of the language from the previous draft, substituting all mention of 'interactive computer services' with the more timely jargon 'social media platforms,' and introducing new provisions that updated the previous language of 'censorship' to involve specific demands relating to 'complaint procedures and disclosure requirements.'[18] It also now included a 'private right of action,' where any user could bring lawsuits against social media platforms for potential violations of SB 12.

In particular, this private right of action was something being advocated by Adam Candeub, a law professor at Michigan State University who had previously worked in the Trump administration in 2019 as Deputy Assistant Secretary of Commerce for Telecommunications and Information and, in that capacity, had played an important role in Trump's anti-Twitter executive order (Bokhari, 2021a). After Trump's electoral defeat, Candeub had become one of an increasingly influential group of legal academics on the right that were re-interpreting First Amendment doctrine as well as jurisprudence around Section 230 immunity in an effort to make their desired forms of regulatory change institutionally possible.

Via a constellation of both new and established conservative think-tanks, policy networks, and legal advocacy organizations, ranging from the Heritage Foundation and Heartland Institute to the Federalist Society and Columbia law Professor Philip Hamburger's New Civil Liberties Alliance, a growing number of these voices were advancing the argument that certain readings of the US Constitution, as well as existing American telecommunications precedent, could perhaps permit government regulation of platform content moderation, maybe by branding them 'akin to common carriers' like interstate telegraph operators or the postal service (Federalist Society, 2021; Hamburger, 2021). This rising coalition was seeking to galvanize state action around content moderation, seeing the states as a path to potential policy change—and a way to shift the general policy discourse in the United States nationally—given federal gridlock (and Democrat control of the House and Senate). Heartland Institute President James Taylor noted in 2021 that their "government relations staff personally discussed tech censorship with legislators in all 50 states this year, giving them the ammunition to go on the offensive against Big Tech censorship" (Taylor, 2021, n.p.), providing alternative policy advice and guidance on bills to fill the void that would have traditionally been provided by ALEC and similar pro-Industry organizations.

In a legislature which is so rarely in session, one would anticipate that the timing of bill introduction, and the logistics around the committee calendar, floor readings, and other general procedural matters, become hugely important. Texas policymakers face an additional unique institutional wrinkle that makes these politics even more difficult: a clause in its state Constitution that only permits bills to be passed after 60 days, meaning that there are only really 80 days where floor votes can happen (Samuels, 2019). Given that more than ten thousand bills have been introduced in the last few Texas legislative sessions, Democrat representatives that are otherwise relatively powerless to affect policy can seek to obfuscate and delay bill passage through various procedural tricks.[19] For example, one of Governor Abbott's priority bills, SB 7, branded by him as crucial 'election reform' legislation—and as 'voter suppression' and 'voter intimidation' legislation by Texas Democrats—was derailed when Democrats in the House left the House chambers, breaking the legislature's quorum and bringing an early end to the proceedings (Lindell, 2021). Industry organizations were able to similarly galvanize Democratic members in the House to use procedural tactics to make the passage of anti-tech bills more difficult. As the session drew to a close, the content moderation-focused SB 12 did not make it back to the Senate in time for final votes, due to a last minute point of order called by Democrats (Bokhari, 2021b):

> All Senate bills needed to be read a second time on the House floor before midnight, and in the early evening Tuesday, lawmakers were still pages away from the social media censorship bill. The legislation was postponed multiple times after Democrats in the chamber used delay tactics to slow down debate on that bill and other Republican priorities.
> (Glynn, 2021, n.p.)

The road for bill SB 12 may have ended there, and this could have been a story of veto points and institutional maneuvering cannily deployed by Texas Democrats to successfully impede some of the Republican policy agenda. However, Governor Abbott had an ace up his sleeve: another clause in the state Constitution which allows the Governor to call special 'emergency' legislative sessions. Because Democrat stalling tactics had helped the Democrats block a number of Abbott's priority bills, especially on "Election Integrity and Bail Reform [as] must-pass emergency items," the Governor announced that he would call an additional 30-day session to ensure adequate time for these laws to be passed (G. Abbott, 2021, n.p.). Under this framework, the Texas Governor can choose to keep the legislature active, calling multiple 30-day sessions to help fulfill the party's policy agenda—a powerful institutional workaround to be deployed against delay tactics. (In 1989, Governor William Clements called a record six consecutive special sessions, keeping the legislature working for almost another full year.)[20]

A little over a week after this announcement, a press release from Abbott's office included the topics to be considered in the special session, slated to begin on July 8. The previously mentioned bail reform and election laws topped the list, but they were now followed by border security as well as 'social media censorship' (Office of the Texas Governor, 2021a). The 'must-carry' 'non-viewpoint discrimination' bill was back in play, repackaged as Senate Bill 5 and introduced by Senator Hughes on the first day the session opened. The companion bill, House Bill 20, was introduced into the House by Representative Briscoe Cain on July 13. That week, Texas House Democrats flew en masse to Washington, DC, vowing to stay out of the state to try and prevent quorum from being reached in the House as part of their effort to get some negotiating power on the voting restriction bill at the heart of Abbott's special session agenda. They were partially successful on this, indeed killing enough time in the first special session for it to expire without major victories for the Governor (Livingston and Ura, 2021). But a number of Democrats broke ranks and began trickling back in August, as a second special session was called by Abbott (Barragán, 2021).

At this point, as the legislature reconvened and it began looking increasingly likely that SB 5/HB 20 would be passed, national attention around it intensified. To help expedite the passage of it and other key bills, House Speaker Phelan formed a new special committee, the 'Select Committee on Constitutional Rights and Remedies.' HB 20 was heard again by this new committee on August 23rd, with the same trio of representatives from NetChoice, TechNet, and the Internet Association testifying against the bill, along with the head of a local free-market-oriented think-tank, the Institute for Policy Innovation.[21] Notably, a few local civil society groups also registered their opposition at the meeting, including the ACLU of Texas and Public Citizen, a consumer protection advocacy group. By this time, the Florida law had gone through the first layer of the American legal system, with a judge deeming it unconstitutional on multiple grounds. TechNet and the other industry associations circulated the ruling to committee members, noting that "if HB 20 passes, it will most certainly be challenged and found to be unconstitutional for similar reasons."[22] They also marshaled polling figures, which they deployed to argue that the measure was going to be electorally unpopular.

Despite the resistance of industry groups, and their apparently strong legal arguments, they could not swing enough of the committee members or exert influence sufficient to convince enough Republican representatives to kill the bill. House Democrats Howard and Rosenthal sought to introduce amendments which would make vaccine misinformation and anti-Semitic content exceptions to the types of 'viewpoints' that platforms would now be forced to carry if the regulation came into effect, but this last-ditch effort to communicate issues relating

140 FROM COAST TO COAST

to the legislation to potentially sympathetic legislators fell flat. On September 2nd, the last day of the Special Session, HB20 passed in the House. It was signed by the Governor a week later.

7.4 Discussion

Shortly after the bill was signed, NetChoice and CCIA once again brought a lawsuit seeking to get the legislation overturned. They had a strong legal argument, and were able to coordinate a huge array of parties from civil society, academia, and industry as 'amici' against the Texas law. While there was some expert disagreement on certain minor provisions of the law (especially around the question of whether narrower transparency mandates, as opposed to the broader 'must-carry' provisions) might be permitted as constitutional, on balance, the case seemed relatively clear for the courts. The Texas and Florida laws were evidently problematic, violating not just the platform firms' First Amendment rights but also aspects of the Constitution that related to federal precedent and the regulation of interstate commerce. So the question stands: how and why has there been such a torrential influx of state-level bills—with Texas and Florida only marking the first to pass—being pursued not just on general trust and safety-related questions, but also, as of 2023, on a host of more targeted questions, such as those at the intersection of platform policies and child safety?

To my mind, the most logical answer involves a combination of demand-side incentives for the range of political actors at play, as well as the narrow set of supply factors that allow state legislators to pass such bills, if not actually implement or enforce them. There appear to be a range of powerful local drivers for state legislators to pursue such policies, and to see them as relatively low-cost and potentially high-reward: as one interviewee remarked, nearly all of the key figures directly pushing Big Tech bills in Texas and Florida can be said to have higher political aspirations. Both Governor Ron DeSantis and Governor Greg Abbott are potential US presidential candidates; there was speculation that Texas Attorney General Ken Paxton, who also played a role in advocating for the legislation, was hoping to run for Texas Governor (a dream that now seems unlikely given his impeachment for fraud in May 2023). Another interviewee speculated that Texas Senator Bryan Hughes has hopes of running for Lt. Governor, and in the next election cycle he will be able to proudly campaign on having introduced bills not just making abortions far more dangerous and difficult to procure but also on generally 'fighting to keep Big Tech accountable.' The same can be said for all the other Republicans involved in these efforts in both states, seeking to ride the policy shock of the Capitol riots to communicate their dissatisfaction with the status quo to the media and to their constituents.

Given the complexity and nuances of tech policy, and perhaps the high degree of wonkiness it demands from the public, policy signaling seems to be a logical strategy for state legislators, who can pursue deceptively simple policies, betting that they will be seen as doing something by constituents, and—as the judicial review process to have their bills overturned or invalidated takes a long time— that they will not be held accountable if their efforts ultimately fail. It is clear that DeSantis was especially effective at using simplistic Big Tech-related arguments to influence the national-level policy discourse and help position himself as a viable Trump 2.0 candidate for the Republican party in 2024.

Beyond these very direct micro-level preferences, there are a growing number of motivated coalitions conducting policy entrepreneurship via the states as part of a long-term strategy to foment regulatory change at the federal level. Part of this involves agenda setting and issue framing, with a growing number of conservative legal intellectuals airing the argument that platforms might indeed be akin to common carriers, for instance. But another aspect of this strategy involves the recognition that the US judiciary is not a static institution and itself can be shifted over time. Was Trump able to shift the ideological character of the judiciary significantly through his hundreds of appointments? Will his judges, many of whom are members of the Federalist Society, break from the ideological mainstream on key issues pertaining to tech policy?

These judges appear to be part of the strategy for groups on the right like Heartland actively lobbying state legislatures to pursue a particular vision of platform regulation. If enough legislation is passed, and then appealed, could these groups get an opportunity to argue their case in front of sympathetic judges with an opportunity to reverse precedent? Something like this happened in Texas. After losing the initial complaint about the constitutionality of HB 20 in the district court, it was appealed by the state to the 5th Circuit Court, where the judge—a Federalist Society Trump appointee—argued that the policy was in fact justified. The opinion, written by Judge Andrew Oldham (who happened to previously be the General Counsel for Texas Governor Greg Abbott), echoed the language of the Texas and Florida laws, brashly "reject[ing] the idea that corporations have a freewheeling First Amendment right to censor what people say."[23] One leading content moderation commentator observed that this opinion sought to "rewrite a century of First Amendment law" (Masnick, 2022a, n.p.).

The 11th Circuit, considering Florida's SB 7072, also featured a panel of three Republican judges. But its opinion—written by Judge Kevin Newsom, also a Trump appointed Federalist member—struck much closer to the case law, ruling that Silicon Valley's platform firms were still private actors with protected speech under the US Constitution. The Court argued that the bill was indeed generally unconstitutional, although it suggested that some of its transparency provisions were less onerous and could be upheld. The split between the appeals courts on the similar Texas and Florida bills has provided an opportunity for the Supreme Court to intervene when it hears the cases in 2024 (R. Barnes and Marimow, 2022).

Other research will need to deploy different methodologies to study the extent to which the demand for changes to the content moderation regulatory status quo in these states came from the top-down (the executive branches of the Texas and Florida governments; key policy officials), the bottom-up (constituents making their voices heard), or from somewhere in the middle (interest groups channeling, or purporting to channel constituent demand into new policy priorities). But counterfactuals from other states help illuminate potential points where things could have been different for Florida SB 7072 and Texas HB 20. Utah, for example, is another Republican trifecta state that saw a deplatforming bill similar to Florida and Texas passed by the legislature in 2021. However, the Republican Governor of Utah ended up vetoing the bill, even though his brother-in-law was its main champion, at least partially due to the successful deployment of arguments around fiscal prudence: the bill's opponents consistently communicated that the bill would be bogged down in very expensive litigation and likely overturned in the Florida and Texas mold if it were to be introduced, wasting significant state resources in the process (Gehrke, 2021). This argument—which did not appear to gain traction in Texas or Florida—was cited by the Utah Governor in his veto announcement (Schott, 2021).

In 2022 and 2023, a number of more subtle content moderation-related bills were also passed in the blue-state trifecta governments of California and New York. Whereas the New York 'hateful conduct' bill is a contested platform regulation strategy following a classic template outlined in this book—a response to policy shock, in this case, a live-streamed mass shooting in Buffalo, NY. California's Age Appropriate Design Code legislation, on the other hand, offers something unique: the successful mobilization of transnational civil society and 'tech reform' interest groups to drive regulatory change in a key jurisdiction. That same extremely savvy coalition—which unified parents, youth organizations, child safety groups, and other actors—appears to have executed an effective combination of policymaker-focused inside advocacy as well as public-facing awareness campaigns (5Rights Foundation, 2022). After an initial success in California, the Age Appropriate Design Code Coalition, which is spearheaded by the UK organization 5Rights and US-based tech regulation advocacy group Reset, also sought to get their model bill passed in other US states, including the blue trifectas of Maryland and Minnesota, but to no avail thus far (Praiss, 2023).

Both New York and California laws have been subject to legal challenges, with the New York bill being defeated on First Amendment grounds in a New York court and NetChoice seeking to overturn the Age Appropriate Design Code in California (Winterton, 2023; Goldman, 2023). Much going forward will depend on how the courts—especially the Supreme Court—rule on this multitude of state-related platform regulation cases that are coming their way.

Part Three

LOOKING FORWARD

8

Platform Regulation and the Majority World

Not only high-income electoral democracies are seeking to shape how global platform businesses conduct online content moderation. While robust data on the emergence and diffusion of different types of platform regulation at the global level does not yet exist,[1] the best existing data looking at the general landscape of intermediary liability policy demonstrates a steady, ongoing increase in the amount of relevant formal laws being enacted to govern online content globally (see Figure 8.1).

Although a growing number of jurisdictions are pursuing data protection reform or competition remedies that might impact certain types of platforms, looking regionally suggests that a smaller number of countries are doing so in the global context than may be expected. In the realm of user-generated online content, many countries—especially on the African continent, in Latin America, and in Asia—are instead maintaining the status quo and convincing, working within the established channels enacted by companies rather than seeking to layer new rules on top of the regulatory status quo. Why is this the case?

Unfortunately, in-depth analyses of all manner of jurisdictions and the factors that lead them to *not* pursue change to the platform governance status quo must be left to future work. This book's framework, however, provides researchers with a toolbox with which to do so. (Are the countries that have yet to pursue collaborative or coercive platform regulation not doing so because of demand-side factors—such as a lack of issue salience among policymakers and the public, or perhaps successful lobbying efforts from firms?—or supply-side factors, such as issues with regulatory capacity or transnational institutional strictures?)

There are at least a dozen countries that have pursued various legislative approaches seeking to crack down on 'harmful content' in recent years. Not all of these would be considered platform regulation under my definition, as

The Politics of Platform Regulation: How Governments Shape Online Content Moderation. Robert Gorwa, Oxford University Press. © Oxford University Press 2024. DOI: 10.1093/oso/9780197692851.003.0008

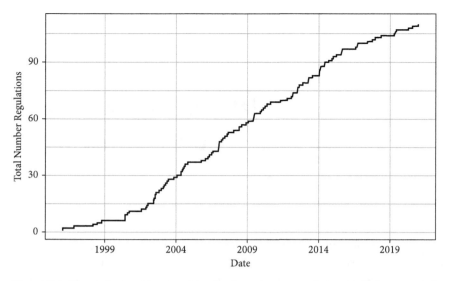

Figure 8.1 The evolution of national-level online content regulation, excluding copyright and intellectual property-related laws. Data from the Stanford World Intermediary Liability Map.

many simply seek to bolster measures for obtaining content takedowns via orders to ISPs and other content providers rather than actually shape platform moderation practices. Regardless, these jurisdictions are often under-examined in global platform policy conversations due to their distance from the European and North American markets, or only attract major attention when something goes really wrong. These countries vary in size, market power, and regulatory capacity, ranging from the high-income yet undersized Singapore to the lower-per-capita-income but extremely populous state of India, both of which have been important actors in this policy arena both domestically and transnationally. Furthermore, there is China: an information environment largely cut off from internationally headquartered user-generated content firms, but nonetheless an important and unique player in the global platform governance conversation.

I hope that future research can investigate these vital jurisdictions in the empirically informed detail that they deserve. Nevertheless, in what follows, I provide a short exposition of important recent regulatory developments in three countries that have become particularly important in the global platform regulation discourse: China, India, and Brazil. While these are not full case studies driven by newly collected original data as in Part II of this book, I draw upon burgeoning scholarship on 'comparative platform capitalism,' as well as analyses of media coverage, publicly released primary source documents, and policy papers to show the plausibility of the book's framework for thinking about the politics of platform regulation in a variety of different contexts.

Table 8.1 **Notable recent international content-focused regulation developments.**

Jurisdiction	Initiative	Date	Status (2023)
Brazil	Law of Liberty, Responsibility and Transparency on the Internet (PL 2630/2020)	2020, 2023	Draft
China	Provisions on Ecological Governance of Network Information Content	2020	In Force
India	Information Technology (Intermediary Guidelines and Digital Media Ethics Code) Rules	2021	In Force
Indonesia	Ministerial Regulation 5	2020	In Force
Malaysia	Anti-Fake News Act	2018	Repealed
Malaysia	Emergency (Essential Powers) Ordinance Bill no. 2	2021	In Force
Nigeria	Code of Practice for Interactive Computer Service Platforms/Internet Intermediaries	2022	Draft
Pakistan	Citizens Protection against Online Harm Rules	2020, 2021	In Force
Russia	Federal Law on Information, Information Technologies, and Information Protection	2020	In Force
Singapore	Protection from Online Falsehoods and Manipulation Act	2019	In Force
Turkey	Regulating Internet Publications and Combating Crimes Committed by Means of Such Publications (No. 5651)	2020	In Force

8.1 China

As one of the world's most populous countries, a rapidly growing economy, and the central rising power in international politics, the question of China always lingers behind globally oriented accounts of internet policy. It has become common to argue, as French President Emmanuel Macron did at the 2019 Internet Governance Forum, that recent years have seen the emergence of three different 'internets,' or different technology governance models: a Californian unregulated internet, a Chinese tightly controlled internet, and a European middle ground of sorts (Haggart, Tusikov, and Scholte, 2021; Bradford, 2023). While arguments like Macron's may tend towards a caricature of 'internet fragmentation' and overemphasize differences between these purported regulatory models rather than their similarities, it is certainly true that China exhibits a number of special characteristics.

Firstly, China has the world's second largest tech industry, and is really the only country with companies that can rival the United States' giants. Key players like Baidu and WeChat have more than a billion global users each, and there is a rich ecosystem of Chinese video, image, and text-oriented user-generated content platforms enmeshed in the lives of hundreds of millions of others.[2] However, most of these firms are firmly oriented towards the domestic Chinese market, which due to a combination local economic, regulatory, and institutional factors—including state-firm interlinkages (Rolf and Schindler, 2023), public investment, and a lack of meaningful competition from foreign firms, many of which do not operate in the country or have left the country due to their unwillingness to be seen complying with regulatory demands (MacKinnon, 2013)—is dominated by these companies. It is safe to say that no country other than the United States has such a high concentration of domestic market share, across various platform sectors, taken by its own homegrown firms.

Secondly, the Chinese government has long taken a highly interventionist and proactive attitude to content governance across a variety of media, which has been extended to today's user-content-oriented-platforms. "In China, both the governance of platforms and the governance by platform (or platform governance) are in most cases combined into one word, Pingtai Zhili, which literally means platform governance," write Cai and Wang (2022, p. 246), noting that in China platform governance is seen as both a form of economic market management as well as a key matter to maintain governance capacity in a digitized society. The Chinese executive seems to have been effective in bringing together multiple arms of the regulatory state in an effort to police content across the internet stack. For instance, Liu and Yang (2022, p. 309) describe the 'Net Clean Action' coordinated by the Chinese Administration of Cyberspace (CAC), which launched in 2011 and involves a range of regulatory authorities including the National Office for Combating Pornography and Illegality, the Ministry of Public Security, the State Internet Information Office, the Ministry of Industry and Information Technology, and the Ministry of Culture, as well as various state-level authorities.

Chinese regulatory efforts are wide-ranging, blurring administrative law, informal pressure, and general industry-norm setting, with Liu and Yang (2022, p. 313) noting that "by June 2021, the CAC had issued 24 effective departmental regulations and normative documents related to content governance" across a range of platform types, including live-streaming, Twitter-esque microblogging, direct messaging, and a host of other online forums. One of the most important frameworks appears to be the 2020 Provisions on Ecological Governance of Network Information Content; the CAC produly claims that this regulation prompted domestic platforms like Weibo, Toutiaou, and Baidu to remove hundreds of millions of instances of improper or illegal user content (Liu and Yang, 2022). As part of these frameworks, firms have been subjected to range of compliance structures, including physical inspections of facilities and company operations, as well as various forms of obligatory transparency reporting and audits.

8.1.1 ANALYSIS

China has successfully brought a combination of collaborative and contested platform regulation to bear on the tech companies active in its jurisdiction. This has been driven on the demand side by a huge amount of state interest in content governance. On the supply side, it has been enabled by high levels of regulatory capacity and ample executive power and single-party control. The Chinese government faces relatively few domestic (normative, institutional) or international constraints on this policymaking ability (e.g., trade agreements, or other institutional channels for foreign governments to exert pressure on regulators to soften their approach).

The relationship between firms and the state in China is certainly complicated, and an especially difficult matter for non-experts to disentangle. Critical accounts complicate the classic narrative of pure authoritarian control over the Chinese media ecosystem, emphasizing the Chinese struggle against the British and American empires in the nineteenth and twentieth century and how the media system and the state co-evolved during efforts to modernize the country and "shape the contours of Chinese modernity" (Zhao 2012, cited in M. Davis and Xiao, 2021). Historically, China has adopted a more mercantilist form of corporate organization, with state-owned enterprises, close firm-state ties in many sectors, and since at least the 1990s, hybrid institutional forms like the 'mixed ownership reform' structures that further blurred the distinction between private and public capital (Zhang and Chen, 2022).

Despite this, Chinese platform firms in many cases have slightly different origins as private enterprises, where their growth was fostered through an initially laissez-faire attitude on behalf of government in the name of economic growth and innovation. Even when they may have competed with state-owned enterprises (Zhang and Chen, 2022), "regulators did not enforce non-compete agreements, introduce rules against preferential treatment of affiliated operations, holding companies, or adjudicate disputes in ways that might restrain the expansion of digital platforms" (Jia and Kenney, 2022, p. 16). However, this began to change in the 2010s, as economic dependence on the platform firms began to be perceived by policymakers as a potential risk (Zhang and Chen, 2022). The interests of Chinese officials thus shifted towards more intensive control over platform operations in general, including by pursuing more muscular competition policies. When it comes to the regulation of online content moderation specifically, however, government oversight and control is a much longer-standing norm, drawing from the tradition in the media and information media sector as well, with platform governance seen as an extension of "the conventional news policy, with the principle of the [Communist party of China] in charge of the media" (Liu and Yang, 2022, p. 318).

This demand for tighter rules for platforms, including for platform content moderation and content governance operations, is enabled by an institutional context that scholars have called "administrative dominance" (Liu and Yang, 2022, p. 313). There are far fewer constraints on executive power to set rules in China, and enough bureaucratic capacity to enforce them, given a whole of government approach that can combine the resources and expertise of different regulatory authorities across various departments and offices. This capacity is enabled in many cases by direct branches of governmental contacts and compliance departments directly inside the organizational structures of firms. Penalties for potential non-compliance are high, with fines, firm closure, and the imprisonment or banishment of executives all on the table. Twitter and Facebook had their licenses to operate in China revoked in 2009, after their services were used to share coverage of protests in Xinjiang (Barry, 2022). International firms which surreptitiously complied with the Chinese government's moderation and data sharing policies have exited the country to save face back at home (as famously in the case of Google), but doing so means that they must bear the cost of missing out on one of the world's largest markets.

For domestically headquartered platforms, non-compliance with the structures of content-oriented platform regulation is a highly risky proposition. Instead, in a context of 'administrative dominance,' regulation becomes part of the cost of doing business for domestic industry, rather than a potential threat to profitability or core business model. If powerful domestic stakeholders are aligned in favor of the status quo, there are fewer opportunities for meaningful opposition from business interests (although theoretically there could be some interesting cases of industry elites seeking to subtly shape policymaker preferences in the long term).

Importantly, there do not appear to be many strong constraints on government interests in platform regulation, or their ability to supply this regulation domestically. One potential source of push-back against government regulation could involve public perception and preferences. While it is very difficult to properly and empirically understand the extent to which these policies are popular and representative of public wishes, work from Chinese scholars has suggested that there is support for regulation focused on content governance, with tens of millions of 'tips' to remove certain accounts or instances of content from platforms claimed to have been made by citizens to government authorities each month (Liu and Yang, 2022). Although there have been high-profile instances of public dissent from the Chinese platform policy status quo by academics and activists (as by workers in the platform-mediated economy), and these can get significant public traction (Lei, 2021), substantial 'glasnost' on the content governance front remains unlikely as long as the executive views information control as both normatively acceptable and politically essential.

A second potential constraint on the Chinese government's ability to pursue binding or voluntary platform regulation would involve the existence of transnational linkages to other states or firms that might tie policymaker and/or industry hands in some way. Much has recently been written about the potential of these linkages to be 'weaponized' as a mode for other governments to exert control (Farrell and Newman, 2019b), but in this context, most of the relevant firms are domestically based, don't have foreign supply chains or contracting relationships that would meaningfully impact their decisionmaking, and as a result have yet to be exploited in this way. These linkages are scarce in terms of formal international agreements or trade agreements, but do exist in terms of financial networks: for instance, there has been much investment in Chinese companies from global venture capital firms (Zhang and Chen, 2022). However, it seems overall as if these international investors have accepted that China's domestic platform governance system is a necessary part of firm operations and profits, and are willing to swallow the free expression issues that may be the result.

The final innovation of the major Chinese platforms is their flexible adaptation to foreign preferences internationally. As Liu and Yang (2022, p. 320) write, describing what they call a "dual track" trust and safety strategy, "ByteDance adapted to the world's two major content governance systems in a 'one company, two systems' approach, creating the Douyin and TikTok twins." Chinese domestic firms can spin off an international company that operates in non-Chinese markets and works with platform governance practices and policies that are otherwise the global norm, allowing companies like TikTok to compete globally without needing to adhere to Chinese content moderation practices that might be seen as unacceptable for consumers in other countries.

Due to the adaptiveness of Chinese industry, the discrete political context and depth of state-firm interlinkages, as well as the lack of meaningful channels for multi-party competition, the Chinese state can pursue both collaborative and contested platform regulation strategies to meet its goals almost at will.

8.2 India

Neck-and-neck with China in the race to be the most populous country in the world, India is one of the largest, fastest growing, and—increasingly—most important markets for global technology companies. It is the largest market for both Facebook and Instagram users (400–500 million each), a staggering number considerably greater than the total population of the United States. So many Indians are on YouTube that their numbers are comparable to the amount of YouTube users in the United States and the European Union combined. Across a range of user-generated platform types, from the business-focused LinkedIn to messaging services like WhatsApp, India is either the primary or second largest market for most technology firms operating globally oriented platform services.[3] The Indian tech economy is especially notable in that it features a vibrant mix of the usual multinational corporate suspects that dominate European and North American markets, but also offerings from domestic players (Bhat, 2022), including powerful 'megacorp' national champions, like the sector-straddling Reliance Jio (Athique and Kumar, 2022).

India is also the world's largest democracy, a hugely complex political system with a distinct regulatory tradition. And it has become increasingly assertive on digital policy matters in recent years, leading to adversarial showdowns with various international platform firms. In 2020, an executive order sought to ban TikTok, WeChat, and other apps developed by Chinese platform firms from App Stores accessible in India (BBC Newsdesk, 2020). A few months later, the government also went head to head with Amazon (M. Singh, 2021), as the Ministry of Commerce and Industry announced new foreign direct investment rules that sought to prevent major e-commerce platforms from self-preferencing their own products (e.g., via the Amazon Basics brand). In May 2021, Twitter's Indian headquarters were raided by the Delhi Police, following a months-long showdown revolving around the companies' reticence to comply with government requests to remove accounts critical of the Modi administration (Daniyal, 2021).

In the realm of content moderation and trust and safety, India has steadily moved away from a regulatory approach once modeled on the European e-Commerce Directive and towards its own unique (and far more strict) model (Devadasan, 2022). Updates to the Indian Intermediary Liability rules made in 2021 and 2022 give regulators and government officials far more tools to pressure companies to obtain content takedowns (Chacko, Misra, and Mishra, 2021). The Indian executive is increasingly insisting that user-generated content platforms make controversial technical interventions (e.g., proactive content screening and takedown, weakened encryption) and comply with novel but potentially problematic bureaucratic structures, such as 'grievance councils' that issue notices for the takedown of specific instances of content (Press Trust of India, 2021). All of this is happening in a context where the Hindu-nationalist government of Narendra Modi is consolidating power and, it seems, increasingly seeking to pressure social media firms to censor activists, journalists, and those in the opposition (Bhat, 2023). It is a difficult environment for firms to navigate, and for the past few years, a growing number of observers have been calling attention to the potential global knock-on effects to how platforms behave in India (Sherman, 2019).

8.2.1 INTERMEDIARY GUIDELINES 2021–2022

The core regulatory framework impacting the companies operating user-generated content platforms in India was laid out in the IT Act of 2000 (Majithia, 2019). Here, safe harbor protections were offered for intermediaries unless they could be found to have 'actual knowledge' of certain content being illegal, a provision that gave firms wide latitude to set standards and police their services according to their business interests. This framework was made more stringent in 2008, following an amendment to the law that resulted in the implementation of a notice-and-takedown framework that increased the pressure on providers to remove illegal content in the 36 hours following a complaint (Arun, 2014). But it was then de facto loosened in 2015, after a high-profile Supreme Court ruling established that only a judicial court order should be understood to constitute 'actual knowledge' on the part of a platform—meaning that firms could not be found criminally liable for failing to act (or acting too slowly) on complaints managed by non-judicial channels (Devadasan, 2022). This decision was hailed by civil society and free expression advocates as a major victory (Panday, 2015), especially given concerns that other outcomes would increase the incentive for platform firms to over-remove legitimate speech and user activity when enforcing and designing their policies.

In 2018, however, discussions began at various levels of the Modi government to amend the IT Act again to create a number of new obligations for platform companies. These included the deployment of mandatory automated content screening tools, as well as pressure on end-to-end encrypted services to institute new technical features that would allow investigators to determine the originator of certain widely shared messages (B. Medeiros and P. Singh, 2020). Through a non-legislative rule-setting process under the auspices of the Ministry of Electronics and Information Technology, a coercive platform regulation strategy was deployed.

The ensuing 'Intermediary Guidelines and Digital Media Ethics Code Rules' of 2021 have been called a "paradigm shift" in Indian platform regulation (Devadasan, 2022, p. 9). The new rules were suddenly substantially more interventionist than previous Indian regulatory efforts, pushing the boundaries of what is technically possible (in terms of operating secure encrypted platforms) and mandating firms to comply with takedown requests for content issues by various non-judicial government actors. These rules have been challenged by civil society groups and media organizations through the courts, and their constitutionality is unclear; at time of writing, the Modi administration is seeking to enshrine this more interventionist mode of shaping industry content governance practices into law through a new omnibus 'Digital India Act' (Sharwood, 2023).

8.2.2 ANALYSIS

The demand of Indian policymakers for changes to how platform companies are governed in India appears to be driven by a combination of technological developments, the 'policy shocks' of certain local crisis events, policy signaling in the context of domestic elections, as well as a general desire to maintain domestic political control on behalf of the ruling BJP party.

Indian Minister for Electronics and IT Rajeev Chandrasekhar told media in early 2023 that changes in the digital environment were necessitating new regulatory frameworks, as early internet intermediaries "have now morphed into multiple types of participants and platforms on the internet, functionally very different from each other, and requiring different types of guardrails and regulatory requirements" (NDTV News Desk, 2023, n.p.). The current government has also been pursuing regulatory initiatives that affect firms operating e-commerce, local service delivery, and other platforms (Majithia, 2019). In the context of user-generated content, the increasing reliance of Indians on services like WhatsApp, and the potential role that these services play in public mobilization and information diffusion appears to be a particularly large concern. The specter of mob violence in rural Indian communities, and the role of rumors or disinformation spread via WhatsApp in facilitating these incidents, have played an outsized role in the policy debate around platform regulation, rapidly raising the public awareness of WhatsApp as a potentially irresponsible or under-regulated intermediary—and according to some reporting, spurring the government to be seen as actively seeking to respond to this issue through stronger regulation in the lead-up to the 2019 general elections (B. Medeiros and P. Singh, 2020).

The Modi government has publicly been linked to a highly repressive form of politics, cracking down on various forms of dissent and protest across the country (S. Sinha, 2021; Sud, 2022). It has displayed its aim of asserting more control over the Indian information and media environment, of which platforms operated by foreign multinationals play a key part. This desire has been enabled by close ties between the government and internet service providers, as well as a normative focus on public security and safety over free expression in many contexts. India has an unusual history of internet shutdowns, especially in response to protest or separatist mobilization: the country "is one of the few democracies to have exercised the power to shut down communication networks" (Rydzak, 2019, p. 21).

The Bharatiya Janata party (BJP) has steadily been increasing its vote share in the federal elections since 2014. In the 2019 elections it won 302 out of 543 possible seats in the Lok Sabha, the country's main legislative body. With additional support from smaller and regional right-wing parties, the government has a commanding majority in this chamber. The BJP has also been steadily increasing its share of seats in the Rajya Sabha, the upper house of the Indian legislature, which is designed to represent the interests of India's twenty-eight states and eight union territories, although it has never held a majority in both houses. Without such a double majority, there are checks on the Modi government's ability to pass legislation at will, especially on controversial topics, and coalitional politics and compromise then become politically necessary although the government has been creative in deploying various institutional workarounds— such as 'voice votes' and 'money bills' which provide the government with some tools to bypass the veto points inherent in the two-chamber system.[4] As of now, the Rajya Sabha can serve as a curb on the government's executive rulemaking power, although the BJP has hopes of winning their first ever double-chamber majority in the 2024 national elections.

Although there are some commonly cited features of the Indian regulatory state—that it is too large, too disorganized, and in some cases too corrupt (Sukhtankar and Vaishnav, 2015; Gupta, 2017)—literature on state capacity suggests that in many cases the Indian government actually has significant regulatory capacities, especially when it comes to managing large and discretely time-bound projects (Shaffer, Nedumpara, and A. Sinha, 2015; Kapur, 2020). Although India is the world's largest democracy, and "a significant part of the Indian state is served by a closed well-paid professional bureaucracy, recruited meritocratically through highly competitive formal examinations, with career stability and secure tenure, strong ties among the members of the bureaucracy, special laws for public employment (as opposed to standard labor laws), and internal promotion" (Kapur, 2020, p. 49), the regulatory state, especially at the federal state and local levels, is actually much smaller in terms of staffing and resources than countries like the United States, China, or Germany. This can limit the effectiveness of governance, and also lead to some paradoxical tensions underlying the effectiveness of Indian institutions—an ability to coordinate impressive infrastructure projects and smoothly deliver daunting administrative efforts at scale (such as the census, or elections) on one hand, while also failing at more basic local service delivery in the other (Bussell, 2010). One potential feature of the Indian context is that as an "imperfect democracy" policymakers "emphasize the provision of goods that are visible and can be provided quickly, like infrastructure, over long-term investments, like human capital or environmental quality" (Kapur, 2020, p. 43)—something that could lend itself to more symbolic tech policy initiatives as well.

There are also a number of constraining factors on the ability of the Indian executive to pursue regulatory change through measures like the IT Guidelines of 2021 and 2022. Alongside the aforementioned legislative checks on executive rulemaking power inherent in India's unique dual-chamber system, also important is the Indian judiciary, which has wide reaching authority and has perhaps the world's most powerful court (Khaitan, 2020). Scholarship has noted the unusually hands-on role that the Indian judiciary plays in the country's regulatory system, noting that it has been especially interventionist in the realm of telecommunications regulation, seeking to intervene strategically in order to build a "constructive contribution to the development of a sound regulatory culture" (Thiruvengadam and Joshi, 2012, p. 329). Through their judgments (for instance, by deciding whether the recently promulgated Ministerial IT Rules are within the acceptable remit of action for the Modi-led government) the judiciary will effectively decide upon whether the government's contested platform regulation strategy is enforceable. The specific tenor of the Supreme Court can vary depending on who is serving on it; certain Chief Justices can be more constitutionalist,' vocally oriented around maintaining the Supreme Court as an check on government power, but others have tended to side more with the establishment, and have received cushy government appointments as a reward after their terms end.[5]

With no meaningful trade agreement or other transnational legal framework that would constrain Indian policymaking in the tech policy space, the main counter-pressure against regulatory demand and supply thus has taken the form of actor-based resistance, especially from civil society organizations, which have been loud advocates against the government's coercive platform regulation strategies (Access Now, 2022). Meanwhile, the positions of the major multinational tech players on the new Indian rules have not been entirely clear. Facebook in particular has long cultivated close ties to the BJP government, placing former BJP affiliates in key policy roles at Facebook India (Perrigo, 2020). Nevertheless, Meta subsidiary WhatsApp has declined so far, at least as far as public reporting goes, to implement a legally mandated 'traceability' framework (via hashing of message metadata or other means), and is engaged in an ongoing legal fight against the provisions mandated in the newest amendments to the IT Rules

(Menn, 2021). Twitter has also refused in a number of cases to comply with the government's content takedown requests and other moderation requirements, although the tenor of this dynamic has shifted considerably since Elon Musk's takeover and the ensuing mass layoffs of policy employees around the world (Field and Vanian, 2023).

Interestingly, public statements from the major tech industry business associations active in India appear supportive of the new changes to the IT rules, including on the creation of 'grievance councils' that will allow government representatives to request content takedown without a court order (Press Trust of India, 2021). Most members of associations like the Internet and Mobile Association of India appear to be Indian firms of varying sizes rather than the national subsidiaries of giants like Google, Meta, Apple, and Microsoft. This could either indicate (1) that domestic industry is careful to not oppose the government plans in public to avoid a backlash from the many Indians that appear to be supportive of the Modi government's policies or (2) there are cleavages between the preferences of different domestic and multinational players involved. As India increasingly is seeing its own domestically grown platform competitors, it's feasible that rising local alternatives to the US platforms—for instance, Indian messaging app ShareChat and their short video platform Moj (Bansal, 2020; Bhat, 2022)—are perfectly happy to comply with the mandated regulatory frameworks in exchange for potential market share. Indeed, following this logic, one would even expect for the burgeoning domestic tech sector to lobby hard for more stringent regulation that might lead to Big Tech's exit, potentially adding to domestic demand for regulatory change if these elites are sufficiently embedded in policy circles.

Overall, the matter does not seem likely to be settled anytime soon, with future Supreme Court intervention on the horizon and what is sure to be active policy contestation in the lead-up to the 2024 elections. India is also actively jostling with platform services, convincing as well as contesting: in recent years, the government has made many tens of thousands of requests for content takedown to a range of platform firms (Reuters Newswire, 2022), constantly engaging policy representatives to publish transparency reports, make their rules more stringent, and resource up their content enforcement pipelines with more local language expertise. Some of this pressure seems to be yielding concrete results: in the summer of 2023, WhatsApp was reported to have made their trust and safety flagging tools and community guidelines available in multiple additional Indian languages, including Hindi, Punjabi, Tamil, Telugu, Malayalam, Kannada, Bengali, Marathi, Urdu, and Gujarati (Business Standard, 2023). As these informal strategies continue to play out alongside more formal efforts to take back some control over online content governance in the country, the stakes are high: not just for Big Tech in one of their largest markets, but also crucially for the hundreds of millions of Indians that use major platform services each day.

8.3 Brazil

The largest country in Latin America in terms of both size and population—which at approximately 215 million residents is almost double that of second-place Mexico—Brazil has for the past twenty years been discussed as a rapidly growing "emerging" economy in the global context. Analysts in the early 2000s predicted it would be increasingly important in international economic matters in the years to come, part of the BRICS club with Russia, India, China, and South Africa (Stuenkel, 2020). While these visions may not have all materialized as predicted, in tech-related discussions, Brazil is still described as a potentially lucrative jurisdiction for business, perhaps the fastest growing tech market that is not located on the African continent (Elliott, 2023).

Brazil is also a country with an important history of involvement in technology policy matters, in particular through its contestation of the transnational institutions of internet infrastructure and protocol governance. As Hurel and Rocha (2018) note, despite having until the mid-2010s comparatively low rates of internet penetration and a lack of major domestically or internationally oriented technology firms, the country has long had a vibrant civil society sector focused on digital policy issues like copyright and open source, and a history of productive interlinkages between civil society and government officials. Following the Snowden revelations of widespread US government-led internet surveillance, Brazil vocally pushed back against the ostensibly multistakeholder but in practice US-dominated global internet governance regime (Musiani and Pohle, 2014). Their efforts eventually involved the organization of the NETmundial Meeting on the Future of Internet Governance in 2014 (Almeida, 2014; Fraundorfer, 2017).

These internationally oriented conversations about the future of a free and open internet at the NETmundial summit became intertwined with Brazil's own domestic policy landscape (F. A. Medeiros and Bygrave, 2015). After multiple years of campaigning by civil society groups to reform a punitive domestic intermediary liability status quo, new legislation, the Marco Civil da Internet (Federal Law No. 12965/2014) was enacted in 2014 (Affonso Souza, Steibel, and Lemos, 2017).

The Marco Civil, which was drafted as part of a hitherto unprecedented multistakeholder effort, with a period of extensive public engagement (including the possibility of online contributions), explicitly carved out a number of freedom of expression and privacy protections for users (Zingales, 2015). The law embedded human rights and open internet language into the platform liability status quo, both discursively and practically: alongside its use of various constitutional metaphors, it also tried to keep firms from over-removing legal content by limiting liability generally only to platforms that failed to act appropriately when faced with a court order (Iglesias Keller, 2020).

Since 2014, however, a number of domestic and international events have raised the salience of platform regulation issues in Brazil, seemingly also increasing the demand for more stringent amendments to the pro-civil society (but also pro-industry) Marco Civil. In 2018, the far-right Jair Bolsonaro was elected to the Brazilian presidency, sending shockwaves through a political elite trying to understand how "a niche congressman [...] a member of a small party (PSL) with almost no registered supporters, who had been relatively unknown until some four years earlier, when he started to make appearances on popular and comic TV shows, on which he combined extremist rhetoric with praise for the military dictatorship" could have ascended to the country's highest office (Evangelista and Bruno, 2019, p. 2). Following a highly politicized and polarizing campaign that drew natural comparisons to Trump's election in the United States just two years prior, domestic and international observers began to hone in on the unique strategies that the Brazilian conservative movement generally—and the Bolsonaro campaign specifically—had deployed to harness various user-generated content platforms for political mobilization.

In particular, Bolsonaro and his family were, like Trump, savvy social media communicators, and Bolsonaro allies were extremely effective at producing persuasive and polarizing content on YouTube and Instagram and galvanizing new and established WhatsApp networks (e.g., evangelical church groups) to push their message (S. Davis and Straubhaar, 2020). Some of this content consisted of intentionally false rumors spread with the intention to deceive or mislead the electorate, bringing to the fore the potential issue of 'disinformation' spread via WhatsApp and other platforms used in the country (Recuero, Soares, and Vinhas, 2021; Chagas, 2022). From rumors that the previously in office Worker's party (PT) were trying to change the sexual orientation of conservative children to more targeted efforts at voter suppression and misinformation about voting procedures (S. Davis and Straubhaar, 2020; Chagas, 2022), the election was perhaps the first instance where platform firms were fully aware of their role as an international discursive battleground. In Brazil, Facebook rolled out its first election 'war room' combating election-related misinformation, and began experimenting with automated tools to help detect and remove hateful or otherwise harmful content, a step unusual for languages other than English at the time (Leander et al., 2023).

These politics did not die down after the election ended. Bolsonaro's official communication team continued to deploy many of the same tactics during his time in office, leading to complaints from the opposition about government-sanctioned disinformation campaigns conducted under the auspices of the President's 'office of hatred' (Ozawa et al., 2023). While opposition parties sought to mobilize platform firms to intervene more explicitly against the political hate speech and disinformation of the Brazilian right, Bolsonaro in turn sought to prevent industry from doing so. In September 2021, he signed an executive order to penalize industry for removing user content without receiving a court order to specifically do so (in effect seeking to prevent industry from acting against purported disinformation, with a few exceptions; see Perrigo, 2021). The order, which echoed the 'deplatforming' and 'anti-censorship' must-carry language of bills introduced in Texas and Florida a few months earlier, could only be in effect for 120 days without legislative approval, but was promptly dubbed unconstitutional and overturned by the Brazilian Supreme Court (Nicas, 2021b).

8.3.1 ANALYSIS

During Bolsonaro's term, other political actors in the Brazilian system stepped in with efforts to push content moderation-related initiatives as well. In 2020, legislators introduced a wide-ranging set of rules pertaining to disinformation and other forms of content moderation, including by mandating a transparency framework. There was insufficient agreement in the governing coalition to pass these rules, however (Mello, 2022). In 2022, the country's electoral authorities (Tribunal Superior Eleitoral, or TSE) began to take a more assertive role in domestic platform regulation, for instance by issuing takedown orders for certain forms of electoral disinformation (Dib and Froio, 2022). Also, in the lead-up to the presidential election in 2022, this electoral authority (which features a number of high-ranking Brazilian judges, including serving Supreme Court justices) negotiated with industry to obtain voluntary commitments, with the input of civil society, into platform's election related content enforcement (Iglesias Keller and Arguelhes, 2022; Regattieri, 2023).

In October 2022, Luiz Inácio Lula da Silva beat Bolsonaro in a run-off Presidential election, bringing the left—and the embattled PT—back into power. In another stunning parallel to the American showdown between Trump and Biden, Bolsonaro contested the election results, citing fraud, and in January 2023, his supporters vandalized the national capitol buildings in Brasilia. As Kira (2023) notes:

> Lula's government became convinced that the brutality of the events was assisted by the circulation of online content. This content was allegedly produced and disseminated by extremist groups in the days leading up to the attack. There were also allegations that platforms

did little to prevent the dissemination of this content and adopted only minimum measures to deal with the systemic risks generated by harmful posts.

The combination of the experience of the Bolsonaro years, the Brasilia riots, and other ongoing events—including a spate of troubling school shootings apparently linked to online extremism (Froio and Andrade, 2023)—have galvanized policymakers on the left and center-left to demand that Brazil layer new rules for platform moderation on top of the laissez-faire status quo established through voluntary agreements and the auspices of the Marco Civil (Hendrix and Mello, 2023). Although the executive has proposed new legislation, parliamentarians have instead gravitated back to the previously proposed 'Fake News Bill' from 2020 (PL2630/2020). The bill has incorporated a wide range of features from the international platform regulation debate (Barata, 2023), including some notion of a duty of care (clearly inspired by the UK Online Safety Bill), a risk assessment framework drawn from the European Union's DSA, and a mandatory crisis response framework akin to that put in place voluntarily by platforms in some contexts as part of the Christchurch call process.

The platform regulation conversation in Brazil continued to heat up in early 2023. In April 2023, the Brazilian Ministry of Justice and Public Safety issued an order seeking to get industry to follow a number of commitments that have not yet been successfully passed through the Brazilian legislature in PL2630 and other proposed bills (Kira, 2023). The Brazilian Supreme Court, an increasingly politicized actor in this whole debate, is also expected to rule on the constitutionality of the immunity provisions of the Marco Civil's Article 19 (Barata, 2023). PL2630 has been defeated in legislative votes thus far, due to active mobilization against it from the right—which has argued that the bill would curb religious free expression—as well as from industry, which has resorted to consumer-facing lobbying techniques (Culpepper and Thelen, 2019) to try and mobilize the public against it.

The demand side of platform regulation in Brazil is on one hand being driven by a number of 'shock' crisis events from the Brasilia riot and beyond, as well as partisan politics (the perception on the left that the existing laissez-faire platform governance status quo benefits Bolsonaro's far right). It also appears to be hotly opposed by both policymaker-facing and public-facing industry lobbying seeking to depress that demand. The bill is also enmeshed within the countervailing forces of party politics, with the right seeking to mobilize their supporters against the bill, despite the claims of some observers that more and more of Brazilian right also wants to regulate platform moderation (Hendrix and Mello, 2023). As mentioned, Brazil has a longstanding and well-connected set of digitally active civil society organizations, and many of these are already opposing these types of proposed legislation on free expression grounds, although keen observers will note that many civil society groups would be willing to compromise on some of their positions if the right regulatory structures were put in place.[6]

Crucially, on the supply side, Lula's PT government has some important constraints on their rulemaking power. They do not hold an absolute majority in the lower house of the federal legislature, meaning that they will need to persuade independents to vote with them to pass PL2630 or any other related policies. This provides an attractive veto point for interest groups to exploit, making deals and exercising persuasion to keep independents from voting with the PT coalition on this issue. Additionally, despite the more central role that the court is now playing in content moderation issues in the country (Iglesias Keller, 2020), it could still feasibly rule to maintain the Marco Civil liability framework over changes to the status quo, if PL2630 is passed but has potentially unconstitutional freedom of expression provisions (although some type of at least partial reforms seem the most likely). Overall, the stakes are clearly high, both for Brazilian residents as well as the global tech sector. The active contestation from industry—Telegram has been direct messaging Brazilians to oppose the legislation, Google has changed its landing page and emailed advertisers in an effort to galvanize them against the new proposed policies (Elliott, 2023)— signals that the rules are perceived as especially threatening, or that industry believes that it can successfully pressure policymakers and the public in the country into changing their preferences. Along with India, Brazil is a jurisdiction to watch closely moving forward.

9

Conclusion

This book has explored the politics of platform regulation: the policy drivers, political dynamics, and institutional characteristics that shape the development of platform regulation in different jurisdictions. In particular, I have sought to reflect upon the questions of *how*, *why*, and *where* platform regulation emerges.

One of my key claims is that the policies and practices of harmful content governance—'trust and safety,' content moderation, platform governance—are worthy of study from a policy and politics perspective, and not just purely as a legal question or issue of computational infrastructure development. Policy outcomes are shaped through battles between governments at various levels, global civil society organizations, foreign multinational firms, and other actors. They are influenced not only by local and transnational institutional factors, but also hyper-local dynamics of partisan electoral politics.

Platform regulation does not occur in a vacuum, or manifest as a simple reflection of shifting public opinion; it is shaped by varying degrees of government demand, constrained or enabled by a wealth of potential domestic and transnational institutions, and influenced by a normative environment that shapes both the scope of possible regulatory intervention as well as how far policymakers are willing to go. This perspective matters because it can not only help us understand the world of platform policy as it exists today, but helps us deploy empirical observation to drive strategic action seeking to change it. For policymakers, advocates, and citizens fighting for more just, equitable, and rights-respecting digital spaces and societies, where should consumer or policymaker-facing advocacy strategies be deployed? Which jurisdictions are the likeliest to be able to secure meaningful policy change? How can governments increase their capacity to meaningfully withstand private platform resistance and lobbying? The analysis presented in the preceding pages, supported by an explicitly political, process-oriented framework, provides a first step towards better understanding the past and future of platform regulation—who wins, who loses, and what the stakes are going forward.

The Politics of Platform Regulation: How Governments Shape Online Content Moderation. Robert Gorwa, Oxford University Press. © Oxford University Press 2024. DOI: 10.1093/oso/9780197692851.003.0009

9.1 Case Studies: A Closing Reflection

In Chapter 4, I argued that government actors seeking to shape how platform companies govern their services can do so by following three broad strategies, that I dubbed contest, collaborate, and convince. I investigated the pursuit of these strategies in-depth in Germany (Chapter 5), Australia and New Zealand (Chapter 6), and the United States (Chapter 7), also applying the conceptual 'demand-and-supply' model for explaining change in platform regulation through micro-cases looking at China, India, and Brazil (Chapter 8).

There are some notable similarities across these cases. First, all of these episodes of eventual regulatory change occurred in a context where there had been some kind of external 'shock' event that raised the profile and salience of platform governance as a pressing policy issue. From the Syrian Civil War to the Christchurch shooting or the Capitol riot, these shocks empowered motivated local policy entrepreneurs to seize the moment and pursue changes to the regulatory status quo (or to frame the ensuing political battles in certain powerful ways). These events presented actors with an opportunity for policy signaling, where they could to demonstrate their commitment on an issue (to their constituents from the policymaker side, or to regulators from the industry side) by pursuing specific regulatory strategies of contestation or collaboration.

Second, electoral factors came into play in all cases where a contested platform regulation strategy was pursued. In both the German and Australian examples, the executive had high levels of demand for change, and sought to achieve that change in a relatively short period of time bounded by an election campaign. It is particularly notable that the German NetzDG and the Australian AVM Act were both passed through Parliament on the last day it sat before an election. In the United States, the electoral pressure was more temporally diffuse, although key policy entrepreneurs in Texas and Florida appeared to be synthesizing their platform regulation policy ideas into their longer-term strategies of self-branding and electioneering.

Third, the case studies suggest that institutions clearly matter for the development of platform regulation, but that these institutions do not necessarily create path-deterministic outcomes. Although institutional capacities and capabilities heavily influence the playing field upon which the contestation around platform regulation proposals take place, motivated actors with the right blend of power resources may be able to get their desired outcomes—against apparently stacked institutional odds—under certain conditions. In the German case, the executive was able to overcome EU resistance, despite (1) the apparent tensions their proposed rules created with existing EU legal frameworks and (2) the various veto points that the Commission could have used to prevent Germany from passing the NetzDG. In the United States, the exceptionally strong normative and institutional constraints of the First Amendment and existing telecommunications law frameworks are both being actively challenged by both policymakers and interest groups on both sides of the aisle, from the anti-tech conservative actors pushing for common carriage or other arguments justifying government regulation of platform content-oriented decisionmaking to the more progressive groups seeking action in narrower areas like child safety. All this contestation has meant that aspects of state laws like those passed in Florida, Texas, and California could potentially be judged as legitimate by courts at some point in the near to medium-term future—spurring longer-term institutional change.

Finally, close readers of the case studies will notice the relatively minimal role played by various forms of actor-based resistance in the narratives I presented. For various reasons, lobbying from industry did not successfully depress policymaker demand for contested platform regulation strategies in Germany, Australia, or the United States (although civil society intervention seems to have an important early framing role in the New Zealand example discussed). In Germany, industry chose not to battle the NetzDG through the judicial system, even though it may have led to the law being overturned, while in the United States, platforms seem to have delegated most of the most antagonistic legal challenges to industry groups like NetChoice and CCIA—which may indeed be successful in having the new state-led policy frameworks overturned. In all of the cases we looked at, international government actors did not play much of a lobbying role: I did not find evidence that the 'home states' of platform firms mobilized against prospective regulation in any of the case studies by threatening retaliatory tariffs, trade measures, or other measures against the government seeking to change the regulatory status quo.

Does this relative absence of geopolitically inflected contestation follow from the recent weakness of the coalition between US platform firms and the White House (and perhaps should be expected in the future)? Or does it suggest that for the largest firms, the international regulatory efforts discussed in this book are not perceived as costly enough to warrant serious expenditures of political capital? As lucrative, high-stakes platformized markets emerge for 'generative' AI applications and related systems (Gorwa and Veale, 2024), and as the platform regulation landscape continues to become more complex, geopolitically inflected contestation between states could be a game-changing development.

9.2 Future Research and the Years Ahead

This book has sought to intervene in a set of fast-moving and rapidly developing debates that sit at the intersection of many disciplines. Platform regulation is a complex policy field and interesting field of study, one which, on one hand, exhibits many similarities to other regulatory debates in technology policy domains and beyond, while, on the other, may be said to have a number of unique characteristics. There are few other regulatory issue areas where the site of political struggle is also simultaneously a space of technically-mediated public expression and interaction. For that reason, the effects and outcomes of content-oriented platform regulation will feed into democratic processes, and in the long term, likely also impact the politics, dynamics, and drivers of platform regulation. This all leads to some distinct challenges for policy and research (such as monitoring and evaluating the effects of policy in a particularly 'black-boxed' and privately led multi-sided socio-technical ecoystem), and distinct political dynamics. Nevertheless, this complexity offers countless potential avenues for related politically-oriented scholarship going forward. I would like to briefly highlight a few promising analytical and empirical avenues for further work.

Bringing political science concepts and methods into internet studies and technology policy areas can yield a range of helpful insights. Remembering that platform companies are, in fact, *companies* opens many possibilities for productive intervention from regulatory politics scholars, international political economists, and others in other political science subfields who deal with corporate actors in social, political, and economic life. There has been some recent work channeling an explicitly "regulatory politics approach to platform governance" (Gorwa, 2021), including the work of Medzini (2021) on platform's self-regulatory regimes and that of Haggart and Iglesias Keller (2021) on the legitimacy of recent governance efforts. Nevertheless, there is an opportunity to go much further in terms of looking at the politics of platform regulation in an even more granular and discrete way, exploring empirically some of the political drivers that underpin the theoretical framework developed in this book.

For instance, political scientists frequently run national and subnational surveys of regulators and policymakers, assessing their preferences on major issues of the day (N. Lee, Landgrave, and Bansak, 2023). Why not run similar surveys on technology policy issues, or piggyback on existing surveys to include questions that could help not only empirically assess the preferences of regulators for specific types of policy change, but also (eventually) illustrate these preferences in a historical and comparative sense? Could similar efforts be launched inside of industry, perhaps via emerging organizations like the Trust and Safety Professionals organization? Generally, given the notable lack of robust, large-scale, and open data on virtually all matters of platform regulation (whether it be in terms of macro-level policy tracking, or efforts to build archives of interviews with policymakers in industry or government for posterity), I believe that more efforts to create and share qualitative and quantitative data among researchers would be massively helpful.[1]

Relatedly, there is more room for internationally oriented comparative work on platform regulation. If states are increasingly seeking to intervene in trust and safety and related platform governance domains, can we find similarities in the strategies pursued by countries with small markets, located in certain regions, or with various institutional commonalities? To what extent are policy approaches developed in one jurisdiction actually diffusing globally, and what are the mechanisms that appear to drive/constrain this diffusion? These types of research projects could help nuance our understanding of regulatory demand and supply-side factors in this context, and I would be thrilled if others opted to pursue similarly focused case studies of policy development in their jurisdictions of expertise.

The general research agenda outlined in this book also provides a toolkit that could be used to look more widely at other technology policy areas in the platform realm and beyond. What are the strategies deployed by local-level government in response to 'locally tethered' service delivery platforms like Uber, Bolt, Lyft, Gorilla, and Airbnb? How do local institutional contexts shape these politics, perhaps giving them some unique demand and supply side features not seen at the federal level? What about online marketplaces and e-commerce sites? Or increasingly platformized 'artificial intelligence' services, available to easily download and deploy via a multitude of third-party intermediaries? How will regulatory contestation play out in the especially complex and varied domain of AI services, which potentially implicates a multitude of industry and government systems and therefore interests (Veale, Matus, and Gorwa, 2023)?

Overall, this remains a tremendously dynamic field of study. New regulatory initiatives, whether orchestrated by states or by firms, seem to be an almost monthly, if not weekly occurrence, and there are many prospective case studies (of regulatory emergence, or also crucially, non-emergence) that would be worth examining in depth. The current trend towards increasing public contestation in the platform governance domain seems only likely to intensify, especially as the European Union's Digital Services Act goes into effect with potentially global impact. On top of this we can add a growing number of proposals being developed in multistakeholder policy forums or by international organizations that are also seeking to intervene in this policy area. In the coming years, observers can certainly expect to have their hands full.

The future seems to promise a far greater, and far more existential, degree of firm-state contestation over the parameters of large platforms' global rulemaking authority. But might models like the Christchurch Call become more prevalent as some states, driven by normative considerations or other types of power constraints, seek instead to incentivise firms to develop their own initiatives like the Facebook Oversight Board or the Global Internet Forum to Counter Terrorism? Or will governments continue to deploy blunt political will and power in an effort to 'take back control' over the private standards that are having major political, social, and economic impacts on the lives of their citizens?

The trend appears to be more collaboration and more contestation—in effect, more efforts to change the platform regulation status quo—from governments around the world. Will the outcome be fairer, more accountable, and more transparent systems of platform governance, with better due process and enhanced rights for users? Or will the outcome be territorialization and fragmentation, as firms are pulled to splinter their services and rules to comply with a vastly increased regulatory burden across jurisdictions, perhaps with deleterious effects for vulnerable populations, political mobilization, and free expression around the globe? Will government efforts to intervene in this space empower a new set of third parties, such as the auditing firms which are likely to be delegated compliance and reporting requirements under an increasing number of national (or even subnational) platform regulation frameworks?

The stakes are high, but the consequences for both platform and state power are not yet fully clear. Nonetheless, the global political economy of platform regulation is just beginning to unfold, and promises to become an increasingly salient, important, and impactful space of transnational politics in the years ahead.

APPENDIX A

Methods Appendix

This appendix provides a more comprehensive discussion of methods than included in the introductory chapter. Part 1 features a more detailed breakdown of the qualitative interview process I underwent, including a discussion of ethical issues and the project's ethics approval, and a list of the interviewees that agreed to have their names publicly listed in this appendix. Part 2 discusses all other types of data deployed, including the strategy for obtaining new documents via freedom of information requests, and a list of archived links at which all of the obtained documents are available.

A.1 The Interview Process

A good portion of the original empirical material assessed in this book consists of qualitative interview data, collected in semi-structured conversations with participants in the regulatory episodes scrutinized as case studies. Interview data can be extremely rich as a source of new, previously under- or unreported information, but also comes with a special set of questions, concerns, and potential pitfalls. Major questions for a researcher to tackle include: who does one talk to, how does one convince them to talk, and how is interview data handled, parsed, and attributed?

These questions are part of mainstream political science methods discussions (Morris, 2009; Mason-Bish, 2019), but are potentially even more acute when studying an area as characterized by both corporate and government secrecy as the one tackled by this book. Platform companies were for a long time shrouded in secrecy, operating as closed 'black-boxes' despite their ostensibly public-facing nature and self-professed belief in workspace transparency (Gorwa and Garton Ash, 2020). As Maréchal and S. T. Roberts (2018, p. 2) outline, these firms "tend not to have a culture of transparency, and resist sharing what

172   METHODS APPENDIX

their consider to be their proprietary data," making qualitative research into company practices especially difficult. While there have been a few examples of researchers in the last few years managing to negotiate extraordinary access to companies like Facebook (e.g., Klonick, 2020), these have been rare, almost one-off occurrences, and researchers who gain access into Facebook's operations are either bound with non-disclosure agreements or committed to staying off the record. On-the-record qualitative interviews with platform company employees remain rare, and notable recent books on content moderation that rely on industry interviews not only usually anonymize their interviews, but even may anonymize the names of the companies in question (S. T. Roberts, 2019).

I wished to also conduct interviews with policymakers and government stake-holders, as well as some key civil society organizations that had sought to influence the policy processes in question. Governments are frequently also cagey about how they interact with platform companies, as negotiations are increasingly politicized and sensitive. However, there is usually a wider range of potential government interview targets (elected representatives and their staff, civil servants in various departments) and I expected current or former policymakers to be slightly more willing to be interviewed than platform employees. Civil society also provides an invaluable source of knowledge, both as in-depth observers of regulatory processes in areas where there is strong digitally oriented civil society and as creators of advocacy and journalism that documents regulatory processes. Using a broad definition of the non-governmental and non-corporate actor category like that outlined by K. W. Abbott and Snidal (2009b), researchers and academic experts that participated in regulatory debates were also considered as interview targets. I figured that this broad set of civil society actors would be the most open to being interviewed, but also unfortunately constituted the least powerful and consequential actor group during regulatory negotiations.

A considerable literature discussing the best practices for various types of interviews exists, tackling important questions such as the kinds of sampling strategies that should be used in the social sciences, and what constitutes an adequate number of interviews (Berry, 2002; Leech, 2002). In some studies, which seek to, for example, interview a representative sample of participants in a particular universe (such as an online forum, or specific social group), an especially precise and careful sampling strategy may be needed (Eynon, Schroeder, and Fry, 2009). Because I had a clearly defined universe of participants (those involved in the regulatory episodes that constituted my case studies), my sampling strategy was a purposive one that effectively came down to an effort to interview as many of the most relevant individuals as possible during the limited amount of time available to me during the research phase of this project. I benefited greatly from my personal networks and 'snowballs' pushed downhill by key interlocutors and colleagues; for this reason, I cannot claim that my interviews represented a complete, or even representative sample of key individuals involved in the policy discussions at the center of each one of my case studies, especially as I was unable to get access to a number of important high-level individuals; nevertheless, I did my best to identify people that played important roles within their respective actor group and sought interviews with them by either contacting them directly or leveraging colleague introductions.

My task was complicated by the COVID-19 pandemic. Many prospective interlocutors fell ill and went on leave, or were unable to participate in an interview due to work-from-home childcare responsibilities and general business. Nevertheless, while I had originally intended to conduct face-to-face interviews where possible, I was forced to shift to a virtual interview strategy due to the stay-at-home situation, which had the major benefit of allowing me to fairly easily conduct multiple interviews with participants in different cities or even different countries in a single day. The work-from-home pandemic situation also normalized home work and videoconference calls to a certain extent, and I was able to secure video calls with some high-level interviewees that, I assume, would have normally not found the time to do so. When starting each case study, I often began by interviewing relevant civil society groups and academics, asking them to also provide me with a shortlist of key individuals involved in the case study events; many were so kind as to directly introduce me to government/industry people that they knew personally, and these direct connections were generally much more likely to yield an interview than a cold email.

This book began as a doctoral dissertation project housed in the Department of Politics and International Relations at the University of Oxford. For that dissertation, upon which this work builds, I conducted 52 semi-structured interviews from the end of 2019 to early 2021. Some of these were quite short, around 30 minutes (often the most that industry sources will be willing to offer researchers out of their busy schedules), and others were much longer, closer to an hour and a half or two hours, with an average length of about an hour. The majority were conducted remotely via videoconferencing software (and in a few cases, with only audio, when the internet connection was unstable or if participants preferred to have their video off). I offered participants the opportunity to choose the platform of their choice, and conducted interviews via secure encrypted services like Jitsi and Signal as well as well as services like Zoom, Google Hangouts, Microsoft Teams, Cisco Webex, and BlueJeans.

After some discussion with my editor at Oxford University Press (Angela Chnapko) and Studies in Digital Politics Series editor Andrew Chadwick, the decision was made to conduct a second wave of additional empirical research, leading to the development of an extra case study looking at the United States. I conducted the research for this chapter in 2022–2023, speaking with an additional 25 stakeholders.

METHODS APPENDIX

Table A.1 **General overview of interview participants, by chapter. (Includes all participants, including anonymous interviews.)**

	Germany	Christchurch	United States	Totals
Government	13	5	7	25
Industry	3	7	6	16
Civil Society	10	14	12	36
Totals	26	26	25	77

A breakdown of the interview participants can be found in Table A.1. This provides a broad overview, where I sought to highlight the main focus point of each interview as well as the main affiliation of participants, although some interviewees had wide-ranging expertise (in both government and industry, for instance), and some interviews touched on multiple case studies.

Despite my relatively strong contacts in this research space, built over more than six years of attending academic, policy, and industry-led conferences and workshops on issues relating to the book, I still found it somewhat difficult to get access to the appropriate industry employees. Partially this is a function of knowing who to talk to: because there is no industry directory of who to contact or general contact points, the entire process is effectively based on personal networks and connections. Many platform employees that I contacted (including those that I had personal connections to) either did not respond or politely let me know that they were too busy in an extremely stressful pandemic time. Many others declined to be interviewed. Nevertheless, a number of high-level individuals in the companies at the global level, as well as key regional representatives, were generous enough to answer some questions.

A.1.1 RESEARCH ETHICS AND ATTRIBUTION

Ethics are an incredibly important part of any research project, especially those that involve qualitative data and human research subjects. Following the best practices in digital research (the Association of Internet Researchers Guidelines 3.0) and political science research (the American Political Science Association Ethics Guidelines), I ensured that my interview subjects and the data collected were treated with an appropriate level of care.

One classic ethical issue involves the re-identification of participants. It has traditionally been the practice in qualitative research to ensure that research-subjects are properly anonymized, given the possible harms and embarrassment that can occur as a result from published material (Markham, 2012), and given that clear processes and guidelines for attribution are followed. However, there is a debate among leading ethnographers, who engage in perhaps the most sensitive and subject-centric qualitative research, as to the best practices for attribution and the anonymization of participants (for an accessible overview, see the research appendix in Nielsen, 2012). While many argue that anonymity is essential for maintaining both the trust and privacy of participants, others have argued that anonymizing subjects permits the researcher to be lazy, less careful, and less accountable when attributing statements to sources (Duneier, 2002).

My specific process for discussing and obtaining consent from participants slightly evolved over the course of the research, eventually crystallizing around two questions: whether they would be willing to have their name listed in this appendix in the published research (and be identified as someone that I spoke with during the course of the research), and what their stance on specific attribution of claims and arguments was. This consent was collected orally after a walkthrough of the project and its aims, or in the cases of participants who preferred written consent, via a digitally signed written consent form. If participants requested it (and a few government—and some industry—participants did), I offered to clear any direct attribution of quotes that I wished to include in this text with them.

I opted for this strategy as I believe that it strikes a balance between credibility (given the centrality of data obtained via interview to my arguments, the reader is in effect required to trust that I was able to obtain access to sufficiently knowledgeable and central participants in these policy discussions; it is therefore helpful to provide a list of people who agreed to be identified as people I spoke with) and participant control. I especially understood the concern that participants could say something candidly only for that quote to have repercussions at their workplace down the line. For this reason, I opted against recording most of the interviews (unless the participant explicitly suggested it, for instance) as I wished to make participants feel comfortable and minimize their worry that sensitive documents (such as interview transcripts) could somehow be shared or improperly handled. Instead, I took detailed notes on each interview, keeping all project data encrypted and anonymized as appropriate. I explored these ethical issues in greater depth in my ethical review application, which was approved at Oxford as CUREC SSH-DPIR-C1A-18-018 and by my current home institution, the WZB Berlin Social Science Center (Research Ethics Committee No. 2022/1/142).

A.1.2 PARTICIPANTS

What kind of people were interviewed? I wished to speak to relevant stakeholders in government, industry, and civil society, but knew that interviews

176   METHODS APPENDIX

are demanding, time-intensive, and often difficult to organize—especially when being conducted with extremely busy people, and on sensitive political topics.

Overall, I believe that I obtained adequate access to policymakers across all three case studies. The types of interviewees that would speak to me varied across the cases; for example, in Germany I was able to get some good access to elected officials and their staff, but could not secure interviews with regulators and civil servants in key ministries. Inversely, in the US chapter, I was able to get better responses from federal-level officials and regulators than political appointees.

I interviewed representatives of the major companies at the center of this book's case studies: Facebook, Google, Twitter, and Microsoft. I also spoke with a few regional industry association representatives, who were able to provide additional context and speak more generally about industry preferences and positions. These interviews involved a mix of high-level 'policymakers' with real decisionmaking power in the companies and regional policy employees on the front lines of certain case studies.

As part of a continuous effort to try and untangle the information provided by interview subjects in government and industry—not just as individuals but also as canny and self-interested actors often (if not always) seeking to shape the narrative around a specific policy debate—I drew heavily on civil society interviews, as well as public documents and reporting that civil society created, to triangulate interview data and help identify potential interlocutors. While civil society groups, NGOs, and academic observers entering these debates naturally also are political, they nevertheless have much knowledge that can help contextualize policy developments from a bird's-eye view. I was especially grateful to colleagues that were able to provide additional local, personal, and historic context underlying my case studies, and to those that took the time to connect me to prospective interviewees in industry and government.

This process was not perfect, of course. Even as I was able to organize some fantastic and extremely informative interviews, I was not always able to get access to some key policymakers. In Australia, I would have liked to have interviewed more political staff in the National/Liberal government, including staff within the Attorney General's Office; in New Zealand, I would have liked to have interviewed more partisan political staff in the governing Labour party and also the opposition. For the United States chapter, it would have been interesting—if perhaps fraught—to speak more directly with the Republican operatives working on the Texas and Florida bills. Part of this access issue may have stemmed from my positionality; a short search of my profile online would have yielded links to the progressive magazines and publications I have written for in the past, and my efforts to set up interviews with certain conservative organizations and interest groups, despite great connections from American colleagues, were generally unsuccessful.

Table A.2 **List of government representatives who agreed to be listed as interviewees. Note that fully anonymous interviews are not included here, and that some preferred for only their position to be disclosed. Titles are current as of time of interview.**

Name	Organization	Title	Interview Date (D.M.Y)
Jörn Pohl	The Green Party of Germany	Chief of Staff, MdB Konstantin von Notz	08.05.2020
Mario Brandenburg	The Free Democratic Party of Germany	Member of the Bundestag (2017–)	18.06.2020
Jens Zimmerman	Social Democratic Party of Germany	Member of the Bundestag (2013–)	02.06.2020
Paul Ash	New Zealand National Cyber Policy Office	Director	15.12.2020
Travis Hall	National Telecommunications and Information Administration	Telecommunications Policy Analyst	10.12.2022
Andrew Learned	Florida House of Representatives	Representative, District 59 (2020–2022)	16.12.2022
Michael Atleson	Federal Trade Commission	Director of Advertising Practices	26.10.2022
Kelly Signs	Federal Trade Commission	Attorney, Bureau of Competition	24.03.2023
Krisha Cerilli	Federal Trade Commission	Deputy Assistant Director, Technology Enforcement Division	24.03.2023
Lubos Kuklis	European Regulators Group for Audiovisual Media Services	Chair	16.06.2020
Felix Reda	European Parliament	Member of the European Parliament (2014-2018), The Greens-European Free Alliance	27.04.2020

Table A.2 **Continued**

Name	Organization	Title	Interview Date (D.M.Y)
Mathias Vermeulen	European Parliament	Staffer, MEP Marietje Schaake (Alliance of Liberals and Democrats for Europe)	02.07.2020
Paul Nemitz	European Commission (DG Justice)	Director for Fundamental Rights	05.06.2020
Prabhat Agarwal	European Commission (DG Connect)	Head of Unit for Online Platforms	15.05.2020
Robert Madellin	European Commission (DG Connect)	Director General (2010–2015)	12.05.2020
Julian King	European Commission	Commissioner for the Security Union (2016–2020)	20.05.2020
	eSafety Commissioner, Australia	Senior Legal and Policy Adviser	16.02.2020
	eSafety Commissioner, Australia	Manager, Online Harms Policy	16.02.2020
Michael Woodside	Department of Internal Affairs, New Zealand	Policy Director—Gambling, Media Content, and Racing	10.03.2020

Table A.3 **List of industry representatives who agreed to be listed as interviewees. Note that fully anonymous interviews are not included here. Titles are current as of time of interview.**

Name	Organization	Title	Interview Date (D.M.Y)
Christiane Gillespie-Jones	Communications Alliance LTD	Director, Program Management	1.12.2020
Ali Sternburg	Computer and Communication Industry Association	Vice President, Information Policy	18.04.2023
Jordan Rodell	Computer and Communication Industry Association	State Policy Manager	27.04.2023
Khara Boender	Computer and Communication Industry Association	State Policy Director	27.04.2023
David Sullivan	Digital Trust and Safety Partnership	Executive Director	25.05.2023
Tony Close	Facebook	Director of Content Regulation (Global)	20.04.2021
Josh Machin	Facebook Australia	Head of Public Policy	28.01.2021

Table A.3 **Continued**

Name	Organization	Title	Interview Date (D.M.Y)
Samantha Yorke	Google Australia	Government Affairs and Public Policy Manager	19.01.2021
Lutz Mache	Google Germany	Public Policy and Government Relations Manager	30.04.2020
Ross Young	Google New Zealand	Head of Government Relations and Public Policy	26.02.2021
Courtney Gregoire	Microsoft	Chief Digital Safety Officer	02.02.2021
Owen Bennett	Mozilla Corporation	Internet Policy Manager	29.04.2020
Servando Esparza	TechNet	Executive Director, Texas and the Southeast	15.12.2022
Nick Pickles	Twitter	Global Head of Public Policy Strategy and Development	27.01.2021
Jonathan Lee	WhatsApp	Head of Global Public Policy	25.04.2023

Table A.4 **List of non-governmental individuals interviewed. Titles are current as of time of interview.**

Name	Organization	Title	Interview Date (D.M.Y)
Duncan McCann	5Rights	Head of Accountability	05.05.2023
Nichole Rocha	5Rights	State Policy Lead	25.05.2023
Javier Pallero	Access Now	Head of Policy	25.01.2021
Wolfgang Schulz	Alexander von Humboldt Institute for Internet and Society	Director	9.04.2020
Mackenzie Nelson	Algorithm Watch	Project Manager, Governing Platforms Project	28.04.2020
Matthias Spielkamp	Algorithm Watch	Director	30.06.2020
Simone Rafael	Amadeu Antonio Stiftung	Executive Director	5.06.2020
Barbara Docklova	Article 19	Senior Campaigner	6.05.2020
Gabrielle Guillemin	Article 19	Digital Rights Lead	2.07.2020
Rita Jabri-Markwell	Australian Muslim Advocacy Network	Chief Advisor	19.01.2021
Emma Llanso	Center for Democracy and Technology	Director, Free Expression Project	18.11.2022
Alexander Ritzmann	Counter Extremism Project	Fellow	10.06.2020
David Green	EFF	Senior Staff Attorney and Civil Liberties Director	26.10.2022
Joe McNamee	European Digital Rights	Executive Director (2009–2019)	15.05.2020
Anupam Chander	Georgetown University	Professor	09.03.2023

Name	Organization	Title	Interview Date (D.M.Y)
Ian Barber	Global Partners Digital	Legal Officer	18.12.2020
Richard Wingfield	Global Partners Digital	Head of Legal	18.12.2020
Matthias Ketteman	Hans Bredow Institute	Head of Research, Online Regulation	22.04.2020
Evelyn Douek	Harvard Law School	Lecturer	30.10.2020
Tom Giovanetti	Institute for Policy Innovation	President	02.12.2022
Jordan Carter	Internet NZ	Chief Executive	9.12.2020
Ellen Strickland	Internet NZ	Chief Policy Advisor, International	9.02.2021
Spencer Overton	Joint Center for Political and Economic Studies	President	08.12.2022
Alex Abdo	Knight First Amendment Institute	Litigation Director	05.12.2022
Scott Wilkens	Knight First Amendment Institute	Senior Counsel	05.12.2022
Alexander Fanta	Netzpolitik	Brussels Correspondent	8.04.2020
Nicolas Suzor	Queensland University of Technology	Professor	3.11.2020
Matt Nguyen	Reset Australia	Policy Lead	9.02.2021
Eric Goldman	Santa Clara University	Professor	06.04.2023
Berin Szoka	TechFreedom	President	25.11.2022
Terry Flew	University of Sydney	Professor	9.12.2020
Peter Thompson	Victoria University Wellington	Lecturer	24.11.2020

A.2 Freedom of Information Requests

Journalists, civil society groups, and activists have for at least a few decades actively used access to information/freedom of information access requests (FOIA) to obtain various documents from, and about, governments. Nevertheless, FOIA requests remain a relatively obscure qualitative method in the social sciences, despite the significant opportunities they present for researchers interested in understanding policy processes (Savage and Hyde, 2014; Walby and Luscombe, 2017). Because most internal government activity is in effect textual—involving the creation, discussion, and debate of various textual material—"Much of what is said and done in government organizations is written down or otherwise documented, and despite a range of limitations, and barriers to access, much of this material is accessible through ATI/FOIA" requests (Walby and Larsen, 2012, p. 39). A small literature on the use of FOIA requests as qualitative data exists, and this work highlights (1) the advantages to using FOIA requests to bolster and triangulate interview data, especially longitudinally; (2) the new types of documents that FOIA requests make available, including special process documents that include "unofficial texts that are never intended for public circulation, such as the notes and the internal memos and the emails of government employees" (Walby and Larsen, 2012, p. 33); and (3) the active role that the researcher plays as part of the FOIA process of 'data production' (Walby and Luscombe, 2017), given that FOIA requests require very precise wording and in some cases direct negotiation with FOIA coordinators within governments.

For this book, I took additional advantage of the latest open-source tools for making and archiving FOIA requests that have been recently developed by civil society and government transparency advocacy groups. New platforms like Avatelli provide an open source back end that have allowed for national-level FOIA websites to easily pop up in multiple countries (such as FYI New Zealand, Right to Know Australia, and Ask the EU). These platforms are in effect web portals that mediate the relationship between the FOIA requestee and the FOIA target, seeking to make the FOIA request process more accessible and externally transparent, bringing FOIA requests between targets and requesters out of the realm of private communication and into an archived and searchable public format. The FOIA platforms additionally host and archive any documents provided by the FOIA target, making them easily accessible to others. For this reason, these services are fantastic for research: they are user friendly (providing a searchable directory of authorities/contact points, and a searchable directory of past requests made via the platform), transparent (allowing others to 'see your work,' including the communication and specific language of requests which is generally hidden in a request performed via private correspondence), and offer built in archiving and citability features (each request has a URL, where others can also publicly access the relevant documents).

There is certainly a learning curve involved with making successful FOIA requests. As Walby and Larsen (2012) write, the language of the request and its scope is essential as to determining its success; they advise keeping a research diary and carefully monitoring what kind of language is successful in obtaining the types of documents one wishes to obtain. Using AsktheEU and the German platform FragDenStaat, I was able to search for past relevant requests (and see what language had successfully yielded results, what documents were being withheld by agencies to past requests) and tweak my language accordingly. I also spoke with a few experts (a German investigative journalist who uses FOIA requests daily in his work, and one of the founders of the FragDenStaat portal) to get some additional tips.

In total, I made use of ten FOIA request clusters, some of which constituted multiple requests to various government agencies. I filed two requests to the European Commission, and three to the German Ministry of Justice. I also filed a request each to various Australian government departments and to the New Zealand Ministry of Foreign Affairs and Trade. Because New Zealand only allows citizens and permanent residents to file requests, I asked a colleague to file the request which would then be publicly archived on the FYI NZ website for me to access later. I also sent FOIA requests to the Texas Attorney General's Office, the chief sponsor of Texas HB 20, the House Select Committee responsible for overseeing the debates around HB 20 in 2021, and similarly to the Florida House records office for documents related to SB 7072.

Not all these requests were successful: in a few instances in the European context, the agency in question said that it did not have the documents I was looking for or cited a very high administrative charge for processing the request. The majority of these documents were digitized and shared simply in a reply via email, and publicly archived on the FOIA platform used to make the request; however, the two longest disclosures sent the documents separately, with the German Ministry of Justice deciding to send instead a giant shoebox filled with documents (perhaps intentionally, making them much more difficult for me to search and archive). The exception was in the United States, where I only discovered the MuckRock platform at a late stage in the research. I sent these FOIA requests via email, and most of the US actors that I sent requests to at the state level simply refused to acknowledge my request. As I was not physically located in the United States while researching that chapter, it was not possible for me to follow up in person, to escalate these requests through legal challenge, or take other measures.

Table A.5 **Public FOIA requests, with links to archived documents where available.**

Actor	Department	Date (D.M.Y.)	Pages	Link to Documents
EU	DG GROW, DG CNECT, DG JUST	20.04.2020	33	https://www.asktheeu.org/en/request/member_state_comments_on_netzdg#incoming-29856
EU	DG GROW	20.04.2020	0	https://www.asktheeu.org/en/request/notification_on_netzdg_amendment#incoming-26403
Germany	Ministry of Justice and Consumer Protection	09.06.2020	98	https://fragdenstaat.de/anfrage/netzdg-notifizierung/
Germany	Ministry of Justice and Consumer Protection	09.06.2020	260 (mail)	https://fragdenstaat.de/anfrage/bmjv-task-force/
Germany	Ministry of Justice and Consumer Protection	15.07.2020	0	https://fragdenstaat.de/anfrage/breife-an-internetkonzerne/
Australia	eSafety Commissioner, Attorney General's Department	08.06.2020	359	https://www.righttoknow.org.au/request/abhorrent_violent_material_act#incoming-18083
New Zealand	Ministry of Foreign Affairs and Trade	05.08.2020	33	https://fyi.org.nz/request/13466

APPENDIX B

Regulatory Context Appendix

This appendix provides some additional background context on the political systems being explored and analyzed in the case studies.

B.1 Germany

B.1.1 KEY ACTORS

The main political actor in Germany is the executive branch of the government, which was from 2013 to 2017 composed of a 'grand coalition' between the country's two largest federal parties, the center-left Social Democrats (SPD, 193 seats) and the center-right Christian Democrats (311 seats including those of its Bavarian counterpart, the CSU, which operates together with the CDU at the federal level). These two parties shared ministerial appointments (with SPD Foreign, Justice, and Labor Ministers) and also generally voted together as a bloc in parliament. In 2013–2017 there were two opposition parties: the Greens (*Die Grüne*, 63 seats), a socially, economically, and environmentally progressive party born out of the 1970s student movements; and the Left (*Die Linke*, 64 seats), a left-wing group founded in 2007 with ties to the former governing party of the East German Democratic Republic.

Additionally, there are a number of regulatory agencies composed of non-elected civil servants that play an important role in drafting, implementing, and enforcing rules. After the scope of a legislation is determined by the executive branch of government (the Federal Chancellery, and the cabinet) the text of the draft law is written up by officials inside the competent ministry involved in a policy issue. Because Germany has no ministry for digital policy issues, the competent ministry over digital issues is usually the Ministry of Justice and Consumer Protection (BMJV). Issues relevant to security and the economy might also feature the Federal Criminal Police Office (BKA), the Federal

Intelligence Service (BND), or the Federal Ministry of Economic Affairs and Energy (BMWI). While these ministries may have their own specific policy agendas, I conceive of their core preference broadly as the supply of rules to meet the demand put upon them by the executive branch.

Because Germany is part of the European Union, a few political actors at the EU level are important as well. While the broad thrust of EU policy is increasingly being dictated by the European Council of (member state) Ministers, the European Commission maintains the broad policymaking remit for the European Union, especially in more technical areas (Rauh, 2019). The Commission is structured into around thirty directorate generals (DGs) which cover various policy areas. On digital policy, the most important ones are DG Communications Networks, Content, and Technology (CNECT), DG Justice and Consumers (JUST), DG Competition (COMP), and DG Internal Market, Industry, Entrepreneurship and Small-to-Medium Enterprises (GROW). While the politics of EU policymaking, and of the Commission in particular, are hugely complex, work has established that each DG is motivated by its "own competence-seeking motives, varying stakeholder networks, and Commissioners with different national and partisan backgrounds" (Rauh, 2019, p. 352; see also Hartlapp, Metz, and Rauh, 2014). Nevertheless, one can generally assume, following EU regulatory politics scholarship, that the overarching preferences for the Commission and its DGs are the maintenance of a single European Market, and the prevention of regulatory fragmentation across member states (Vogel, 2003; Bradford, 2020).

B.1.2 POWER RESOURCES & INSTITUTIONAL CONSTRAINTS

In traditional, power-based terms, Germany would likely be said to wield significant market power. In 2015, Germany had the fourth largest GDP in the world on nominal terms.[1] The largest country by population in Europe, its approximately 80 million residents in 2015 put it within the top twenty of the world's most populous countries. However, the penetration of major platform companies was not as high as in the United States or other leading markets; while precise statistics are difficult to come by, less than 40% of the German population is active on various user generated content platforms. For instance, in 2015 there were only about 25–30 million Facebook users in Germany, making the country roughly their 19th largest market.[2] The best estimates of Twitter usership in Germany put it at about 5 million users in 2021; YouTube has become more popular in the past few years, according to some recent estimates, with 2019 figures suggesting it is used by almost 75% of German social media users.[3] According to some estimates, platform companies like Facebook also glean about five times less revenue per user on average in Europe, as North America is far bigger and a more lucrative advertising market, minimizing the policy impact of EU countries on platform companies.[4] Despite the large GDP of Germany, Germany's market power vis-à-vis platform companies might be considered moderate rather than substantial.

That all said, and as outlined in Chapter 4, market size is not the only important factor in shaping the ability of a state actor to intervene and supply new rules. Germany can potentially punch above its market power weight by exerting its considerable influence on the supranational bloc of the European Union, a global regulatory power and frequent exporter of regulatory standards which has its policy preferences shaped by the preferences of leading member states (Bradford, 2012). Germany thus has some influence on shaping regulatory outcomes in the large EU market—which, for example, represented approximately 320 million Facebook users in 2015, a significant proportion of Facebook's approximately 1.45 billion users in the second half of 2015.

Today, Germany is known for having a highly competent and powerful bureaucratic state, with well-funded and capable regulators (Müller, 2001)—in a major development from the 1980s and 1990s, where the country did not yet have independent or sophisticated regulatory agencies for many sectors (Bach and Newman, 2007). However, Germany notably does not have a federal ministry tasked with digital policy or digitization issues, nor does it have a federal media regulator, meaning that both the relevant expertise and competencies are diffused across various state-level and federal ministries.

Also important to consider for a state's power to intervene are any institutional constraints that are shaping a state's ability to supply new rules. While Germany's role within the European Union can provide an amplifying effect, allowing it to potentially steer EU policy and tap into broader EU competencies (and the tens of thousands of regulators working at the European Commission), Germany's membership in the European Union also presents it with a number of transnational institutional constraints. The most important one of these is that the German government must generally adhere to existing EU laws and regulatory frameworks when developing new rules. Under a series of measures designed to ensure harmonization of the European single market, codified into European law by Directive 1998/34, and most recently updated in the Single Market Transparency Directive 2015/1535, the European Union has a procedure for notification of technical regulations and of rules on products and services, including 'information society services' (e-commerce, media, and internet services). The 2015/1535 Directive sets out a process through which member states must notify the European Commission of any changes to the rules they wish to impose upon certain products or services, including electronic ones, setting up a formalized mechanism through which member states must submit draft laws for review by the Commission and other member states before they are adopted.

The procedure requires a three-month 'standstill' period, in which the member state must wait to receive comments from the Commission and other member states; during this period, the Directorate General for the Internal Market (DG GROW) spearheads a consultation with other DGs, and conducts a legal analysis intended to "help Member States ascertain the degree of compatibility of notified drafts with EU law."[5] This means that an individual member state cannot simply decide to regulate an issue tomorrow, whip up a draft law, and push it through parliament immediately; it must formally notify the Commission (where the draft law is placed in a publicly available database) and wait three months for the input of the Commission and other member states. The Commission, as well as the other member states, can choose to do nothing, issue a comment to be taken into consideration by the proposing party, or issue a so-called 'detailed opinion': if this occurs, the standstill period is further extended by a month, and the member state must formally respond to the issues raised by the complainant. Through this notification and harmonization process, the Commission can veto proposed member state draft regulations if it has its own concrete plans to regulate in that area:

> The Commission can block a draft technical regulation if it announces its intention of proposing an EU act (directive, regulation or decision) or its finding that the draft legislation concerns a matter which is covered by a proposal for an EU act presented to the Council. In the case of draft technical regulations containing rules on services, the Commission can block such draft acts only when it announces its finding that the draft legislation concerns a matter which is covered by a proposal for an EU act presented to the Council.[6]

According to the TRIS database, since 1999, 305 national-level regulations pertaining to 'information society services' have been notified to the Commission, with detailed opinions issued on around 10 percent (30) of the proposals. According to the text of EU 2015/1535, any regulatory initiative that changes the rules of operation for businesses—even less formalized processes like voluntary regulations or codes of conduct—should be notified to the commission. If a government fails to notify the law and yet implements it anyway, it can be deemed invalid by the European Court of Justice (see Case C-194/94 CJEU).

B.1.3 NORMATIVE LANDSCAPE

What is the German attitude to regulation more generally, and relating to channels of information distribution and dissemination more specifically? What is the normative landscape shaping the willingness of policymakers to intervene with rules that might have an impact on free expression?

Generally, Germany is known for being a neoliberal state with an unusually high, ordoliberal or 'new corporatist' degree of government intervention in markets (Witt, 2002; Streeck, 2009). It has a relatively high appetite for intervention in media, communications, and information sectors generally, although this has been structured in an intentionally decentralized and slightly quixotic fashion. Media policy in Germany is complex, and was born in the aftermath of the Second World War as part of a broader effort to avoid politically dangerous concentrations of power and the likelihood of vital communications infrastructure being captured by anything akin to the Nazi regime. Information and communication policy is thus largely decentralized and placed under the remit of the federal states, as established in the German Interstate Broadcasting Treaty (*Rundfunkstaatsvertrag*, or RStV) of 1991. Beginning in the 1990s, pressure was placed on media companies and the emerging telecommunications industry to embrace certain self-regulatory measures, especially in the realm of youth protection, and Germany has a long tradition of self-regulatory and co-regulatory management of information distribution sectors (Hoffmann-Riem, 2016). The German Association for Voluntary Self-Regulation of Digital Media Service Providers (*Freiwillige Selbstkontrolle Multimedia-Diensteanbieter*, or FSM) was established in 1997 and eventually became a major part of the regulatory framework for youth protection in the media that was codified by the German states in the Interstate Treaty on the Protection of Human Dignity and the Protection of Minors in Broadcasting and in Telemedia (*Jugendmedienschutz-Staatsvertrag*, JMStV) of 2002. FSM works within the tradition of 'regulated self-regulation,' a German regulatory approach which involves self-regulatory associations of companies being overseen by some body that meets criteria set out by regulation (e.g., the institution must meet legal criteria, be licensed by the state and monitored by the Federal Office of Justice). This approach emerged in the early 2000s and has been a major way through which Germany has regulated new media industries (Schulz and Held, 2002; Hoffmann-Riem, 2016). FSM has developed a number of code of conducts for its members, including a code on self-regulation for search engines in 2005 (Google, ask.de, MSN, Searchteq, T-Online, and Yahoo!) and a code for major mobile phone providers in 2007.[7] In 2009, FSM spearheaded a code of conduct with the largest social networks then active in Germany (VZnet Netzwerke, Lokalisten, and wer-kennt-wen), all of which would eventually be made irrelevant by the rise of giant American alternatives.

Germany also has a historically distinct position on freedom of expression. In all European Union countries, freedom of expression is encoded under the 1950 European Convention on Human Rights (ECHR)—the first paragraph of Article 10 of the ECHR notes that "Everyone has the right to freedom of expression.... This right shall include freedom to hold opinions and to receive and impart information and ideas without interference by public authority and regardless of frontiers" (Benedek and Kettemann, 2014, p. 23). The European human rights treaties also include provisions which describe the conditions under which the right to freedom of opinion and expression can be restricted, which include the prevention of crimes, disorder, and incidents which lead to the violations of the rights of others. Nevertheless, Germany is known for having a more restrictive environment for free expression than many other democracies, even though freedom of expression is enshrined as a fundamental individual right in Article 5(1) of the Constitution, the Basic Law (*Grundgesetz*) (Karpen, Molle, and Schwarz, 2007). While the Basic Law notes that "there shall be no censorship," which is understood as restriction on certain types of restrictions rather than a blanket US-style free speech exceptionalism (Jouanjan, 2009), Article 5 also notes how the right to expression may be limited by certain general laws and youth protection statutes.

In the German Criminal Code (*Strafgesetzbuch*, or StGB), a wide array of offenses that disturb the public peace and the concept of the 'free democratic basic order' are prohibited (Appleman, 1995). Under the StGB, it is famously illegal to disseminate the propaganda or symbols of unconstitutional organizations, such as those associated with the German Nazi party (Sec. 86 and 86a); to defame the state and its symbols, including its flag, colors, or anthems (Sec. 90a); to engage in criminal insult or defamation (Sec. 185 and 186); or to incite hatred against national, racial, or religious groups (Appleman, 1995, p. 413). Evidently, this is a far less absolutist position on free expression than encoded in other legal approaches, and many different types of harmful speech restrictions are legally justifiable in the German context, even when they come into tension with the broader European legal frameworks (ARTICLE 19, 2018).

As Tworek (2021, p. 115) outlines in a historical analysis of the connection between the NetzDG and older German principles of speech regulation, Germany has long tradition of "seeing speech law as a political solution to democratic problems, especially concerns about the inability of citizens to protect themselves from dangerous [material]." In effect, Tworek argues that successive German governments since the Wiemar era have held an interventionist position on governing information channels, seeing the creation of rules for books, radio, television, and now digital media, as part of the core competency of a democratic government. The specific history of Germany, forged out of two world wars, have led to the country to have an interventionist norm, although one which, paired with Germany's specific regulatory tradition, seems to often favor co-regulatory governance solutions.

B.2 Australia

B.2.1 KEY ACTORS

There are three groups of actors that played important roles in the development of the AVM Act. These consisted of two substate groupings within the Australian government (the executive branch of the elected Liberal/National coalition government, and the various regulatory agencies and ministries that play a role during the policy development process) and the platform companies.

The executive branch of the Australian government is formed following elections that, in the past 50 years, have led to governments being led by either the center-left Labor party, or by a coalition of the two major parties on the right: the Liberal party and the National party. In 2016, the Liberal/National coalition narrowly won the election, and Malcolm Turnbull was elected as Prime Minister with a one-seat majority. After an internal leadership challenge, Scott Morrison became Prime Minister in 2018 after Turnbull stepped down. In the lead-up to the Christchurch Attack, the governing coalition carried a narrow majority in the 150 seat House of Representatives, with Labor holding 69 seats, and a host of minor parties and independents holding the remaining 5 seats. Federal elections in Australia are held every three years, and an election was slated for mid-2019. Although Morrison had been consistently behind in the polling, which steadily predicted a Labor victory (Gauja, Sawer, and Simms, 2020), one can assume that he was heavily motivated by a desire to be elected Prime Minister and stay on as Liberal party leader.

The elected party forms the cabinet. Cabinet ministers serve as the head of the various ministries and departments that play an important role in the development, implementation, monitoring, and enforcement of rules. The most relevant of these actors in the development of the Australian Christchurch response were the Attorney General's department, headed at the time by Attorney General (AG) Christian Porter. The AG's department often leads on legislative drafting and is broadly concerned with matters of law and justice, but also has responsibilities over criminal law/law enforcement, and national security. Other relevant ministries included the Department of Communications and the Arts, which had policy responsibilities over the digital economy, telecommunications policy,

194   REGULATORY CONTEXT APPENDIX

broadcasting policy, and 'content policy relating to the information economy.'[8] The Department of the Prime Minister and Cabinet, led by the Prime Minister and his direct staff, generally determines the broad thrust of policy and also has competencies relating to the coordination of digital and 'cyber policy.' One final substate actor relevant in the enforcement of the AVM Act is the eSafety Commissioner, an independent regulatory agency that was created in 2015 to work on digital child safety issues. Their remit was expanded in 2017, and they have some competencies relating to online content, including the fight against the proliferation of child sexual abuse material online.[9]

B.2.2 POWER RESOURCES & INSTITUTIONAL CONSTRAINTS

In market-size-based accounts of state power, Australia would be considered a moderately powerful actor in global regulatory politics. The country has a population of approximately 25 million, making it the around the 50th most populous in the world, slightly less populous than Madagascar, Venezuela, Nepal, and Yemen, and slightly larger than North Korea, Cameroon, and Taiwan.[10] However, it has a large economy, with a nominal GDP that would make it about the 13th largest in the world.[11] It has a high degree of internet penetration, with a steady 89% of residents estimated to have an internet connection of some sort in 2015–2020.[12] In 2019, around 40% of Australia's population, or around 11 million people, were estimated to be active Facebook users.[13] Estimates made by social media marketing agencies put Twitter usage at about 4.6 million people, and YouTube at 15 million Australians in 2019.[14] These kinds of imperfect figures would lead us to estimate that, for the global user-generated content platform companies, the Australian market is small in the global context, although potentially more valuable from an advertising perspective given advertising revenue per user. Australia represents about 0.014% of Twitter's global user base, 0.008% of YouTube's global user base, and 0.006% of Facebook's global user base.[15]

Australia is a G20 country known to have a capable and competent bureaucracy. According to the World Bank's 'Worldwide Governance Indicators' dataset, which has various measures seeking to estimate "the capacity of a government to effectively formulate and implement sound policies" (Kaufmann, Kraay, and Mastruzzi, 2010, p. 4) Australia ranked in the world's 98th percentile in 2019 in terms of its 'regulatory quality.' According to the same indices, which feature an estimate of 'government effectiveness' which measure "perceptions of the quality of public services, the quality of the civil service and the degree of its independence from political pressures, the quality of policy formulation and implementation, and the credibility of the government's commitment to such policies" (Kaufmann, Kraay, and Mastruzzi, 2010, p. 4), Australia ranked in the global 92nd percentile in 2019.[16] Australia is perceived to have high regulatory capacity, with highly competent, well-resourced civil servants, at least when considered in the global context. The Department of Communications and the Arts had 550 staff in 2018–2019, and one of the regulatory agencies under its purview, the Australian Communications and Media Authority, a converged regulator with an influence in broadcast, television, and internet policy, had an additional 427 staff (Commonwealth of Australia, 2018).

The government in Australia's Westminster-style system also has significant capacities to set domestic legislation and pursue-wide ranging policy reforms. Power is fairly concentrated in the executive: even though the Liberal/National governing coalition only had a one-seat majority after the 2016 election, it still had a huge degree of executive power, with an ability to basically pass legislation at will as long it was able to maintain control of party members (Kumarasingham, 2013). Legislative studies scholars, discussing the similar systems of Canada and Australia, have quipped that these countries represent 'elected dictatorships' with an unusually high degree of centralization in government, not seen in systems like the United States, where parties often control only part of a bicameral legislature (Sayers and Banfield, 2013). This means that in Australia there are few domestic institutional constraints in place to bind the hands of a majority government that strongly demands new policies.

Transnationally, the only major institutional constraint on Australia's ability to supply new platform-related rules was a preferential trade agreement with the United States, the Australia-United States Free Trade Agreement (AUS-FTA), signed in 2004. The agreement does contain some provisions pertaining to telecommunications policy and the digital economy, including stipulations that the signatories do not impose customs duties on digital products and do not discriminate against the 'digital products' of their trading partners (Given, 2004). This is an older trade agreement that slightly pre-dated the rise of major American user-generated content businesses (Burrell and Weatherall, 2008); it does not have more specific considerations directly mandating the types of intermediary liability provisions that the signatories should implement or maintain, as seen in the 'NAFTA 2.0' US-Mexico-Canada Trade Agreement of 2018 (Krishnamurthy and Fjeld, 2020). AUSFTA thus provided a relatively weak constraint that the Australian government could likely overcome as long as they were able to make a coherent argument that any new rules they supplied did not merely discriminate against American firms.

B.2.3 NORMATIVE LANDSCAPE

What is the attitude to regulation in Australia more generally and relating to channels of information distribution and dissemination more specifically? What is the normative landscape shaping the willingness of policymakers to intervene with rules that might have an impact on free expression?

Scholars of Australian regulation have used various conceptual tools to explain the evolution of its regulatory philosophy in the past 50 years, but it appears as if Australia has historically embodied a more interventionist 'regulatory state' approach to regulating firms and markets than many other G20 countries. Rather than total neoliberalization and de-regulation, the 1980s and 1990s were associated with (often large-scale) reforms in key economic sectors such as finance, leading to a certain degree of "regulatory liberalisation and privatisation" (Allen et al., 2021, p. 118). In the media and broadcasting sectors, there has always been significant state involvement: as B. Goldsmith and Thomas (2012, p. 2) note, it has been observed that "the history of Australian content in broadcasting has been a history of regulation," and there is a long tradition of Australian governments intervening in information distribution channels for social and cultural reasons.

Part of the story is likely that the absence of constitutionally guaranteed rights in Australia has meant that the balance of limits to rights (including to expression and speech) versus security has been frequently tilted towards security, especially by conservative governments (Mann, Daly, and Molnar, 2020). This has included an interest in online safety, including attempts to set limits on the types of online content that Australian residents are able to access and the things that they can say and do via platform services. In 2011, a report by the Australian Law Reform Commission, an independent regulatory authority that conducts periodic assessments into existing Australian legal frameworks, recommended new legislation that required internet intermediaries to "block or remove 'prohibited' content available on or through their networks" (Pappalardo and Suzor, 2018, p. 470). In 2015, the Tony Abbott-led Liberal/-National government implemented the Enhancing Online Safety Act, which created the Office of the eSafety Commissioner (eSafety), which advertises itself as "the world's first government agency committed to keeping its citizens safer online."[17] eSafety's mandate was initially confined to child safety, and issues like cyberbullying and child abuse material, but in 2017 Prime Minister Malcolm Turnbull's Liberal/National government expanded its remit to include "online safety for all Australians."[18] In the lead-up to the Christchurch attack, eSafety had a reporting mechanism for online content, and had the power to issue takedown requests to companies in certain cases.

This is all to say that one can argue that policy debates in Australia are underpinned by a relatively interventionist normative frame about the appropriate scale of government intervention in the (digital) public sphere. While this landscape is constantly evolving and being contested—there are also political actors within the country seeking to move towards a more libertarian,

US-style model of free expression that have sought to secure the repeal of the most recent iteration of Australian hate speech legislation passed by Labor in 1995 (Gelber and McNamara, 2013)—the last three Liberal/National governments have been very muscular on security policies and terrorism, especially on its intersections with the digital, and have been willing to sacrifice both privacy and free expression as a result. In 2015, the Turnbull Liberal/National government enacted a set of serious telecommunications rules requiring that service providers retain metadata (information about calls, who called whom, etc.) about their customers for two years for possible counter-terrorism investigations (Sarre, 2017). Relatedly, as Mann, Daly, and Molnar (2020) describe, Prime Minister Turnbull quipped that in June 2017 that "the laws of mathematics are very commendable, but the only law that applies in Australia is the law of Australia," setting off a broad national debate about end-to-end encryption that culminated in significant legislative reforms seeking to increase the ability of security agencies to conduct counter-terrorism and intelligence operations by intercepting communications on Australian networks. These comments about the unequivocal primacy of Australian law over all else (including perhaps the natural world) presaged the very similar arguments made by other Australian political leaders around platform companies and their content moderation practices in mid-2019.

B.3 New Zealand

B.3.1 KEY ACTORS

The executive, rulemaking branch of the New Zealand government is formed following elections which have historically led to governments headed by one of the two major mainstream political parties, the center-right National party and the center-left Labour party. A little over two months after the German Bundestag voted through the NetzDG, and in the same week in September 2017 that voters in Germany were going to the polls to re-elect the Merkel-led CDU/SPD governing coalition, voters in New Zealand split the majority of the vote between National (which earned 56 seats) and Labour (46). Interestingly and unusually, one of the 'minor parties' of New Zealand's politics, New Zealand First, a party commonly described as populist and nationalist that had broken off from National in the 1990s (Denemark and Bowler, 2002), received enough seats (9) to make it a potential kingmaker in the post-election scrum. It decided to form a coalition with Labour, propelling Labour to a Minority government additionally backed by the Green party (8 seats). Labour's Jacinda Ardern, elected head of the Labour party only eight weeks before the election, became Prime Minister, with New Zealand First's Winston Peters the Deputy

Prime Minister; New Zealand First received four seats in the 20-member Cabinet with the Greens granted three other ministerial positions outside of Cabinet. As Vowles and Curtin (2020, p. 3) describe, this surprising turn of events "was the first time in the history of the mixed member proportional system [implemented in New Zealand in 1996] that a party with the second-most votes gained the position of leading a government."

While this elected branch sets the broad policy direction, New Zealand has various regulatory agencies and government ministries that provide input into the development, implementation, monitoring, and enforcement of rules. The central one tapped to lead the internationally collaborative response post-Christchurch was the Ministry of Foreign Affairs and Trade (MFAT); other relevant ministries involved in digital policy issues included the Department of Internal Affairs (DIA), which had a team working on issues relating to online safety, the Office of Film and Literature Classification (a government agency that reviews movies, video games, and some online content), and the Ministry of Business, Innovation, and Employment, which has a mandate over telecommunications policy.

B.3.2 POWER RESOURCES & INSTITUTIONAL CONSTRAINTS

In market-size-based accounts of power, New Zealand would not be considered a powerful actor in international regulatory politics. The country has a population of about 5 million, putting it roughly around the 120th most populous country in the world, comparable to Ireland, Costa Rica, or Liberia.[19] It has a larger economy than most countries of its size, however, with a nominal GDP that would put it at about the 50th largest economy in the world. It has a very high degree of internet penetration, with 94% of residents said to be 'active internet users' in 2021,[20] as well as a extraordinarily high degree of user-generated platform penetration: according to 2018 statistics from Statista, 76% of the country's population used YouTube, 75% used Facebook, and about 30% used Instagram.[21] Microsoft's Bing search has about 3% of the New Zealand search market, which is dominated by Google Search.[22] To put these numbers in a global perspective, New Zealand's Facebook user-base in 2019 corresponded to less than one-tenth of 1 percent of the company's global user total.[23]

Despite its small size, New Zealand has fairly strong levels of regulatory capacity. According to the World Bank's 'Worldwide Governance Indicators' dataset, which has various measures seeking to estimate "the capacity of a government to effectively formulate and implement sound policies" (Kaufmann, Kraay, and Mastruzzi, 2010, p. 4) New Zealand ranks in the world's 99th percentile in terms of its 'regulatory quality.' According to the same indices, which feature an estimate of 'government effectiveness' which measures "perceptions of the quality of public services, the quality of the civil service and the degree of its independence from political pressures, the quality of policy formulation and implementation, and the credibility of the government's commitment to such policies" (Kaufmann, Kraay, and Mastruzzi, 2010, p. 4), New Zealand ranks in the global 96th percentile in 2019.[24] While these are imperfect heuristic estimates and thus must be taken with a grain of salt, it is evident that New Zealand is seen to have high regulatory capacity, with highly competent, well-resourced civil servants.

New Zealand, however, does not have a traditionally construed media or internet regulator; instead it has an Office of Film and Literature Classification, an independent regulator headed by a 'Chief Censor' and a small staff of fewer than 20 civil servants charged with reviewing, parental rating, and potentially barring content from New Zealand (such as films, television shows, and video games; it can also make it illegal to possess certain forms of online content, such as terrorist manifestos or depictions of terrorist violence; Graham-McLay, 2020). As well, in 2019 the New Zealand government had a small office of about a dozen people within the Department of Internal Affairs charged with unearthing and combating child sexual exploitation material accessible in New Zealand (Kenny, 2019). This lack of large and discrete regulatory authorities with general competencies in media and tech policy (Germany has 14 media state-level authorities with some experience dealing with online content, for example), likely helped shape the decision to tap the MFAT to end up leading the Christchurch response in partnership with the Prime Minister's department. MFAT has about 1,800 employees, more than double that of the German Ministry of Justice and Consumer Protection in charge of the NetzDG process (760 employees), although the German BMJV has a considerably larger budget than the MFAT (around 900 million Euros annually, to the MFAT's approximately 600 million Euros). MFAT does not appear to ordinarily work on technology policy issues, although it would be involved in negotiating the digitally relevant (e.g., intellectual property) provisions of international trade agreements, for example.[25]

Institutionally, there are few formal transnational institutional constraints shaping the ability of New Zealand to intervene and supply new rules for platforms operating in the country. New Zealand is not part of a regional regulatory bloc like Germany; it also does not have any trade agreements or bilateral or multilateral agreements with the United States that place limits on the type of rules the government can deploy domestically for internet intermediaries.

B.3.3 NORMATIVE LANDSCAPE

What is the attitude to regulation in New Zealand more generally, and relating to channels of information distribution and dissemination more specifically? What is the normative landscape shaping the willingness of policymakers to intervene with rules that might have an impact on free expression?

In the mid-1980s, New Zealand began a rapid process of economic liberalization, deregulation, and commercialization (Easton, 1997). Political scientists writing in the 1990s observed the growing 'rolling back' of traditional state functions, and a move towards more minimal government intervention in the market, to the extent that the country became a "free market laboratory" for experimentation with neoliberal governance concepts (Kelsey, 1993, p. 65). In terms of media policy, as Thompson (2011, p. 11) notes, "The programme of neoliberal macroeconomic reforms in New Zealand from the mid 1980s through the 1990s saw the emergence of one of the most heavily commercialised and deregulated broadcasting sectors in the OECD," as a BBC-esque model of state-led public broadcasting was slowly dismantled. This intentionally 'light-handed' regulatory approach was also deployed in the telecommunications sector, which was 'partially de-regulated' in 1987 with the passage of the Telecommunications Act (Blanchard, 1994). Overall, even in the early 2010s, the country was still being described as having a 'laissez-faire' regulatory culture across a wide range of policy issues, especially those relating to digital policy (Barrett and Strongman, 2012), though there was an increase in state intervention in the media and telecommunications sectors and a partial roll-back of the almost completely hands-off model of the 1990s (Hansen and Jones, 2017).

As mentioned previously, New Zealand does not have a traditionally construed media or internet regulator. It does have a long history of limited oversight in various media and content via the—pragmatically named—Chief Censor, an independent and government-appointed official that leads on the implementation of the various film and media censorship laws that have existed in the country since 1916 (Anderson, 2017). The Chief Censor can append parental warnings and create new categories of 'viewer discretion advised' interstitials for films, movies, video games, and 'computer files,' and has the power to render certain forms of 'objectionable' content illegal to own or share publicly.[26] However, the Censor's office is small and its true power in the online environment is limited; it was largely set up for professionally produced content, for example for screening content to be shown at cinemas in the country. While the Censor can make online content illegal (such as a specific video, file, or piece of content, creating criminal repercussions for New Zealand citizens that download or upload this content), it did not under the legal framework in place in 2019 have the power to issue takedown notices to platform companies hosting content in other jurisdictions.[27]

Another set of newer regulations passed in 2015 also sought to tackle the issue of cyberbulling and online harassment by creating a complaints-handling body to which users can submit complaints (Panzic, 2015), with the body, NetSafe, "intended to deal with complaints in the first instance" (Síthigh, 2020, p. 18) and helping intermediate between users and the platform companies that host or facilitate content. This Harmful Digital Communication Act (HCDA) does not properly constitute platform regulation, however, as the offenses target ordinary New Zealanders and not platform companies; the new criminal offenses apply to individuals that "post a digital communication with the intention that it cause harm to a victim" (Post, 2017, p. 211), and not to firms.

While the combination of New Zealand's Chief Censor and the HCDA may make it seem as if New Zealand has a generally interventionist set of speech norms, the government has been more comfortable potentially intervening in areas such as pornography, indecency, and harassment than it is around the broader and more contentious areas of political speech. The New Zealand Bill of Rights Act of 1990 states that "everyone has the right to freedom of expression, including the freedom to seek, receive, and impart information and opinions of any kind in any form," without significant qualifications for dangerous and dehumanizing speech (Elers and Jayan, 2020). After a number of racist incidents in the early 2000s, Prime Minister Helen Clark's Labour government considered a set of hate speech laws in 2004, but dropped the project after political pressure and a public consultation in which the "overwhelming majority of submissions were opposed to implementing a new, general hate speech law" (Harrison, 2006, p. 71). Critics of New Zealand's laissez-faire norm around political speech note that it harms minoritized groups, underplaying the fact that "the right to free speech may negatively impinge upon the right of targeted communities to be free from discrimination, including discriminating hate speech" and that this is "a dehumansing by-product of Whiteness, racism and coloniality reflected in New Zealand's freedom of expression laws" (Elers and Jayan, 2020, p. 240).

Notes

Chapter 1

1. @ThierryBreton, 19.01.2023, https://twitter.com/ThierryBreton/status/148378651021 4303744.
2. A brief note on terminology: in past work, I have theorized platform governance as seeking to encompass both 'governance by platforms' (what industry does in terms of rulemaking, enforcement, and other softer forms of governance—see in particular Gillespie, 2018) and 'governance of platforms' (how other stakeholders seek to intervene in this process, or influence the activities of platform companies more generally). My work has sought to explore the interlinkages between these two facets of governance, and how, for instance, industry practices are deeply shaped by while simultaneously informing government policy responses (Gorwa, 2019a; Gorwa, Binns, and Katzenbach, 2020). Here, I envision 'platform regulation' as a narrower concept located on the 'governance of platforms' side of this spectrum.

Chapter 2

1. Here, I'm talking about what has become the global status quo, in the context of US-headquartered multinational tech companies. The less globally pervasive but increasingly important Chinese model obviously features fewer US-trained policy staff in the domestic context, and has a number of other distinctive features given the level of government involvement. See the work of China scholars such as M. E. Roberts (2018) for more insight into this system.
2. Facebook Community Stanards, Adult Nudity and Sexual Activity, Sep. 29, 2022. https://transparency.fb.com/en-gb/policies/community-standards/adult-nudity-sexual-activity, archived at https://perma.cc/HV4H-YAAM.

Chapter 3

1. For that reason, the chapter focuses predominantly but not exclusively on the European Union and the transatlantic EU-US relationship. This may be the logical outcome of the European Union experimenting more widely with policy initiatives in the platform domain than any other country; however, it also leads to a focus on the markets where platform firms invest the most resources—high-income democracies, mainly in the Global North—and not where platforms have the most users. A more global discussion of content moderation-focused platform regulation can be found in Chapter 8.

204   NOTES

2. Estimates based upon data from Statista; see https://www.statista.com/statistics/1032154/microsoft-employees-by-location/ and https://www.statista.com/statistics/938614/number-of-employees-in-europes-largest-banks/.

3. Content moderation is the notable exception to this, with social media firms indirectly employing tens of thousands of contractors. Firms also generally prefer to publicly downplay the importance of this work; see the excellent work of Sarah Roberts and Tarleton Gillespie overviewed in earlier chapters.

4. See for instance https://www.aboutamazon.com/news/operations/amazon-ramps-hiring-opening-100-000-new-roles-to-support-people-relying-on-amazons-service-in-this-stressful-time.

5. About the Clean IT Project', archived at http://web.archive.org/web/20120109073856/http://www.cleanitproject.eu/abouttheproject.html

6. Similar processes have long been the purview of intellectual property and copyright debates, which I would consider as 'content undesirable for economic' rather than national stability/democracy reasons. Copyright features its own distinct historical dynamics, different stakes and players (e.g., Hollywood, content producers, global brands) and has unique politics that have been well described by scholars like Haggart (2014), Tusikov (2016), and Meyer (2017).

Chapter 5

1. Interview with CDU policy staffers that requested anonymity, July 2020.

2. Maas's statement to begin the press conference is available online at: https://www.youtube.com/watch?v=TZdWdrfDnug.

3. Partial agenda summaries are available on an archived Ministry webpage: https://web.archive.org/web/20170930061101/http://www.fair-im-netz.de/WebS/NHS/DE/Home/home_node.html.

4. Very little public information was released about the project, and detailed meeting minutes were not kept. In response to a freedom of information request to the BMJV seeking obtain the meeting minutes for the task force, the Ministry responded that they did not exist (Fraag den Staat, 2017).

It seems as if the BMJV created a website (no longer online) which had more details about the task force, with brief summaries of the meetings and the main commitments made, but this was only archived in July 2017 (suggesting it was created during that key legislative moment and then later taken down in July 2019): https://web.archive.org/web/20170930061101/http://www.fair-im-netz.de/WebS/NHS/DE/Home/home_node.html.

5. These were jugendschutz.net, klicksafe.de, the Amadeu Antonio-Stiftung, and Gesicht Zeigen. While the Amadeu Antonio foundation and Gesicht Zeigen are independent civil society organizations, Jungendschutz and Klicksafe are probably better understood as governmental actors or quasi-governmental actors with close ties to the German state and federal governments. Klicksafe is a EU-funded project of the state media regulators of Rhineland-Palatinate and North Rhine-Westphalia.

6. Interview held via videoconference with Simone Rafael, Executive Director of the Amadeu Antonio-Stiftung, June 2020.

7. Interview conducted in April 2020 with Lutz Mache, Public Policy and Government Relations Manager, Google Germany.

8. These quotes are from p. 1 of Ministry's official English translation, obtained by European Digital Rights and available here: https://edri.org/eu-internet-forum-document-pool/ The German version is archived here: https://perma.cc/J35T-DGC6.

9. The tweet is available at https://twitter.com/HeikoMaas/status/676739434239426561.

10. Interview with member of the Bundestag Jens Zimmerman, SPD Digital Policy Spokesman, June 2020; interview with Alexander Ritzmann, Counter Extremism Project, June 2020.

11. Interview with Jens Zimmerman.
12. Interview with Green party policy staffer, May 2020.
13. These targets were defined broadly as "service providers who operate platforms on the Internet with the intention of making a profit which enable users to exchange, share or make available to the public any content with other users (social networks)," with the exclusion of journalistically curated services where an editor is responsible for content under existing legal frameworks (e.g., newspapers, broadcasters).

    The first draft is available at: https://cdn.netzpolitik.org/wp-upload/2017/03/1703014_NetzwerkDurchsetzungsG.pdf, author translation.
14. Interview with FDP member of the Bundestag, June 2020.
15. Interview with Lutz Mache, Google; interview with anonymous platform policy staffer.
16. Gorwa FOIA to DG GROW, 2020. Document received June 9, 2020; document dated April 3, 2017. Available at https://www.asktheeu.org/en/request/7872/response/26398/attach/3/Document%205.pdf
17. Gorwa FOIA to DG JUST, 2020. Document received June 16, 2020, and dated June 8, 2017. https://www.asktheeu.org/en/request/member_state_comments_on_netzdg#incoming-26570, p. 5.
18. Ibid.
19. Article 3 of the ECD is legally complex and has been interpreted slightly differently by various member states in their implementations of the ECD. See Hellner (2004) for a detailed discussion.
20. Interview with DG Connect Staffer, 2020.
21. Interview with Mathias Schindler, Office of member of the European Parliament Felix Reda (The Greens/European Free Alliance), April 2020.
22. Gorwa FOIA to DG GROW, 2020. Document received June 9, 2020; document dated July 6, 2017. https://www.asktheeu.org/en/request/member_state_comments_on_netzdg#incoming-26398.
23. See contributions from Petra Sitte (Die Linke) and Konstantin von Notz collected by Reuter (2017).
24. See Jacob (2018).
25. Interview held via videoconference with major platform policy manager, summer 2020. They requested that both their name and the name of their employer be anonymized.
26. Gorwa FOIA to DG CNECT, 2020. Document received July 10, 2020, and dated May 24, 2017. https://www.asktheeu.org/en/request/member_state_comments_on_netzdg#incoming-27094.
27. Interview held via videoconference with Paul Nemitz, Director for Fundamental Rights, DG Justice, June 2020.
28. Interview with DG CNECT Staffer, 2020.
29. See Gorwa FOIA to DG GROW, 2020. Germany's Response to Sweden, recieved June 9, 2020; document dated July 28, 2017. https://www.asktheeu.org/en/request/7872/response/26398/attach/2/Document%203%20EN.pdf
30. As German law professor Marc Leisching established through correspondence with the Ministry of Justice, the Jungendschutz team that conducted the monitoring was not composed of lawyers, and given the complex nature of some German criminal statutes, it is probable that "legal laypersons" were not actually able to identify precisely what exactly constituted illegal content under the German Criminal Code (Liesching, 2017). Likewise, the content was never archived before flagging by Jungendschutz, so it is unclear whether the flagged content was actually illegal in Germany or just removed or not removed under the platforms broader 'community standards.'

Chapter 6

1. Interview with Michael Woodside, Policy Director, NZ Department of Internal Affairs, October 2020.

206   NOTES

2. See the published parliamentary transcript at: https://www.parliament.nz/en/pb/hansard-debates/rhr/combined/HansDeb_20190319_20190319_08.

3. Interview held via videoconference with Paul Ash, Director, New Zealand National Cyber Policy Office, December 2020.

4. Microsoft's business model is more enterprise-oriented and business-facing than the other firms engaged in this discussion, but it, and Brad Smith specifically, have deployed this type of policy advocacy strategically in since 2016 as part of an apparent effort to portray their company as more responsible than its competitors. Smith is very active on information security issues and had previously called for a 'Digital Geneva Convention' that resulted in a similar Paris-based declaration to the Christchurch Call, the 'Paris Call for Trust and Security in Cyberspace.' See Gorwa and Peez (2020) for more.

5. Interview with Jordan Carter, Chief Executive, InternetNZ, December 2020.

6. Interview with Paul Ash, December 2020.

7. In 2019, the Labour government would have needed support from its coalition partner, NZ First, to pass new rules. NZ First leader Winston Peters frequently re-iterated in the post-Christchurch conversation that the "Prime Minister speaks for the coalition Government" (and that the party did not wish to advocate separate policy positions, especially on the sensitive post-Christchurch issues). While the counterfactual is not possible here, and I was unfortunately unable to interview any NZ First policymakers to ascertain their position on the Call or its alternatives, it appears likely that they would have supported the government had Ardern and the executive pursued a contested response. See https://www.parliament.nz/en/pb/hansard-debates/rhr/combined/HansDeb_20190319_20190319_08.

8. All quotes from this section taken from the Gorwa FOIA to the Australian Attorney General's department, Document 1.

9. Gorwa FOIA to the Australian Attorney General's department, Document 3.

10. Ibid., Document 4.

11. Ibid., Document 30.

12. Ibid., Document 16.

13. Ibid.

14. Ibid.

15. Ibid., Document 8.

16. Ibid.

17. Interview with Christiane Gillespie-Jones, Director (Program Management), Communications Alliance, December 2020.

18. According to statistics from the Parliament of Australia, approximately 95 percent of proposed laws are first introduced in the House (site of most amendments, debate, and discussion) before going to the Senate for approval. See the documentation at https://www.aph.gov.au/About_Parliament/House_of_Representatives/Powers_practice_and_procedure/Practice7/HTML/Chapter10/Bills%E2%80%94the_parliamentary_process.

19. Senate Hansard for April 3, 2019, p. 819.

20. See https://www.openaustralia.org.au/senate/?id=2019-04-03.225.1&s=Sharing+of+Abhorrent+Violent+Material.

21. As Douek (2020b, p. 3) outlines, this material is that which depicts a "terrorist act, murder, attempted murder, torture, rape, or kidnapping ... however, content only meets the definition where the material is recorded or streamed by the perpetrator or their accomplice."

22. See the legislation at https://www.legislation.gov.au/Details/C2019A00038.

23. See https://www.openaustralia.org.au/debates/?id=2019-04-04.15.1&s=Sharing+of+Abhorrent+Violent+Material#g15.2.

24. Ibid.

25. This following section is largely based upon an interview conducted with Paul Ash, December 2020.

26. FOIA to the New Zealand Ministry of Foreign Affairs and Trade, August 2020. Documents recieved December 10 2020. Available at https://fyi.org.nz/request/13466, henceforth NZ FOIA 2020.
27. Ibid.
28. Annotated copy of the Christchurch Call circulated to potential supporters. NZ FOIA 2020, p. 12.
29. Ibid.
30. Ibid.
31. See https://www.christchurchcall.com/supporters.html.
32. Pip Mclachlan and Elizabeth Thomas, 'Christchurch Call: Ministerial Progress Update.' Obtained via NZ FOIA 2020, p. 20. Redactions in the document I obtained.
33. Ibid.
34. See https://gifct.org/about/story/
35. Interview held with anonymous platform policy manager, February 2021.
36. Ministerial Progress Update on the Christchurch Call, cont. Obtained via NZ FOIA 2020, pp. 25–26.
37. More than forty prominent global civil society organizations were part of this network, and as part of that, civil society groups were able to attend this meeting and were offered some opportunity to speak (York and McSherry, 2019). However, as other civil society members of the network described in interviews, their capacity and resources to actively contribute to the Network varies significantly. Civil society has been themselves organizing formal principles and rules for members of the advisory network, and the New Zealand government has been in conversations to equip them with a secretariat that could help offset some of the capacity burden they are facing.
38. The full text of the speech is available at https://www.newsroom.co.nz/full-text-pms-speech-to-the-united-nations.
39. See https://gifct.org/about/story/#june-2020.
40. Despite these changes, the GIFCT is still frequently critiqued by researchers and civil society groups. Douek (2020b) has called it a "content cartel," and the Center for Democracy and Technology in Washington has coordinated multiple civil society statements expressing their concerns with the GIFCT re-organization and mandate (Llansó, 2020).
41. Interview with Paul Ash.

Chapter 7

1. Tweet by Jim Jordan, https://twitter.com/Jim_Jordan/status/1102650387096629248.
2. Interview with Michael Atleson, FTC Bureau of Consumer Protection, October 2022.
3. Interview with FTC Staff, Bureau of Competition, March 2023.
4. All figures from the 2021 data available at federalpay.org.
5. Interview held with Democrat tech policy adviser who requested anonymity, December 2022.
6. See the CPAC web archive at https://web.archive.org/web/20230425233805/https://www.conservative.org/cpac/
7. Session recording available at https://thefloridachannel.org/videos/3-15-21-house-appropriations-committee/ and https://web.archive.org/web/20210320183033/https://thefloridachannel.org/videos/3-15-21-house-appropriations-committee/; Fine's remarks begin at the 09:35 mark.
8. Ibid.; Geller's statement begins at the video's 27 : 40 mark.
9. The Heartland Institute is part of the Atlas Network, an influential group of neoliberal think-tanks working in the climate space (Plehwe, 2014); a group of German researchers tracking this network called Heartland the "the world's most prominent organization denying man-made climate change": https://lobbypedia.de/wiki/Heartland_Institute.
10. See the official record at https://www.flsenate.gov/Session/Bill/2021/7074.

208 NOTES

11. Interview with former member of Florida House of Representatives, winter 2023; employment figures from https://business.orlando.org/wp-content/uploads/sites/3/2020/02/Top-75-Employers.pdf.
12. See the official record at https://www.flsenate.gov/Session/Bill/2021/7072/Amendment/811008/HTML.
13. This exception led to a few humorous exchanges between lawmakers as the final bill was being read on the House floor. After Democrats asked if the provision meant that Facebook or Google could purchase theme parks in Florida to become exempt from it, Representative Ingoglia grudgingly agreed that yes, a hypothetical 'ZuckLand' would bring Facebook/Meta outside of the legislation's legal purview (Eskamani, 2021).
14. See the archive of court documents available at Netchoice.org: https://netchoice.org/wp-content/uploads/2021/06/NetChoice-v.-Moody-PI-decision.pdf.
15. Interview with Tom Giovanneti, President, Institute for Policy Innovation (IPI), December 2022.
16. Interview with industry association staffer working on the Texas bills, December 2022.
17. Gorwa FOIA to Texas Senate, fall 2022.
18. See the Committee Substitute bill of TX87 SB 12 of March 22, 2021 at https://legiscan.com/TX/text/SB12/id/2343916.
19. See aggregate data at https://openstates.org/tx.
20. See the list of all special sessions at https://www.lrl.texas.gov/sessions/specialsessions/index.cfm.
21. Hearing documents, including a list of speakers, are available on the Texas.gov website: https://capitol.texas.gov/tlodocs/87R/witlistmtg/pdf/C0902021082308001.PDF.
22. TechNet letter to House Select Committee Chairman Ashby, Gorwa FOIA.
23. NetChoice v. Paxton, No. 21-51178 (5th Cir. 2022), p. 2

Chapter 8

1. There is very little exhaustive, comparative regulatory work that has been undertaken on the broad issue of online content regulation (Gillespie et al., 2020), and comprehensive data on regulatory and institutional emergence in this domain does not currently exist. However, there are some repositories of intermediary liability laws and court decisions more generally; in particular, a resource compiled by researchers at Stanford Law School's Center for Internet and Society, the World Intermediary Liability Map (WILMap), is the best publicly available source of data on intermediary liability policies and content-related internet regulation. The WILMap is a volunteer-driven project with more than a hundred listed contributors, seeking to map all "law discussing obligations and liability of online intermediaries due to (infringing) activities undertaken by their users," covering "almost one hundred jurisdictions in Africa, Asia, the Caribbean, Europe, Latin America, North America and Oceania" (Frosio, 2017, p. 3). The WILMap's main strength is its coverage: the team of researchers and volunteers assembling the data harnessed country and regional expertise to include all relevant laws they could. It contains "case law, statues, and proposed laws" across the wide range of content-related policy sub-areas, from copyright, trademark, and intellectual property infringement, to hate speech, defamation, terrorism, and more (Frosio, 2017, p. 3). It has the major limitation of focusing primarily on statutory law, rather than informal instruments.
2. Estimates derived from Statista 2023.
3. Estimates derived from Statista 2023: General Overview, YouTube, LinkedIn.
4. The Indian money bill procedure has some similarities to the US budget reconciliation procedure mentioned in Chapter 7. It allows the executive to bypass the Rajya Sabha in certain cases, and controversially, was used to pass the 2016 Aadhar Act despite

opposition resistance. See https://www.barandbench.com/columns/aadhaar-money-bill-controversy. My thanks to Pranav Bidare for feedback on this section and for raising this point specifically.

5. See for example the discussion about a former Chief Justice of India being nominated to the Rajya Sabha: https://thewire.in/law/cji-ranjan-gogoi-rajya-sabha-nomination.

6. I would like to thank Clara Iglesias Keller for her helpful feedback on this section, and for bringing up this point specifically.

Chapter 9

1. I applaud ongoing efforts to create datasets of digital policy decisionmaking (as for instance done by Arregui and Perarnaud, 2022; cf. Perarnaud, 2021, in the EU context), as well as some ongoing work seeking to more robustly archive changes in industry community guidelines (Katzenbach et al., 2023). I hope that negotiated tools for researcher data access, like under the Digital Services Act, will likewise seek to provide some 'outside of the box' tools that could be used to inform policy-oriented research (for some creative ideas, see Karanicolas, 2021).

Appendix-B

1. See the data from the World Bank, available at https://data.worldbank.org/country/DE.
2. See Statista Research Department (2016).
3. See Content Works (2019) and Tankovska (2021).
4. See Tankovska (2021).
5. A full description is available at https://ec.europa.eu/growth/tools-databases/tris/en/about-the-20151535/the-aim-of-the-20151535-procedure/.
6. Ibid., n.p.
7. See https://www.fsm.de/en/voluntary-commitments for a detailed discussion.
8. See the Administrative Arrangements order of 2015, which outlines the scope and functions of the various departments: https://www.legislation.gov.au/Details/C2015Q00006.
9. See the documentation at https://www.esafety.gov.au/about-us/who-we-are/our-legislative-functions.
10. https://en.wikipedia.org/wiki/List_of_countries_and_dependencies_by_population.
11. See https://en.wikipedia.org/wiki/List_of_countries_by_GDP_(nominal).
12. See https://www.statista.com/statistics/680142/australia-internet-penetration/.
13. See https://www.statista.com/statistics/304862/number-of-facebook-users-in-australia/.
14. See https://www.fiber.com.au/post/social-media-statistics-worldwide-australia.
15. Calculation based upon 317 monthly active Twitter users in 2019; 2 billion monthly logged-in YouTube users in 2019, and 1.8 monthly active users for Facebook in 2019.
16. Data available at https://databank.worldbank.org/reports.aspx?source=worldwide-governance-indicators.
17. See http://web.archive.org/web/20210302074810/https://www.esafety.gov.au/about-us.
18. See http://web.archive.org/web/20210304070612/https://www.esafety.gov.au/about-us/who-we-are/our-legislative-functions.
19. See estimates available at https://en.wikipedia.org/wiki/List_of_countries_and_dependencies_by_population.
20. See https://www.statista.com/statistics/680688/new-zealand-internet-penetration/.
21. See https://www.statista.com/statistics/681512/new-zealand-facebook-users-by-age/.
22. See https://gs.statcounter.com/search-engine-market-share/all/new-zealand.
23. Calculation based upon roughly 3.75 million FB users in NZ in 2019 (Statista figures) and 1.8 billion global FB users in 2019.

210 NOTES

24. Data available at https://databank.worldbank.org/reports.aspx?source=worldwide-governance-indicators.
25. See https://www.mfat.govt.nz/en/about-us/who-we-are/treaties/.
26. See the documentation available at https://www.classificationoffice.govt.nz/about-nz-classification/classification-and-the-internet/.
27. Ibid.

References

5Rights Foundation. 2022. "New Hope for a Global Standard of Children's Data Protection as Californian Age Appropriate Design Code Is Signed into Law." *5Rights Newsroom*, September 15.

Abbott, Greg. 2021. "Governor Abbott Statement on 87th Legislative Session." *Texas.Gov*, May 31.

Abbott, Kenneth W., David Levi-Faur, and Duncan Snidal. 2017. "Theorizing Regulatory Intermediaries: The RIT Model." *The ANNALS of the American Academy of Political and Social Science* 670.1, pp. 14–35.

Abbott, Kenneth W. and Duncan Snidal. 2000. "Hard and Soft Law in International Governance." *International Organization* 54.3, pp. 421–456.

Abbott, Kenneth W. and Duncan Snidal. 2009a. "Strengthening International Regulation through Transnational New Governance: Overcoming the Orchestration Deficit." *Vanderbilt Journal of Transnational Law* 42, pp. 501–578.

Abbott, Kenneth W. and Duncan Snidal. 2009b. "The Governance Triangle: Regulatory Standards Institutions and the Shadow of the State." *The Politics of Global Regulation*. Ed. Walter Mattli and Ngaire Woods. Princeton, NJ: Princeton University Press, pp. 44–88.

Access Now. 2022. "Indian IT Ministry's Amendments to the 2021 IT Rules: Not Enough to Protect Rights and Freedoms." *Access Now Blog*, June 6.

Affonso Souza, Carlos, Fabro Steibel, and Ronaldo Lemos. 2017. "Notes on the Creation and Impacts of Brazil's Internet Bill of Rights." *Theory and Practice of Legislation* 5.1, pp. 73–94.

Ahmad, Sana and Martin Krzywdzinski. 2022. "Moderating in Obscurity: How Indian Content Moderators Work in Global Content Moderation Value Chains." *Digital Work in the Planetary Market*. Ed. Mark Graham and Fabian Ferrari. Cambridge, MA: MIT Press.

Alberta, Tim. 2018. "The Deep Roots of Trump's War on the Press." *POLITICO Magazine*, April 26.

Albrecht, Jan Philipp. 2016. "How the GDPR Will Change the World." *European Data Protection Law Review* 2.3, pp. 287–289.

ALEC. 2018. *Resolution Protecting Online Platforms and Services*. Arlington, VA: American Legislative Exchange Council.

Alizadeh, Meysam et al. 2022. "Content Moderation as a Political Issue: The Twitter Discourse around Trump's Ban." *Journal of Quantitative Description: Digital Media* 2, pp. 1–44.

Allen, Darcy W. E. et al. 2021. "The Political Economy of Australian Regulatory Reform." *Australian Journal of Public Administration* 80.1, pp. 114–137.

Allyn, Bobby, Shannon Bond, and Alina Selyukh. 2020. "Heads of Amazon, Apple, Facebook and Google Testify on Big Tech's Power." *NPR*, July 29.

Almeida, Virgilio A. F. 2014. "The Evolution of Internet Governance: Lessons Learned from NETmundial." *IEEE Internet Computing* 18.5, pp. 65–69.

REFERENCES

Alon-Beck, Anat. 2020. "Times They Are A-Changin': When Tech Employees Revolt!" *Maryland Law Review* 80.1, pp. 120–165.

Anand, Meghan et al. 2021. "All the Ways Congress Wants to Change Section 230." *Slate*, March 21.

Anderson, Duncan. 2017. "Film and Video Censorship in New Zealand, 1976–1994." PhD thesis. Wellington, NZ: Victoria University Wellington.

Andersson Schwarz, Jonas. 2017. "Platform Logic: An Interdisciplinary Approach to the Platform-Based Economy." *Policy & Internet* 9.4, pp. 374–394.

Angelopoulos, Christina and Stijn Smet. 2016. "Notice-and-Fair-Balance: How to Reach a Compromise between Fundamental Rights in European Intermediary Liability." *Journal of Media Law* 8.2, pp. 266–301.

Appleman, Bradley A. 1995. "Hate Speech: A Comparison of the Approaches Taken by the United States and Germany." *Wisconsin International Law Journal* 14.2, pp. 422–439.

Aranguiz, Ane. 2021. "Platforms Put a Spoke in the Wheels of Spain's 'Riders' Law.' " *Social Europe*, September 2.

Arregui, Javier and Clément Perarnaud. 2022. "A New Dataset on Legislative Decision-Making in the European Union: The DEU III Dataset." *Journal of European Public Policy* 29.1, pp. 12–22.

ARTICLE 19. 2018. *Self-Regulation and 'Hate Speech' on Social Media Platforms*. London, UK.

Arun, Chinmayi. 2014. "Gatekeeper Liability and Article 19 (1)(a) of the Constitution of India." *NUJS Law Review* 7, pp. 73–87.

Arun, Chinmayi. 2018. "Rebalancing Regulation of Speech: Hyper-Local Content on Global Web-Based Platforms." *SSRN Scholarly Paper 3108238*. Rochester, NY.

Arun, Chinmayi. 2022. "Facebook's Faces." *Harvard Law Review Forum* 135, pp. 236–265.

Athique, Adrian and Akshaya Kumar. 2022. "Platform Ecosystems, Market Hierarchies and the Megacorp: The Case of Reliance Jio." *Media, Culture & Society* 48.8, pp. 1420–1436.

Ausloos, Jef. 2020. *The Right to Erasure in EU Data Protection Law*. Oxford, UK: Oxford University Press.

Ausloos, Jef, Réne Mahieu, and Michael Veale. 2020. "Getting Data Subject Rights Right." *JIPITEC* 10.3, pp. 283–309.

Avant, Deborah D., Martha Finnemore, and Susan K. Sell, eds. 2010. *Who Governs the Globe?* Cambridge, UK: Cambridge University Press.

Bach, David and Abraham L. Newman. 2007. "The European Regulatory State and Global Public Policy: Micro-Institutions, Macro-Influence." *Journal of European Public Policy* 14.6, pp. 827–846.

Bach, David and Abraham L. Newman. 2010. "Transgovernmental Networks and Domestic Policy Convergence: Evidence from Insider Trading Regulation." *International Organization*, pp. 505–528.

Baistrocchi, Pablo Asbo. 2002. "Liability of Intermediary Service Providers in the EU Directive on Electronic Commerce." *Santa Clara Computer & High Technology Law Journal* 19.1, pp. 111–130.

Baldwin, Robert, Martin Cave, and Martin Lodge. 2012. *Understanding Regulation: Theory, Strategy, and Practice*. 2nd ed. Oxford, UK: Oxford University Press.

Bambauer, Derek E. 2015. "Against Jawboning." *Minnesota Law Review* 100.51, pp. 51–126.

Bansal, Varsha. 2020. "Indian Developers Are Racing to Replace TikTok." *Rest of World*, November 27.

Barata, Joan. 2023. "Regulating Online Platforms Beyond the Marco Civil in Brazil: The Controversial 'Fake News Bill.' " *Tech Policy Press*, May 23.

Barnes, Jeb. 2007. "Bringing the Courts Back In: Interbranch Perspectives on the Role of Courts in American Politics and Policy Making." *Annual Review of Political Science* 10, pp. 25–43.

Barnes, Robert and Ann E. Marimow. 2022. "A Landmark Supreme Court Fight Over Social Media Now Looks Likely." *The Washington Post*, September 22.

Barragán, James. 2021. "After a Nearly Six-Week Exodus over GOP Voting Bill, Enough Democrats Return to Texas House to Resume Work." *The Texas Tribune*, August 18.

Barrett, Jonathan and Luke Strongman. 2012. "The Internet, the Law, and Privacy in New Zealand: Dignity with Liberty?" *International Journal of Communication* 6.1, pp. 127–143.

Barry, Eloise. 2022. "These Are the Countries Where Twitter and Facebook Are Banned." *Time*, January 18.

Baum, Lawrence and Neal Devins. 2017. "Federalist Court: How the Federalist Society Became the de facto Selector of Republican Supreme Court Justices." *Slate*, January 31.

BBC Newsdesk. 2020. "India Bans TikTok, WeChat and Dozens More Chinese Apps." *BBC*, June 29.

BBC Newsdesk. 2021. "Capitol Riots Timeline: What Happened on 6 January 2021?" *BBC*, February 10.

Beckedahl, Markus. 2016. "Brief von Maas an Facebook." *Fraag den Staat*, July 17.

Benedek, Wolfgang and Matthias C. Kettemann. 2014. *Freedom of Expression and the Internet.* Strasbourg, FR: Council of Europe.

Bernard, Tim. 2022. "Considering KOSA: A Bill to Protect Children from Online Harms." *Tech Policy Press*, December 1.

Berry, Jeffrey M. 2002. "Validity and Reliability Issues in Elite Interviewing." *PS: Political Science & Politics* 35.4, pp. 679–682.

Bessa, Ioulia et al. 2022. *A Global Analysis of Worker Protest in Digital Labour Platforms.* Geneva, CH: International Labor Organization.

Bhat, Adnan. 2022. "India's Homegrown TikTok Clones Struggle to Replicate Bytedance's Success." *Rest of World*, October 20.

Bhat, Adnan. 2023. "Indian Government Gives Itself the Power to 'Fact-Check' and Delete Social Media Posts." *Rest of World*, April 12.

Binder, Sarah A. 1999. "The Dynamics of Legislative Gridlock, 1947–96." *American Political Science Review* 93.3, pp. 519–533.

Black, Julia. 2001. "Decentring Regulation: Understanding the Role of Regulation and Self-Regulation in a 'Post-Regulatory' World." *Current Legal Problems* 54.1, pp. 103–146.

Black, Julia. 2008. "Constructing and Contesting Legitimacy and Accountability in Polycentric Regulatory Regimes." *Regulation & Governance* 2.2, pp. 137–164.

Blanchard, Carl. 1994. "Telecommunications Regulation in New Zealand: How Effective Is 'Light-Handed' Regulation?" *Telecommunications Policy* 18.2, pp. 154–164.

Bloch-Wehba, Hannah. 2019. "Global Platform Governance: Private Power in the Shadow of the State." *Southern Methodist University Law Review* 1, pp. 27–80.

Bloch-Wehba, Hannah. 2020. "Automation in Moderation." *SSRN Scholarly Paper* 521619. Rochester, NY.

BMFSFJ. 2016. "Hassbotschaften in Sozialen Netzwerken wirksam bekämpfen." *BMFSJF Press Release*, April 11.

Bogost, Ian and Nick Montfort. 2009. "Platform Studies: Frequently Questioned Answers." *Proceedings of the Digital Arts and Culture Conference.* Irvine, CA.

Bokhari, Allum. 2021a. "Texas Big Tech Bill Wins Praise from Trump's Tech Censorship Expert." *Breitbart*, May 7.

Bokhari, Allum. 2021b. "Texas Gov. Greg Abbott Urged to Add Big Tech Bill to Special Session After Democrat Stall Tactics." *Breitbart*, May 28.

Boland, Hannah. 2021. "Unions Push for More Uber Scrutiny after Claims Its Photo ID TechWas Racist." *The Telegraph*, March 2.

Bolton, Alexander. 2022. "Gridlock, Bureaucratic Control, and Nonstatutory Policymaking in Congress." *American Journal of Political Science* 66.1, pp. 238–254.

Bradford, Anu. 2012. "The Brussels Effect." *Northwestern University Law Review* 107.1, pp. 2–64.

Bradford, Anu. 2020. *The Brussels Effect: How the European Union Rules the World.* New York, NY: Oxford University Press.

Bradford, Anu. 2023. *Digital Empires: The Global Battle to Regulate Technology.* New York, NY: Oxford University Press.

Brennen, J. Scott Babwah and Matt Perault. 2022a. *The State of State Platform Regulation.* University of North Carolina: Center on Technology Policy.

Brennen, J. Scott Babwah and Matt Perault. 2022b. *Understanding, Enforcement, and Investment: Options and Opportunities for State Regulation of Online Content.* University of North Carolina: Center on Technology Policy.

Brown, Ian. 2020. *Interoperability as a Tool for Competition Regulation.* Brussels, BE: Open Forum Europe.

Brunton, Finn. 2013. *Spam: A Shadow History of the Internet.* Cambridge, MA: MIT Press.

Buch-Hansen, Hubert and Angela Wigger. 2010. "Revisiting 50 Years of Market-Making: The Neoliberal Transformation of European Competition Policy." *Review of International Political Economy* 17.1, pp. 20–44.

Budzinski, Oliver and Annika Stöhr. 2019. "Competition Policy Reform in Europe and Germany—Institutional Change in the Light of Digitization." *European Competition Journal* 15.1, pp. 15–54.

Burgess, Jean and Joshua Green. 2018. *YouTube: Online Video and Participatory Culture.* 2nd ed. Cambridge, UK: Polity.

Burrell, Robert and Kimberlee Weatherall. 2008. "Exporting Controversy—Reactions to the Copyright Provisions of the U.S.-Australia Free Trade Agreement: Lessons for U.S. Trade Policy." *University of Illinois Journal of Law, Technology & Policy* 8.2, pp. 259–319.

Busch, Christoph. 2020. "The P2B Regulation (EU) 2019/1150: Towards a 'Procedural Turn' in EU Platform Regulation?" *Journal of European Consumer and Market Law* 9.4, pp. 133–178.

Business Standard. 2023. "WhatsApp's New Security Centre Page to Be Available in 10 Indian Languages." *BS*, June 1.

Bussell, Jennifer L. 2010. "Why Get Technical? Corruption and the Politics of Public Service Reform in the Indian States." *Comparative Political Studies* 43.10, pp. 1230–1257.

Cabral, Luís et al. 2021. *The EU Digital Markets Act: A Report from a Panel of Economic Experts.* Brussels, BE: European Commission, Joint Research Center.

Cai, Cuihong and Tianchan Wang. 2022. "Moving toward a 'Middle Ground'?—The Governance of Platforms in the United States and China." *Policy & Internet* 14.2, pp. 243–262.

Cameron, Nadia. 2019. "Industry Warns of Negative Tech, Cultural Consequences as Social Media Violent Material Bill Passes." *CMO*, April 4.

Campbell, John L. 2004. *Institutional Change and Globalization.* Princeton, NJ: Princeton University Press.

Cant, Callum. 2019. *Riding for Deliveroo: Resistance in the New Economy.* Cambridge, UK: Polity.

Caplan, Robyn. 2018. *Content or Context Moderation?* New York, NY: Data & Society Research Institute.

Caplan, Robyn. 2023. "Networked Platform Governance: The Construction of the Democratic Platform." *International Journal of Communication* 17.0, pp. 3451–3472.

Carter, Jordan. 2019a. "How to stop the Christchurch Call on social media and terrorism from falling flat." *InternetNZ Blog*, April 24.

Carter, Jordan. 2019b. "Reporting Back: InternetNZ @ the Christchurch Call in Paris." *InternetNZ Blog*, May 17.

Casper, Jonathan D. 1976. "The Supreme Court and National Policy Making." *American Political Science Review* 70.1, pp. 50–63.

Cennamo, Carmelo. 2019. "Competing in Digital Markets: A Platform-Based Perspective." *Academy of Management Perspectives* 35.2, pp. 265–291.

Center for Democracy and Technology. 2021. "CDT Applauds Biden Revocation of Trump's Unconstitutional Social Media Executive Order." *CDT Blog*, June 14.

Chacko, Mathew, Aadya Misra, and Shambhavi Mishra. 2021. "Accountability, Liability and Intermediaries: A New Set of Rules in India." *International Cybersecurity Law Review* 2, pp. 271–278.

Chagas, Viktor. 2022. "WhatsApp and Digital Astroturfing: A Social Network Analysis of Brazilian Political Discussion Groups of Bolsonaro's Supporters." *International Journal of Communication* 16, p. 25.

Chander, Anupam. 2016. *Internet Intermediaries as Platforms for Expression and Innovation.* Waterloo, ON: Centre for International Governance Innovation.

Chandrasekharan, Eshwar et al. 2018. "The Internet's Hidden Rules: An Empirical Study of Reddit Norm Violations at Micro, Meso, and Macro Scales." *Proceedings of the ACM on Human-Computer Interaction* 2. CSCW, pp. 1–25.

Cini, Michelle and Patryk Czulno. 2022. "Digital Single Market and the EU Competition Regime: An Explanation of Policy Change." *Journal of European Integration* 44.1, pp. 41–57.

Citron, Danielle Keats and Benjamin Wittes. 2017. "The Internet Will Not Break: Denying Bad Samaritans Sec. 230 Immunity." *Fordham Law Review* 86.2, pp. 401–423.

Clark, Mitchell. 2021. "Googler Who Helped Lead 2018 Walkout Is Joining the FTC." *The Verge,* November 2.

Claussen, Victor. 2018. "Fighting Hate Speech and Fake News. The Network Enforcement Act (NetzDG) in Germany in the Context of European Legislation." *Rivista Di Diritto Dei Media* 2.3, pp. 1–27.

Cobbe, Jennifer. 2021. "Algorithmic Censorship by Social Platforms: Power and Resistance." *Philosophy & Technology* 34.4, pp. 739–766.

Coche, Eugénie. 2018. "Privatised Enforcement and the Right to Freedom of Expression in a World Confronted with Terrorism Propaganda Online." *Internet Policy Review* 7.4, pp. 1–17.

Cohen, Julie E. 2019. *Between Truth and Power: The Legal Constructions of Informational Capitalism.* Oxford, UK: Oxford University Press.

Cohen, Julie E. 2019. "Review of Zuboff's *The Age of Surveillance Capitalism.*" *Surveillance & Society* 17.1/2, pp. 240–245.

Coldewey, Devin. 2022. "FTC Challenges Consolidation in Tech with Review of Merger Guidelines." *TechCrunch,* January 18.

Collier, Ruth Berins, Veena B. Dubal, and Christopher L. Carter. 2018. "Disrupting Regulation, Regulating Disruption: The Politics of Uber in the United States." *Perspectives on Politics* 16.4, pp. 919–937.

Commonwealth of Australia. 2018. *Agency Resourcing Budget Paper No. 4, 2018–19.*

Computer Business Review. 2006. "Bush's Tech-Spending Promises Cheer Silicon Valley." *Techmonitor,* February 1.

Content Works. 2019. "Social Media in Germany: The Stats You Need To Know." *Content Works,* October 24.

Cowls, Josh and Jessica Morley. 2022. "App Store Governance: The Implications and Limitations of Duopolistic Dominance." *The 2021 Yearbook of the Digital Ethics Lab.* Ed. Jakob Mökander and Marta Ziosi. Cham, CH: Springer, pp. 75–92.

Coyle, Diane. 2019. "Practical Competition Policy Implications of Digital Platforms." *Antitrust Law Journal* 82.3, pp. 835–860.

Crawford, Kate. 2021. *The Atlas of AI: Power, Politics, and the Planetary Costs of Artificial Intelligence.* New Haven, CT: Yale University Press.

Crawford, Kate and Tarleton Gillespie. 2016. "What Is a Flag For? Social Media Reporting Tools and the Vocabulary of Complaint." *New Media & Society* 18.3, pp. 410–428.

Cremer, Jacques, Yves-Alexandre de Montjoye, and Heike Schweitzer. 2019. *Competition Policy for the Digital Era.* European Commission: Directorate-General for Competition.

Culpepper, Pepper D. and Kathleen Thelen. 2019. "Are We All Amazon Primed? Consumers and the Politics of Platform Power." *Comparative Political Studies* 53.2, pp. 288–318.

Custos, Dominique. 2006. "The Rulemaking Power of Independent Regulatory Agencies" *American Journal of Comparative Law* 54, pp. 615–639.

Cutolo, Donato and Martin Kenney. 2021. "Platform-Dependent Entrepreneurs: Power Asymmetries, Risks, and Strategies in the Platform Economy." *Academy of Management Perspectives* 35.4, pp. 584–605.

Dahl, Robert A. 1957. "Decision-Making in a Democracy: The Supreme Court as a National Policy-Maker." *Journal of Public Law* 6, pp. 279–295.

Daly, Angela. 2017. "Beyond Hipster Antitrust: A Critical Perspective on the European Commission's Google Decision." *European Competition and Regulation Law Review* 3.1, pp. 188–192.

216 REFERENCES

Daniyal, Shoaib. 2021. "Why Is the Government of India at War with Twitter?" *Scroll.in*, July 8.

Davies, Rob and Johana Bhuiyan. 2022. "Uber Used Greyball Fake App to Evade Police across Europe, Leak Reveals." *The Guardian*, July 7.

Davis, Mark and Jian Xiao. 2021. "De-Westernizing Platform Studies: History and Logics of Chinese and US Platforms." *International Journal of Communication* 15, pp. 103–122.

Davis, Stuart and Joe Straubhaar. 2020. "Producing Antipetismo: Media Activism and the Rise of the Radical, Nationalist Right in Contemporary Brazil." *International Communication Gazette* 82.1, pp. 82–100.

Dayen, David. 2016. "Google's Remarkably Close Relationship with the Obama White House, in Two Charts." *The Intercept*, April 22.

Deibert, Ronald J. et al., eds. 2008. *Access Denied: The Practice and Policy of Global Internet Filtering*. Cambridge, MA: MIT Press.

Deibert, Ronald J. et al., eds. 2010. *Access Controlled: The Shaping of Power, Rights, and Rule in Cyberspace*. Cambridge, MA: MIT Press.

Dellinger, A. J. 2021. "The List of Tech Companies That Have Banned Trump and His Supporters Is Staggeringly Long." *Mic*, January 11.

Denemark, David and Shaun Bowler. 2002. "Minor Parties and Protest Votes in Australia and New Zealand: Locating Populist Politics." *Electoral Studies* 21.1, pp. 47–67.

Dernbach, Andrea. 2015. "Germany Suspends Dublin Agreement for Syrian Refugees." *Euractiv*, August 26.

DeSantis, Ron. 2021. "Ron DeSantis At CPAC Highlights Future Of Republican Party Moving Forward: 'Don't Ever Back Down.' " *Daily Wire News*, February 27.

Deutscher Bundestag. 2017. "Bundestag beschließt Gesetz gegen strafbare Inhalte im Internet." *Parliamentary Summary*, June 30.

Devadasan, Vasudev. 2022. *Report on Intermediary Liability in India*. Centre for Communication Governance: National Law University Delhi.

Diamond, Larry. 2010. "Liberation Technology." *Journal of Democracy* 21.3, pp. 69–83.

Dib, Daniela and Nicole Froio. 2022. "Brazilian Authorities Step in to Catch Fake News Faster than Facebook." *Rest of World*, October 28.

Dostal, Jörg Michael. 2015. "The Pegida Movement and German Political Culture: Is Right-Wing Populism Here to Stay?" *Political Quarterly* 86.4, pp. 523–531.

Douek, Evelyn. 2019. "Facebook's Oversight Board: Move Fast with Stable Infrastructure and Humility." *North Carolina Journal of Law and Technology* 21.1, pp. 1–78.

Douek, Evelyn. 2020a. "Australia's 'Abhorrent Violent Material' Law: Shouting 'Nerd Harder' and Drowning Out Speech." *Australian Law Journal* 94, pp. 41–60.

Douek, Evelyn. 2020b. *The Rise of Content Cartels*. Columbia University: Knight First Amendment Institute.

Douek, Evelyn. 2021. "Governing Online Speech: From 'Posts-as-Trumps' to Proportionality and Probability." *Columbia Law Review* 121.3, pp. 759–834.

Douek, Evelyn and Johanna Weaver. 2023. "Everything Is Content Moderation." *Tech Mirror*, August 1.

Dovere, Edward-Isaac. 2020. "Hillary Clinton Says She Was Right All Along." *The Atlantic*. October 9.

Drezner, Daniel W. 2008. *All Politics Is Global: Explaining International Regulatory Regimes*. Princeton, NJ: Princeton University Press.

Driesen, David M. 2018. "President Trump's Executive Orders and the Rule of Law." *UMKC Law Review* 87, p. 489.

Dubal, Veena B. 2017. "Wage Slave or Entrepreneur?: Contesting the Dualism of Legal Worker Identities." *California Law Review* 105.1, pp. 65–123.

Dubal, Veena B. 2022. "Economic Security & the Regulation of Gig Work in California: From AB5 to Proposition 22." *European Labour Law Journal* 13.1, pp. 51–65.

Duckett, Chris. 2019. "Australia's Abhorrent Video Streaming Legislation Rammed through Parliament." *ZDNet*, April 4.

Duneier, Mitchell. 2002. "What Kind of Combat Sport Is Sociology?" *American Journal of Sociology* 107.6, pp. 1551–1576.

Dür, Andreas and Gemma Mateo. 2014. "Public Opinion and Interest Group Influence: How Citizen Groups Derailed the Anti-Counterfeiting Trade Agreement." *Journal of European Public Policy* 21.8, pp. 1199–1217.

Dvoskin, Brenda. 2022. "Representation without Elections: Civil Society Participation as a Remedy for the Democratic Deficits of Online Speech Governance." *Villanova Law Review* 67, pp. 447–508.

Easton, Brian. 1997. *The Commercialisation of New Zealand.* Auckland, NZ: Auckland University Press.

Eberlein, Burkard and Claudio M. Radaelli. 2010. "Mechanisms of Conflict Management in EU Regulatory Policy." *Public Administration* 88.3, pp. 782–799.

Eberlein, Burkard et al. 2014. "Transnational Business Governance Interactions: Conceptualization and Framework for Analysis." *Regulation & Governance* 8.1, pp. 1–21.

Echikson, William and Olivia Knodt. 2018. "Germany's NetzDG: A Key Test for Combatting Online Hate." *SSRN Scholarly Paper* 3300636. Rochester, NY.

Edelman, Gilad. 2020. "Twitter Finally Fact-Checked Trump. It's a Bit of a Mess." *Wired.* May 27.

EDMO. 2022. *Report of the European Digital Media Observatory's Working Group on Platform-to-Researcher Data Access.* Brussels, BE: European Digital Media Observatory.

Elers, Christine Helen and Pooja Jayan. 2020. "'This Is Us': Free Speech Embedded in Whiteness, Racism and Coloniality in Aotearoa, New Zealand." *First Amendment Studies* 54.2, pp. 236–249.

Elliott, Vittoria. 2023. "Brazil Proposed Internet Regulation. Big Tech Dug In Its Heels." *Wired.* May 9.

Englert, Sai, Jamie Woodcock, and Callum Cant. 2020. "Digital Workerism: Technology, Platforms, and the Circulation of Workers' Struggles." *tripleC: Communication, Capitalism & Critique* 18.1, pp. 132–145.

Eskamani, Anna. 2021. "Deplatforming Bill Gets a Theme Park Carve Out." *YouTube,* May 2.

European Commission. 2016. "European Commission and IT Companies Announce Code of Conduct on Illegal Online Hate Speech." *EC Press Release,* May 31.

European Commission. 2020. *Proposal for a Regulation of the European Parliament and of the Council on Contestable and Fair Markets in the Digital Sector (Digital Markets Act).*

European Commission. 2021. *Q&A: Improving Working Conditions in Platform Work.* EC Press Release, December 9.

European Council of Ministers. 2022. *Digital Markets Act (DMA): Agreement between the Council and the European Parliament.* EC Press Release, March 25.

European Digital Rights. 2013. "RIP Clean IT." *EDRi Blog,* January 29.

Evangelista, Rafael and Fernanda Bruno. 2019. "WhatsApp and Political Instability in Brazil: Targeted Messages and Political Radicalisation." *Internet Policy Review* 8.4, pp. 1–23.

Evans, David S. 2003. "Some Empirical Aspects of Multi-Sided Platform Industries." *Review of Network Economics* 2.3, pp. 191–209.

Executive Office of the President. 2020. *Preventing Online Censorship.* Federal Register, June 2.

Eynon, Rebecca, Ralph Schroeder, and Jenny Fry. 2009. "New Techniques in Online Research: Challenges for Research Ethics." *Twenty-First Century Society* 4.2, pp. 187–199.

Fabo, Brian et al. 2017. *An Overview of European Platforms: Scope and Business Models.* Brussels, BE: European Commission, Joint Research Centre.

Fairwork. 2021. "Response to the European Commission's Proposal for a Directive on Platform Work." *The Fairwork Project,* September 12.

Farrell, Henry. 2006. "Regulating Information Flows: States, Private Actors, and E-Commerce." *Annual Review of Political Science* 9.1, pp. 353–374.

Farrell, Henry and Abraham L. Newman. 2014. "Domestic Institutions beyond the Nation-State: Charting the New Interdependence Approach." *World Politics* 66.2, pp. 331–363.

Farrell, Henry and Abraham L. Newman. 2016. "The New Interdependence Approach: Theoretical Development and Empirical Demonstration." *Review of International Political Economy* 23.5, pp. 713–736.

Farrell, Henry and Abraham L. Newman. 2019a. *Of Privacy and Power: The Transatlantic Struggle over Freedom and Security.* Princeton, NJ: Princeton University Press.

218 REFERENCES

Farrell, Henry and Abraham L. Newman. 2019b. "Weaponized Interdependence: How Global Economic Networks Shape State Coercion." *International Security* 44.1, pp. 42–79.

Fay, Robert. 2019. "Digital Platforms Require a Global Governance Framework." *CIGI Online*, October 28.

Federal Trade Commission. 2019. *FTC's Bureau of Competition Launches Task Force to Monitor Technology Markets*. FTC Press Release, February 26.

Federal Trade Commission. 2020. *FTC Sues Facebook for Illegal Monopolization*. FTC Press Release, December 9.

Federal Trade Commission. 2022. *FTC Explores Rules Cracking Down on Commercial Surveillance and Lax Data Security Practices*. FTC Press Release, August 11.

Federalist Society. 2021. "Public and Private Power: Preserving Freedom or Preventing Harm?" *FedSoc Blog*, November 12.

Feiner, Lauren. 2021. "House Republican Staff Outline Principles to Reform Tech's Liability Shield." *CNBC*, April 15.

Fiedler, Kirsten. 2016. "EU Internet Forum against Terrorist Content and Hate Speech Online: Document Pool." *EDRi Blog*, March 1.

Field, Hayden and Jonathan Vanian. 2023. "Tech Layoffs Ravage the Teams That Fight Online Misinformation and Hate Speech." *CNBC*, June 26.

Fiesler, Casey and Nicholas Proferes. 2018. "'Participant' Perceptions of Twitter Research Ethics." *Social Media + Society* 4.1, p. 2056305118763366.

Fink, Jenni. 2022. "Capitol Riot Timeline: From Trump's First Tweet to Biden's Certification." *Newsweek*, January 6th.

Fioretos, Orfeo. 2011. "Historical Institutionalism in International Relations." *International Organization* 65.2, pp. 367–399.

Fisher, Adam. 2018. "Sex, Beer, and Coding: Inside Facebook's Wild Early Days in Palo Alto." *Wired*, July 10.

Fisher, Franklin M. 2000. "The IBM and Microsoft Cases: What's the Difference?" *American Economic Review* 90.2, pp. 180–183.

Fiske, Warren. 2022. "Did Democrats Suggest the 2016 Presidential Election Was Stolen?" *PolitiFact*, October 5.

Fitzpatrick, Alex. 2014. "A Judge Ordered Microsoft to Split. Here's Why It's Still a Single Company." *Time*, November 5.

Fraag den Staat. 2017. "Task Force 'Umgang Mit Rechtswidrigen Hassbotschaften Im Internet.' " *Fraag den Staat*, August 3.

Fraundorfer, Markus. 2017. "Brazil's Organization of the NETmundial Meeting: Moving Forward in Global Internet Governance." *Global Governance* 23, p. 503.

Froio, Nicole and Matheus Andrade. 2023. "Online Extremism Linked to Rise in School Shootings in Brazil, Researchers Find." *Rest of World*, May 17.

Frosio, Giancarlo F. 2017. "From Horizontal to Vertical: An Intermediary Liability Earthquake in Europe." *Journal of Intellectual Property Law & Practice* 12.7, pp. 565–575.

Frosio, Giancarlo F. 2018. "Why Keep a Dog and Bark Yourself? From Intermediary Liability to Responsibility." *International Journal of Law and Information Technology* 26.1, pp. 1–33.

Fujimura, Naofumi. 2016. "Re-election Isn't Everything: Legislators' Goal-Seeking and Committee Activity in Japan." *Journal of Legislative Studies* 22.2, pp. 153–174.

Fuster, Gloria González. 2014. *The Emergence of Personal Data Protection as a Fundamental Right of the EU*. Cham, CH: Springer.

G, Sarah. 2020. "InternetNZ: Government Internet Filtering Not the Answer." *InternetNZ Blog*, June 27.

Garrett, Garrett, Robert T. 2023. "Must-Pass Bills of Dan Patrick, Dade Phelan Show Texas GOP Has Warring Factions." *Dallas News*, March 14.

Gathmann, Florian. 2015. "Heidenau: Sigmar Gabriel besucht Flüchtlingsunterkunft." *Der Spiegel*, October 24.

Gathmann, Florian and Horand Knaup. 2017. "Heiko Maas zu Machtanspruch von Martin Schulz: 'Alles andere wäre armselig." *Der Spiegel*, March 19.

Gauja, Anika, Marian Sawer, and Marian Simms, eds. 2020. *Morrison's Miracle: The 2019 Australian Federal Election.* Canberra, AU: ANU Press.

Gawer, Annabelle. 2014. "Bridging Differing Perspectives on Technological Platforms: Toward an Integrative Framework." *Research Policy* 43.7, pp. 1239–1249.

Gebicka, Aleksandra and Andreas Heinemann. 2014. "Social Media & Competition Law." *World Competition* 37.2, pp. 149–172.

Gehrke, Robert. 2021. "Here Are Four Bills Utah Gov. Spencer Cox Should Veto." *The Salt Lake Tribune*, March 9.

Gelber, Katharine and Luke McNamara. 2013. "Freedom of Speech and Racial Vilification in Australia: 'The Bolt Case' in Public Discourse." *Australian Journal of Political Science* 48.4, pp. 470–484.

Gillespie, Tarleton. 2010. "The Politics of 'Platforms'." *New Media & Society* 12.3, pp. 347–364.

Gillespie, Tarleton. 2015. "Platforms Intervene." *Social Media + Society* 1.1, p. 2056305115580479.

Gillespie, Tarleton. 2018. *Custodians of the Internet: Platforms, Content Moderation, and the Hidden Decisions That Shape Social Media.* New Haven, CT: Yale University Press.

Gillespie, Tarleton et al. 2020. "Expanding the Debate about Content Moderation: Scholarly Research Agendas for the Coming Policy Debates." *Internet Policy Review* 9.4, pp. 1–29.

Given, Jock. 2004. "'Not Unreasonably Denied': Australian Content after AUSFTA." *Media International Australia* 111.1, pp. 8–22.

Glaser, Stefan et al. 2008. *Protection of Minors on the Internet: Jungendschutz Annual Report.* Mainz, DE: Jungendschutz.

Glynn, Maggie. 2021. "Texas House Midnight Deadline Passes without Vote on Social Media Censorship Bill." *KXAN News*, May 25.

Goldman, Eric. 2018. "The Complicated Story of FOSTA and Section 230." *First Amendment Law Review* 17, pp. 279–293.

Goldman, Eric. 2023. "New York's Mandatory Editorial Transparency Law Preliminarily Enjoined Volokh v. James." *Technology and Marketing Law Blog*, February 15.

Goldsmith, Ben and Julian Thomas. 2012. "The Convergence Review and the Future of Australian Content Regulation." *Australian Journal of Telecommunications and the Digital Economy* 62.3, pp. 44.1–44.12.

Goldsmith, Jack L. and Eugene Volokh. 2023. "State Regulation of Online Behavior: The Dormant Commerce Clause and Geolocation." *Texas Law Review* 101.5, pp. 1084–1125.

Gollatz, Kirsten and Leontine Jenner. 2018. "Hate Speech and Fake News—How Two Concepts Got Intertwined and Politicised." *HIIG Digital Society Blog*, March 15.

Gorwa, Robert. 2019a. "The Platform Governance Triangle: Conceptualising the Informal Regulation of Online Content." *Internet Policy Review* 8.2, pp. 1–18.

Gorwa, Robert. 2019b. "What Is Platform Governance?" *Information, Communication & Society* 22.6, pp. 854–871.

Gorwa, Robert. 2021. "Elections, Institutions, and the Regulatory Politics of Platform Governance: The Case of the German NetzDG." *Telecommunications Policy* 45.6, p. 102145.

Gorwa, Robert, Reuben Binns, and Christian Katzenbach. 2020. "Algorithmic Content Moderation: Technical and Political Challenges in the Automation of Platform Governance." *Big Data & Society* 7.1, p. 205395171989794.

Gorwa, Robert and Timothy Garton Ash. 2020. "Democratic Transparency in the Platform Society." *Social Media and Democracy: The State of the Field and Prospects for Reform.* Ed. Nathaniel Persily and Joshua Tucker. Cambridge, UK: Cambridge University Press, pp. 286–312.

Gorwa, Robert and Anton Peez. 2020. "Big Tech Hits the Diplomatic Circuit: Norm Entrepreneurship, Policy Advocacy, and Microsoft's Cybersecurity Tech Accord." *Governing Cyberspace: Behaviour, Power, and Diplomacy.* Ed. Dennis Broeders and Bibi van den Berg. Lanham, MD: Rowman & Littlefield, pp. 263–284.

Gorwa, Robert, and Michael Veale. 2024. "Moderating Model Marketplaces: Platform Governance Puzzles for AI Intermediaries." *Law, Innovation and Technology* 16.2, pp. 1–45.

Graef, Inge. 2018. "When Data Evolves into Market Power-Data Concentration and Data Abuse under Competition Law." *Digital Dominance: The Power of Google, Amazon, Facebook, and*

Apple. Ed. Martin Moore and Damian Tambini. Oxford, UK: Oxford University Press, pp. 72–97.

Graef, Inge. 2019. "Differentiated Treatment in Platform-to-Business Relations: EU Competition Law and Economic Dependence." *Yearbook of European Law* 38, pp. 448–499.

Graham, Mark and Fabian Ferrari, eds. 2022. *Digital Work in the Planetary Market.* International Development Research Centre. Cambridge, MA: MIT Press.

Graham-McLay, Charlotte. 2020. " 'I'm the Last Censor in the Western World': New Zealand's David Shanks Tackles the c-Word." *The Guardian,* January 10.

Gray, Megan. 2018. *Understanding and Improving Privacy "Audits" under FTC Orders.* CIS White Paper. Palo Alto, CA: Stanford Law School.

Greenleaf, Graham. 2022. "Now 157 Countries: Twelve Data Privacy Laws in 2021/22." *SSRN Scholarly Paper 4137418.* Rochester, NY.

Greve, Joan E. 2022. "Senate Passes $739bn Healthcare and Climate Bill after Months of Wrangling." *The Guardian,* August 7.

Grimmelmann, James. 2015. "The Virtues of Moderation." *Yale Journal of Law & Technology* 17.1, pp. 43–109.

Gupta, Akhil. 2017. "Changing Forms of Corruption in India." *Modern Asian Studies* 51.6, pp. 1862–1890.

Haggart, Blayne. 2014. *Copyfight: The Global Politics of Digital Copyright Reform.* Toronto, CA: University of Toronto Press.

Haggart, Blayne and Clara Iglesias Keller. 2021. "Democratic Legitimacy in Global Platform Governance." *Telecommunications Policy* 45.6, p. 102152.

Haggart, Blayne, Natasha Tusikov, and Jan Aart Scholte, eds. "The Return of the State?" (2021). "Introduction: Return of the State?" *Power and Authority in Internet Governance.* Ed. Blayne Haggart, Natasha Tusikov, and Jan Aart Scholte. Abingdon, UK: Routledge, pp. 1–12.

Halliday, Josh. 2012. "Twitter's Tony Wang: 'We Are the Free Speech Wing of the Free Speech Party.' " *The Guardian,* March 22.

Hamburger, Philip. 2021. "The Constitution Can Crack Section 230." *Wall Street Journal,* January 29.

Hanegraaff, Marcel, Jan Beyers, and Iskander De Bruycker. 2016. "Balancing Inside and Outside Lobbying: The Political Strategies of Lobbyists at Global Diplomatic Conferences." *European Journal of Political Research* 55.3, pp. 568–588.

Hansen, Suella and Noelle Jones. 2017. "New Zealand Telecommunications: The Actual Situation-Legislation and Regulations." *Australian Journal of Telecommunications and the Digital Economy* 5.3, pp. 83–88.

Harrison, Joel. 2006. "Truth, Civility, and Religious Battlegrounds: The Contest between Religious Vilification Laws and Freedom of Expression." *Te Mata Koi: Auckland University Law Review* 12, pp. 71–96.

Hartlapp, Miriam, Julia Metz, and Christian Rauh. 2014. *Which Policy for Europe?: Power and Conflict inside the European Commission.* Oxford, UK: Oxford University Press.

He, Danya. 2020. "Governing Hate Content Online: How the Rechtsstaat Shaped the Policy Discourse on the NetzDG in Germany." *International Journal of Communication* 14, pp. 3746–3768.

Heissl, Christina. 2022. "The Legal Status of Platform Workers: Regulatory Approaches and Prospects of a European Solution." *Italian Labour Law e-Journal* 15.1, pp. 13–28.

Heldt, Amélie. 2019. "Reading between the Lines and the Numbers: An Analysis of the First NetzDG Reports." *Internet Policy Review* 8.2, pp. 1–18.

Hellner, Michael. 2004. "Country of Origin Principle in the E-commerce Directive: A Conflict with Conflict of Laws?" *European Review of Private Law* 12.2, pp. 193–213.

Hendel, John. 2020. "Senate Panel Secures Top Tech CEO Testimony for Oct. 28." *Politico,* October 2.

Hendrix, Justin and Anna Lenhart. 2023. "An Exit Interview with a Hill Staffer." *Tech Policy Press,* February 26.

Hendrix, Justin and Patricia Campos Mello. 2023. "Election Disinformation and the Violence in Brazil." *Tech Policy Press*, January 14.

Henley, Jon and Harry Davies. 2022. "Emmanuel Macron Secretly Aided Uber Lobbying Drive in France, Leak Reveals." *The Guardian*, July 10.

Héritier, Adrienne and Dirk Lehmkuhl. 2008. "The Shadow of Hierarchy and New Modes of Governance." *Journal of Public Policy* 28.1, pp. 1–17.

Hertel-Fernandez, Alexander. 2019. *State Capture: How Conservative Activists, Big Businesses, and Wealthy Donors Reshaped the American States—and the Nation*. New York, NY: Oxford University Press.

Hinger, Sophie. 2016. "Asylum in Germany: The Making of the 'Crisis' and the Role of Civil Society." *Human Geography* 9.2, pp. 78–88.

Hoffman, D. Bruce. 2018. "Competition Policy and the Tech Industry—What's at Stake?" *Computer and Communication Industry Association Blog*, April 12.

Hoffmann, Anna Lauren, Nicholas Proferes, and Michael Zimmer. 2018. "'Making the World More Open and Connected': Mark Zuckerberg and the Discursive Construction of Facebook and Its Users." *New Media & Society* 20.1, pp. 199–218.

Hoffmann-Riem, Wolfgang. 2016. "Selbstregelung, Selbstregulierung und regulierte Selbstregulierung im digitalen Kontext." *Neue Macht- und Verantwortungsstrukturen in der digitalen Welt*. Ed. Michael Fehling and Utz Schliesky. Baden-Baden, DE: Nomos, pp. 27–52.

Hoofnagle, Chris Jay. 2016. *Federal Trade Commission Privacy Law and Policy*. Cambridge, UK: Cambridge University Press.

Hurel, Louise Marie and Maurício Santoro Rocha. 2018. "Brazil, China and Internet Governance: Mapping Divergence and Convergence." *Journal of China and International Relations* 6.0, pp. 98–115.

Husovec, Martin. 2023. "How to Facilitate Data Access under the Digital Services Act." *SSRN Scholarly Paper 4452940*. Rochester, NY.

Huszti-Orban, Krisztina. 2017. "Countering Terrorism and Violent Extremism Online: What Role for Social Media Platforms?" *Platform Regulations: How Platforms Are Regulated and How They Regulate Us*. Ed. Luca Belli and Nicolo Zingales. Rio de Janeiro: Fundação Getulio Vargas, pp. 189–212.

Jacob, Lisa. 2018. "87% of Germans Approve of Social Media Regulation Law." *Dalia Research Blog*, April 17.

Jacobi, Tonja and Jeff VanDam. 2013. "The Filibuster and Reconciliation: The Future of Majoritarian Lawmaking in the U.S. Senate." *U.C. Davis Law Review* 47.1, pp. 261–342.

Jardin, Xeni. 2006. "Bush Administration Seeks Google Search Records." *NPR*, January 20.

Jennen, Birgit and Ania Nussbaum. 2021. "Germany and France Oppose Trump's Twitter Exile." *Bloomberg*, January 11.

Jia, Kai and Martin Kenney. 2022. "The Chinese Platform Business Group: An Alternative to the Silicon Valley Model?" *Journal of Chinese Governance* 7.1, pp. 58–80.

Jouanjan, Olivier. 2009. "Freedom of Expression in the Federal Republic of Germany Symposium: An Ocean Apart—Freedom of Expression in Europe and the United States." *Indiana Law Journal* 84.3, pp. 867–884.

Julià-Barceló, Rosa and Kamiel J. Koelman. 2000. "Intermediary Liability in the E-Commerce Directive: So Far So Good, But It's Not Enough." *Computer Law & Security Review* 16.4, pp. 231–239.

Jungendschutz. 2016. "Ergebnisse Des Monitorings von Beschwerdemechanismen Jugendaffiner Dienste." *BMJ Press Release*, March 14.

Jupille, Joseph, Walter Mattli, and Duncan Snidal. 2017. "Dynamics of Institutional Choice." *International Politics and Institutions in Time*. Ed. Orfeo Fioretos. Oxford, UK: Oxford University Press, pp. 118–143.

Just, Natascha and Michael Latzer. 2000. "EU Competition Policy and Market Power Control in the Mediamatics Era." *Telecommunications Policy* 24.5, pp. 395–411.

Juste, Carl. 2022. "Florida Law Targeting Facebook, Twitter Is Unconstitutional, U.S. Appeals Court Rules." *Miami Herald*, May 23.

REFERENCES

Kalra, Aditya, and Munsif Vengattil. 2022. "Google Fined $162 Mln by India Antitrust Watchdog for Abuse of Android Platform." *Reuters*, October 20.

Kaltheuner, Frederike, ed. 2021. *Fake AI*. London, UK: Meatspace Press.

Kalyanpur, Nikhil and Abraham L. Newman. 2019. "The MNC-Coalition Paradox: Issue Salience, Foreign Firms and the General Data Protection Regulation." *JCMS: Journal of Common Market Studies* 57.3, pp. 448–467.

Kang, Cecilia. 2021. "A Leading Critic of Big Tech Will Join the White House." *The New York Times*, March 5.

Kapur, Devesh. 2020. "Why Does the Indian State Both Fail and Succeed?" *Journal of Economic Perspectives* 34.1, pp. 31–54.

Karanicolas, Michael. 2021. "A FOIA for Facebook: Meaningful Transparency for Online Platforms." *Saint Louis University Law Journal* 66, p. 49.

Karpen, Ulrich, Nils Molle, and Simon Schwarz. 2007. "Freedom of Expression and the Administration of Justice in Germany." *European Journal of Law Reform* 9.1, pp. 63–90.

Karpf, David. 2017. "Digital Politics after Trump." *Annals of the International Communication Association* 41.2, pp. 198–207.

Katzenbach, Christian et al. 2023. *Platform Governance Archive (PGA): Dataset PGA v2*. Bremen, DE: University of Bremen.

Kaufmann, Daniel, Aart Kraay, and Massimo Mastruzzi. 2010. *The Worldwide Governance Indicators: Methodology and Analytical Issues*. World Bank Policy Research Working Paper 5430. New York, NY: World Bank.

Kayali, Laura. 2021. "Google Agrees to Advertising Changes after €220M French Antitrust Fine." *Politico*, June 7.

Kaye, David. 2018. *A Human Rights Approach to Platform Content Regulation*. Report of the UN Special Rapporteur on the Promotion and Protection of the Right to Freedom of Opinion and Expression. Geneva, CH: United Nations Human Rights Council.

Kaye, David. 2019a. *"Hate Speech" Regulation in International Human Rights Law*. Report of the UN Special Rapporteur on the Promotion and Protection of the Right to Freedom of Opinion and Expression. Geneva, CH: United Nations Human Rights Council.

Kaye, David. 2019b. *Speech Police: The Global Struggle to Govern the Internet*. New York, NY: Columbia Global Reports.

Keck, Margaret E. and Kathryn Sikkink. 2014. *Activists beyond Borders: Advocacy Networks in International Politics*. Ithaca, NY: Cornell University Press.

Keene, Houston. 2021. "Texas Gov. Abbott Says State "taking a Stand" against Big Tech Censorship." *Fox News*, March 5.

Iglesias Keller, Clara and Diego Werneck Arguelhes. 2022. "How Courts Became a Battlefront against Disinformation: The 2022 Brazilian Elections." *Verfassungsblog*, September 20.

Keller, Daphne. 2018. *Internet Platforms: Observations on Speech, Danger, and Money*. Aegis Series Paper. Palo Alto, CA: Hoover Institution.

Keller, Daphne. 2019. *Dolphins in the Net: Internet Content Filters and the Advocate General's Glawischnig-Piesczek v. Facebook Ireland Opinion*. Palo Atlo, CA: Stanford Center for Internet and Society.

Keller, Daphne. 2022. "Lawful but Awful? Control over Legal Speech by Platforms, Governments, and Internet Users." *The University of Chicago Law Review Online*, June 28.

Keller, Eileen. 2018. "Noisy Business Politics: Lobbying Strategies and Business Influence after the Financial Crisis." *Journal of European Public Policy* 25.3, pp. 287–306.

Kelly, Makena. 2020. "Joe Biden Wants to Revoke Section 230." *The Verge*, January 17.

Kelly, Makena. 2021a. "Democrats Take First Stab at Reforming Section 230 after Capitol Riots." *The Verge*, February 5.

Kelly, Makena. 2021b. "Facebook Declares "Emergency Situation" and Removes Trump Video." *The Verge*, January 6.

Kelsey, Jane. 1993. *Rolling Back the State: Privatisation of Power in Aotearoa/New Zealand*. Wellington, NZ: B. Williams Books.

Kenny, Katie. 2019. "Chief Censor David Shanks Says an Entirely New Media Regulator May Be Needed." *Stuff.nz*, October 22.

Khaitan, Tarunabh. 2020. "The Indian Supreme Court's Identity Crisis: A Constitutional Court or a Court of Appeals?" *Indian Law Review* 4.1, pp. 1–30.

Khan, Lina M. 2017. "Amazon's Antitrust Paradox." *Yale Law Journal* 126.3, pp. 712–805.

Khanna, Parag and David Francis. 2023. "These 25 Companies Are More Powerful Than Many Countries." *Foreign Policy*, June 20.

Kira, Beatriz. 2023. "In Brazil, Platform Regulation Takes Center Stage." *Tech Policy Press*, April 24.

Kirschbaum, Erik. 2015. "German Justice Minister Takes Aim at Facebook over Racist Posts." *Reuters*, August 27.

Klas, Mary Ellen. 2021. "Legislators Move Closer to Imposing Speech Requirements on Social Media Companies." *Miami Herald*, April 20.

Kleine, Mareike. 2013. *Informal Governance in the European Union: How Governments Make International Organizations Work*. Ithaca, NY: Cornell University Press.

Klonick, Kate. 2017. "The New Governors: The People, Rules, and Processes Governing Online Speech." *Harvard Law Review* 131.6, pp. 1598–1670.

Klonick, Kate. 2020. "The Facebook Oversight Board: Creating an Independent Institution to Adjudicate Online Free Expression." *Yale Law Journal* 129.8, pp. 2418–2499.

Klüver, Heike. 2013. *Lobbying in the European Union: Interest Groups, Lobbying Coalitions, and Policy Change*. Oxford, UK: Oxford University Press.

Knibbs, Kate. 2015. "Uber Is Faking Us Out with "Ghost Cabs" on Its Passenger Map." *Gizmodo*, July 28.

Kosseff, Jeff. 2019a. "First Amendment Protection for Online Platforms." *Computer Law & Security Review* 35.5, p. 105340.

Kosseff, Jeff. 2019b. *The Twenty-Six Words That Created the Internet*. Ithaca, NY: Cornell University Press.

Kotzeva, Rossitza et al. 2019. "Recent Developments at DG Competition: 2018/2019." *Review of Industrial Organization* 55, pp. 551–578.

Koutsimpogiorgos, Nikos et al. 2020. "Conceptualizing the Gig Economy and Its Regulatory Problems." *Policy & Internet* 12.4, pp. 525–545.

Krauss, Martin. 2015. "Null Toleranz bei Hassparolen." *Jüdische Allgemeine*, September 22.

Kraut, Robert E. and Paul Resnick. 2012. *Building Successful Online Communities: Evidence-Based Social Design*. Cambridge, MA: MIT Press.

Kreiss, Daniel and Shannon C. Mcgregor. 2019. "The 'Arbiters of What Our Voters See': Facebook and Google's Struggle with Policy, Process, and Enforcement around Political Advertising." *Political Communication* 36.4, pp. 499–522.

Krishnamurthy, Vivek and Jessica Fjeld. 2020. *CDA 230 Goes North American? Examining the Impacts of the USMCA's Intermediary Liability Provisions in Canada and the United States*. Ottawa, ON: Centre for Law, Technology and Society.

Krotoszynski, Ronald J. 2006. *The First Amendment in Cross-Cultural Perspective: A Comparative Legal Analysis of the Freedom of Speech*. New York, NY: NYU Press.

Krutz, Glen S. 2001. "Tactical Maneuvering on Omnibus Bills in Congress." *American Journal of Political Science* 45.1, pp. 210–223.

Krzywdzinski, Martin and Christine Gerber. 2021. "Between Automation and Gamification: Forms of Labour Control on Crowdwork Platforms." *Work in the Global Economy* 1.1–2, pp. 161–184.

Kuczerawy, Aleksandra and Jef Ausloos. 2015. "From Notice-and-Takedown to Notice-and-Delist: Implementing Google Spain." *Colorado Tech Law Journal* 14.2, pp. 219–258.

Kumarasingham, Harshan. 2013. "Exporting Executive Accountability? Westminster Legacies of Executive Power." *Parliamentary Affairs* 66.3, pp. 579–596.

Lapowsky, Issie. 2019. "House Probes Cambridge Analytica on Russia and WikiLeaks." *Wired*, March 4.

Leander, Anna et al. 2023. "Ripples and Their Returns: Tracing the Regulatory Security State from the EU to Brazil, Back and Beyond." *Journal of European Public Policy* 30.7, pp. 1379–1405.

Lee, Dave. 2019. "US Threatens Tax on Champagne and French Cheese." *BBC News*, December 2.

Lee, Nathan, Michelangelo Landgrave, and Kirk Bansak. 2023. "Are Subnational Policymakers' Policy Preferences Nationalized? Evidence from Surveys of Township, Municipal, County, and State Officials." *Legislative Studies Quarterly* 48.2, pp. 441–454.

Leech, Beth L. 2002. "Interview Methods in Political Science." *Political Science & Politics* 35.4, pp. 663–664.

Leerssen, Paddy. 2023. "An End to Shadow Banning? Transparency Rights in the Digital Services Act between Content Moderation and Curation." *Computer Law & Security Review* 48, p. 105790.

Lehdonvirta, Vili. 2022. *Cloud Empires: How Digital Platforms Are Overtaking the State and How We Can Regain Control.* Cambridge, MA: MIT Press.

Lei, Ya-Wen. 2021. "Delivering Solidarity: Platform Architecture and Collective Contention in China's Platform Economy." *American Sociological Review* 86.2, pp. 279–309.

Levi-Faur, David. 2010. *Regulation and Regulatory Governance.* Jerusalem Papers in Regulation and Governance. Jerusalem, IL: Hebrew University.

Li, Siyao and Abraham L. Newman. 2022. "Over the Shoulder Enforcement in European Regulatory Networks: The Role of Arbitrage Mitigation Mechanisms in the General Data Protection Regulation." *Journal of European Public Policy* 29.10, pp. 1698–1720.

Liesching, Marc. 2017. "NetzDG-Entwurf basiert auf Bewertungen von Rechtslaien." *Beck Community Blog*, February 11.

Lindell, Chuck. 2021. " 'Good Trouble': House Democrats Walk, Killing GOP Elections Bill, but Abbott Vows Special Session." *Austin American-Statesman*, May 30.

Liu, Jinhe and Le Yang. 2022. "'Dual-Track' Platform Governance on Content: A Comparative Study between China and United States." *Policy & Internet* 14.2, pp. 304–323.

Livingston, Abby and Alexa Ura. 2021. "Texas Democrats Land in Washington, D.C., and Promise to Stay out of Texas until after Special Legislative Session Ends." *The Texas Tribune*, July 13.

Livingstone, Sonia, Kjartan Ólafsson, and Elisabeth Staksrud. 2013. "Risky Social Networking Practices among 'Underage' Users: Lessons for Evidence-Based Policy." *Journal of Computer-Mediated Communication* 18.3, pp. 303–320.

Livingstone, Sonia et al. 2012. *Towards a Better Internet for Children: Findings and Recommendations from EU Kids Online to Inform the CEO Coalition.* London, UK: EU Kids Online.

Llansó, Emma. 2016. "Takedown Collaboration by Private Companies Creates Troubling Precedent." *CDT Blog*, December 6.

Llansó, Emma. 2020. "Human Rights NGOs in Coalition Letter to GIFCT." *CDT Blog*, July 28.

Lomas, Natasha. 2022. "TikTok Pauses Policy Switch in Europe after Privacy Scrutiny." *TechCrunch*, July 12.

Lynch, Jenna. 2019. "Jacinda Ardern Will Not Follow Australia's Hard-Line Response to Extremist Content." *Newshub*, July 19.

MacKinnon, Rebecca. 2013. *Consent of the Networked: The Worldwide Struggle for Internet Freedom.* New York, NY: Basic Books.

Maclay, Colin Miles. 2010. "Protecting Privacy and Expression Online: Can the Global Network Initiative Embrace the Character of the Net." *Access Controlled: The Shaping of Power, Rights, and Rule in Cyberspace.* Ed. Ronald J. Deibert et al. Cambridge, MA: MIT Press, pp. 87–108.

Maggiolino, Mariateresa and Federico Cesare Guido Ghezzi. 2022. "The Italian Amazon Case and the Notion of Abuse." *SSRN Scholarly Paper* 4288948. Rochester, NY.

Majithia, Vasundhara. 2019. "The Changing Landscape of Intermediary Liability for E-commerce Platforms: Emergence of a New Regime." *Indian Journal of Law and Technology* 15.2, pp. 470–493.

Majone, Giandomenico. 1998. "Public Policy and Administration: Ideas, Interests and Institutions." *A New Handbook Of Political Science.* Ed. Robert E. Goodin and Hans-Dieter Klingemann. Oxford, UK: Oxford University Press, p. 687.

Malhotra, Neil, Benoît Monin, and Michael Tomz. 2019. "Does Private Regulation Preempt Public Regulation?" *American Political Science Review* 113.1, pp. 19–37.

Manjarres, Javier. 2021. "Republicans Drop the Ball On DeSantis' Big Tech Bill." *The Floridian*, March 9.

Mann, Monique, Angela Daly, and Adam Molnar. 2020. "Regulatory Arbitrage and Transnational Surveillance: Australia's Extraterritorial Assistance to Access Encrypted Communications." *Internet Policy Review* 9.3, pp. 1–20.

March, James G. and Johan P. Olsen. 2011. "The Logic of Appropriateness." *The Oxford Handbook of Political Science*. Ed. Robert E. Goodin. Oxford, UK: Oxford University Press, pp. 479–497.

Maréchal, Nathalie and Sarah T. Roberts. 2018. *Researching ICT Companies: A Field Guide for Civil Society Researchers*. Philadelphia, PA: University of Pennslyvania Internet Policy Observatory.

Markham, Annette. 2012. "Fabrication as Ethical Practice: Qualitative Inquiry in Ambiguous Internet Contexts." *Information, Communication & Society* 15.3, pp. 334–353.

Marsden, Christopher. 2011. *Internet Co-Regulation: European Law, Regulatory Governance and Legitimacy in Cyberspace*. Cambridge, UK: Cambridge University Press.

Masnick, Mike. 2021a. "As Expected: Judge Grants Injunction Blocking Florida's Unconstitutional Social Media Law." *Techdirt*, June 30.

Masnick, Mike. 2021b. "Various States All Pile On to Push Blatantly Unconstitutional Laws That Say Social Media Can't Moderate." *Techdirt*, February 4.

Masnick, Mike. 2022a. "5th Circuit Rewrites a Century of 1st Amendment Law to Argue Internet Companies Have No Right to Moderate." *Techdirt*, September 16.

Masnick, Mike. 2022b. "More Than Two Thirds of States Are Pushing Highly Controversial (and Likely Unconstitutional) Bills to Moderate Speech Online." *Techdirt*, July 8.

Mason-Bish, Hannah. 2019. "The Elite Delusion: Reflexivity, Identity and Positionality in Qualitative Research." *Qualitative Research* 19.3, pp. 263–276.

Mattioli, Dana. 2020. "Amazon Scooped Up Data from Its Own Sellers to Launch Competing Products." *Wall Street Journal*, April 24.

Mayer, Kenneth. 2002. *With the Stroke of a Pen: Executive Orders and Presidential Power*. Princeton, NJ: Princeton University Press.

Mayhew, David R. 2004. *Congress: The Electoral Connection*. 2nd ed. New Haven, CT: Yale University Press.

Mayhew, David R. 2005. *Divided We Govern: Party Control, Lawmaking and Investigations, 1946-2002*. New Haven, CT: Yale University Press.

McCarthy, Tom. 2020. "Zuckerberg Says Facebook Won't Be 'Arbiters of Truth' after Trump Threat." *The Guardian*. May 28.

McConnell, Charles. 2022. "Japan Weighs Regulating Apple and Google Following Government Study." *Global Competition Review*, April 27.

McCulloch, Craig. 2019. "Christchurch Call: Tech Companies Overhaul Organisation to Stop Terrorists Online." *Radio New Zealand*, September 24.

McKellar, Katie. 2021. "Has the Internet Become Too Unruly? These Lawmakers Think So." *Deseret News*, July 27.

Medeiros, Ben and Pawan Singh. 2020. "Addressing Misinformation on Whatsapp in India through Intermediary Liability Policy, Platform Design Modification, and Media Literacy." *Journal of Information Policy* 10, pp. 276–298.

Medeiros, Francis Augusto and Lee A. Bygrave. 2015. "Brazil's Marco Civil Da Internet: Does It Live Up to the Hype?" *Computer Law & Security Review* 31.1, pp. 120–130.

Medzini, Rotem. 2021. "Enhanced Self-Regulation: The Case of Facebook's Content Governance." *New Media & Society* 24.10, pp. 2227–2251.

Mello, Patricia Campos. 2022. "An Unholy Coalition Torpedoes Social Media Reform Legislation in Brazil." *Poynter*, May 17.

Menn, Joseph. 2021. "WhatsApp Sues Indian Government over New Privacy Rules—Sources." *Reuters*, May 26.

Meyer, Trisha. 2017. *The Politics of Online Copyright Enforcement in the EU: Access and Control.* Cham, CH: Palgrave Macmillan.

Mia, Valentina. 2020. "The Failures of SESTA/FOSTA: A Sex Worker Manifesto." *Transgender Studies Quarterly* 7.2, pp. 237–239.

Microsoft Corporate. 2017. "Facebook, Microsoft, Twitter and YouTube Announce Formation of the Global Internet Forum to Counter Terrorism." *Microsoft On the Issues Blog*, June 26.

Mikler, John. 2018. *The Political Power of Global Corporations.* Cambridge, UK: Polity.

Moravcsik, Andrew. 1993. "Preferences and Power in the European Community: A Liberal Inter-governmentalist Approach." *JCMS: Journal of Common Market Studies* 31.4, pp. 473–524.

Morris, Zoë Slote. 2009. "The Truth about Interviewing Elites." *Politics* 29.3, pp. 209–217.

Mueller, Milton. 2017. *Will the Internet Fragment? Sovereignty, Globalization and Cyberspace.* Cambridge, UK: Polity Press.

Muldoon, James. 2022. *Platform Socialism: How to Reclaim Our Digital Future from Big Tech.* London, UK: Pluto Press.

Müller, Markus M. 2001. "Reconstructing the New Regulatory State in Germany: Telecommunications, Broadcasting and Banking." *German Politics* 10.3, pp. 37–64.

Musiani, Francesca and Julia Pohle. 2014. "NETmundial: Only a Landmark Event if 'Digital Cold War' Rhetoric Abandoned." *Internet Policy Review* 3.1, pp. 1–9.

NDTV News Desk. 2023. "Centre Reviewing 'Safe Harbour' Clause in Digital India Bill: Minister." *NDTV*, March 10.

Nemacheck, Christine L. 2021. "Trump's Lasting Impact on the Federal Judiciary." *Policy Studies* 42.5–6, pp. 544–562.

NetChoice. 2023. "NetChoice & CCIA v. Moody: Key Resources." *NetChoice Blog*, March 21.

Newman, Abraham L. 2017. "Sequencing, Layering, and Feedbacks in Global Regulation." *International Politics and Institutions in Time.* Ed. Orfeo Fioretos. Oxford, UK: Oxford University Press.

Newman, Abraham L. and David Bach. 2004. "Self-Regulatory Trajectories in the Shadow of Public Power: Resolving Digital Dilemmas in Europe and the United States." *Governance* 17.3, pp. 387–413.

Newsbusters Staff. 2021. "Conservative Leaders: Tech Companies Pose Existential Threat, Must Be Broken Up." *Newsbusters Blog*, January 11.

Nicas, Jack. 2021a. "Apple Says Parler Can Return to iPhones after the App Makes Some Changes." *The New York Times*, April 19.

Nicas, Jack. 2021b. "Brazil's Senate and Supreme Court Overturn Bolsonaro's Ban on Removing Social Media Posts." *The New York Times*, September 21.

Nieborg, David B. and Thomas Poell. 2018. "The Platformization of Cultural Production: Theorizing the Contingent Cultural Commodity." *New Media & Society* 20.11, pp. 4275–4292.

Nielsen, Rasmus Kleis. 2012. *Ground Wars: Personalized Communication in Political Campaigns.* Princeton, NJ: Princeton University Press.

Notley, Tanya. 2019. "The Environmental Costs of the Global Digital Economy in Asia and the Urgent Need for Better Policy." *Media International Australia* 173.1, pp. 125–141.

O'Mara, Margaret. 2020. *The Code: Silicon Valley and the Remaking of America.* New York, NY: Penguin.

Office of Governor Ron DeSantis. 2021a. "Governor Ron DeSantis Signs Bill to Stop the Censorship of Floridians by Big Tech." *FL.Gov*, May 24.

Office of Governor Ron DeSantis. 2021b. "Governor Ron DeSantis, Florida House Speaker Chris Sprowls and Senate President Wilton Simpson Highlight Proposed Legislation to Increase Technology Transparency in Florida." *FL.Gov*, February 2.

Office of the Texas Governor. 2021a. "Governor Abbott Announces Special Session Agenda." *Texas.Gov*, July 7.

Office of the Texas Governor. 2021b. "Governor Abbott Signs Law Protecting Texans From Wrongful Social Media Censorship." *Texas.Gov*, Sep 9.

Owen, Taylor. 2015. *Disruptive Power: The Crisis of the State in the Digital Age*. Oxford, UK: Oxford University Press.

Ozawa, Joao V. S. et al. 2023. "How Disinformation on WhatsApp Went From Campaign Weapon to Governmental Propaganda in Brazil." *Social Media+ Society* 9.1, p. 20563051231160632.

Pallero, Javier. 2020. *What the Facebook Oversight Board Means for Human Rights, and Where We Go from Here*. New York, NY: Access Now.

Panday, Jyoti. 2015. "The Supreme Court Judgment in Shreya Singhal and What It Does for Intermediary Liability in India." *Center for Internet and Society Blog*, April 11.

Panzic, Stephanie Frances. 2015. "Legislating for E-Manners: Deficiencies and Unintended Consequences of the Harmful Digital Communications Act." *Auckland University Law Review* 21.1, pp. 225–247.

Pappalardo, Kylie and Nicolas Suzor. 2018. "The Liability of Australian Online Intermediaries." *Sydney Law Review* 40.4, pp. 469–498.

Park, Kate. 2021. "South Korean Antitrust Regulator Fines Google $177M for Abusing Market Dominance." *TechCrunch*, September 14.

Partridge, Joanna. 2022. "US Bans 'Advanced Tech' Firms from Building Facilities in China for a Decade." *The Guardian*, September 9.

Patrick, Dan. 2021. "Lt. Gov. Dan Patrick Statement: Top Legislative Priorities On-Track." *Homepage of Lieutenant Governor Dan Patrick*, April 16.

Pentzien, Jonas. 2022. "Platform Regulation, Policy Legacies and Institutional Change—Towards a Historico-Institutional Understanding of Platform-Specific Rulemaking in the U.S., Germany, and France." *Politics & Culture of Digital Capitalism Colloquium*. Berlin, DE.

Perarnaud, Clément. 2021. "A Step Back to Look Ahead: Mapping Coalitions on Data Flows and Platform Regulation in the Council of the EU (2016–2019)." *Internet Policy Review* 10.2. pp. 1–21.

Perrigo, Billy. 2020. "Facebook's Ties to India's Ruling Party Complicate Its Fight against Hate Speech." *Time*, August 28.

Perrigo, Billy. 2021. "What Brazil's New Social Media Rules Mean for the Future of the Internet." *Time*, September 10.

Pierson, Paul. 2000. "Increasing Returns, Path Dependence, and the Study of Politics." *American Political Science Review* 94.2, pp. 251–267.

Plantin, Jean-Christophe et al. 2018. "Infrastructure Studies Meet Platform Studies in the Age of Google and Facebook." *New Media & Society* 20.1, pp. 293–310.

Plehwe, Dieter. 2014. "Think Tank Networks and the Knowledge–Interest Nexus: The Case of Climate Change." *Critical Policy Studies* 8.1, pp. 101–115.

Popiel, Pawel. 2018. "The Tech Lobby: Tracing the Contours of New Media Elite Lobbying Power." *Communication, Culture and Critique* 11.4, pp. 566–585.

Post, Savannah. 2017. "Harmful Digital Communications Act 2015." *New Zealand Women's Law Journal* 1.1, pp. 208–214.

Powers, Shawn M. and Michael Jablonski. 2015. *The Real Cyber War: The Political Economy of Internet Freedom*. Champaign, IL: University of Illinois Press.

Praiss, Zach. 2023. "Minnesota's Kids Left Vulnerable, Landmark Online Protections Fail to Pass Legislature." *Minnesota Kids Code Blog*, May 23.

Press Trust of India. 2021. "Internet and Mobile Association of India Sets Up Grievance Council to Ensure OTT Guideline Compliance." *Firstpost*, May 29.

Prime Minister of Australia. 2019. "Tough New Laws to Protect Australians from Live-Streaming of Violent Crimes." *The Office of Hon Scott Morrison MP*, March 30.

PRS Legislative Research. 2024. "Draft Amendments to the Consumer Protection (E-Commerce) Rules." *PRS India Blog*, March 11.

Rahman, K. Sabeel and Kathleen Thelen. 2019. "The Rise of the Platform Business Model and the Transformation of Twenty-First-Century Capitalism." *Politics & Society* 47.2, pp. 177–204.

Rasheed, Ayesha. 2022. "Dormant Commerce Clause Constraints on Social Media Regulation." *SSRN Scholarly Paper 4247006*. Rochester, NY.

228 REFERENCES

Rath, Christian. 2017. "SPD-Politiker über Facebook-Gesetz: 'Legale Posts wiederherstellen.'" *Die Tageszeitung*, July 4.

Rauh, Christian. 2019. "EU Politicization and Policy Initiatives of the European Commission: The Case of Consumer Policy." *Journal of European Public Policy* 26.3, pp. 344–365.

Raymond, Mark and Laura DeNardis. 2015. "Multistakeholderism: Anatomy of an Inchoate Global Institution." *International Theory* 7.3, pp. 572–616.

Recuero, Raquel, Felipe Bonow Soares, and Otávio Vinhas. 2021. "Discursive Strategies for Disinformation on WhatsApp and Twitter during the 2018 Brazilian Presidential Election." *First Monday* 26.1.

Regattieri, Lori. 2023. "January 8 and the Information Crisis in Brazilian Democracy." *Tech Policy Press*, January 18.

Reid, Blake E. 2020. "Section 230 Of . . . What?" *Blakereid.org*, September 4.

Reinbold, Fabian. 2015. "Hetze auf Facebook: Warum der Hass nicht gelöscht wird." *Der Spiegel*, September 9.

Renckens, Stefan. 2020. *Private Governance and Public Authority: Regulating Sustainability in a Global Economy*. Cambridge, UK: Cambridge University Press.

Reuter, Markus. 2017a. "Anhörung zum NetzDG: Mehrheit der Experten hält Gesetzentwurf für verfassungswidrig." *Netzpolitik*, June 19.

Reuter, Markus. 2017b. "Bundestagsdebatte: Maas findet sein Hate-Speech-Gesetz gut, alle anderen wollen Änderungen." *Netzpolitik*, May 19.

Reuter, Markus. 2017c. "Hate-Speech-Gesetz: Geteilte Reaktionen auf den Entwurf des Justizministers." *Netzpolitik*, March 16.

Reuter, Markus. 2017d. "Vorsicht Beruhigungspille: Netzwerkdurchsetzungsgesetz geht unverändert in den Bundestag." *Netzpolitik*, May 18.

Reuters Newswire. 2016. "German Minister Tells Facebook to Get Serious about Hate Speech." *Reuters*, September 26.

Reuters Newswire. 2022. "India Wants Big Tech to Take Content Down More Actively: Report." *Reuters*, February 2.

Roberts, Margaret E. 2018. *Censored: Distraction and Diversion inside Chinas Great Firewall*. Princeton, NJ: Princeton University Press.

Roberts, Sarah T. 2018. "Digital Detritus: 'Error' and the Logic of Opacity in Social Media Content Moderation." *First Monday* 23.3.

Roberts, Sarah T. 2019. *Behind the Screen: Content Moderation in the Shadows of Social Media*. New Haven, CT: Yale University Press.

Rochet, Jean-Charles and Jean Tirole. 2003. "Platform Competition in Two-Sided Markets." *Journal of the European Economic Association* 1.4, pp. 990–1029.

Rolf, Steve and Seth Schindler. 2023. "The US–China Rivalry and the Emergence of State Platform Capitalism." *Environment and Planning A: Economy and Space*, p. 0308518X221146545.

Roose, Kevin. 2021. "In Pulling Trump's Megaphone, Twitter Shows Where Power Now Lies." *The New York Times*, January 9.

Rosenblat, Alex. 2018. *Uberland: How Algorithms Are Rewriting the Rules of Work*. Berkeley, CA: University of California Press.

Ross, Alec. 2011. "Digital Diplomacy and US Foreign Policy." *Hague Journal of Diplomacy* 6, pp. 451–456.

Royal Commission of Inquiry. 2020. *Royal Commission of Inquiry into the Attack on Christchurch Mosques on 15 March 2019*. Wellington, NZ: Department of Internal Affairs, New Zealand Government.

Rudalevige, Andrew. 2021. *By Executive Order: Bureaucratic Management and the Limits of Presidential Power*. Princeton, NJ: Princeton University Press.

Rydzak, Jan. 2019. "Of Blackouts and Bandhs: The Strategy and Structure of Disconnected Protest in India." *SSRN Scholarly Paper 3330413*. Rochester, NY.

Sachdeva, Sam. 2019. "What the Christchurch Call Means for International Law." *Newsroom NZ*, December 2.

Samuels, Alex. 2019. "Why Do the Texas House and Senate Adjourn So Early in the Day at the Beginning of the Legislative Session?" *The Texas Tribune*, January 15.

Sandoval, Greg. 2002. "Bush Shows Support for Tech Industry." *CNET*, April 24.

Sarre, Rick. 2017. "Metadata Retention as a Means of Combatting Terrorism and Organised Crime: A Perspective from Australia." *Asian Journal of Criminology* 12.3, pp. 167–179.

Saurwein, Florian. 2011. "Regulatory Choice for Alternative Modes of Regulation: How Context Matters." *Law & Policy* 33.3, pp. 334–366.

Savage, Ashley and Richard Hyde. 2014. "Using Freedom of Information Requests to Facilitate Research." *International Journal of Social Research Methodology* 17.3, pp. 303–317.

Sayers, Anthony M. and Andrew C. Banfield. 2013. "The Evolution of Federalism and Executive Power in Canada and Australia." *Federal Dynamics: Continuity, Change, and the Varieties of Federalism*. Ed. Arthur Benz and Jörg Broschek. Oxford, UK: Oxford University Press, pp. 185–204.

Schaffner, Brian F. 2022. *Public Demand for Regulating Big Tech: Findings from Recent Polling*. Washington, DC: The Tech Oversight Project.

Schoenebeck, Sarita, Oliver L. Haimson, and Lisa Nakamura. 2020. "Drawing from Justice Theories to Support Targets of Online Harassment." *New Media & Society* 23.5, pp. 1278–1300.

Scholtz, Trebor and Nathan Schneider, eds. 2016. *Ours to Hack and Own: The Rise of Platform Cooperatives*. New York, NY: OR Books.

Schott, Bryan. 2021. "Utah Gov. Spencer Cox Vetoes Controversial Social Media Legislation." *The Salt Lake Tribune*, March 23.

Schulz, Wolfgang. 2018. "Regulating Intermediaries to Protect Privacy Online: The Case of the German NetzDG." *SSRN Scholarly Paper 3216572*. Rochester, NY.

Schulz, Wolfgang and Thorsten Held. 2002. *Regulierte Selbstregulierung als Form modernen Regierens*. Hamburg, DE: Hans-Bredow-Institut.

Schulz, Wolfgang and Thorsten Held. 2004. *Regulated Self-Regulation as a Form of Modern Government: A Comparative Analysis with Case Studies from Media and Telecommunications Law*. Bloomington, IN: Indiana University Press.

Schwemer, Sebastian Felix. 2019. "Trusted Notifiers and the Privatization of Online Enforcement." *Computer Law & Security Review* 35.6, p. 105339.

Seawright, Jason and John Gerring. 2008. "Case Selection Techniques in Case Study Research: A Menu of Qualitative and Quantitative Options." *Political Research Quarterly* 61.2, pp. 294–308.

Seering, Joseph, Geoff Kaufman, and Stevie Chancellor. 2020. "Metaphors in Moderation." *New Media & Society* 24.3, pp. 621–640.

Segal, Jeffrey A. et al. 1995. "Ideological Values and the Votes of US Supreme Court Justices Revisited." *Journal of Politics* 57.3, pp. 812–823.

Seidl, Timo. 2020. "The Politics of Platform Capitalism: A Case Study on the Regulation of Uber in New York." *Regulation & Governance* 16.2, pp. 357–374.

Shaffer, Gregory, James Nedumpara, and Aseema Sinha. 2015. "State Transformation and the Role of Lawyers: The WTO, India, and Transnational Legal Ordering." *Law & Society Review* 49.3, pp. 595–629.

Sharwood, Simon. 2023. "India Set to Regulate AI, Big Tech, with Digital Act." *The Register*, May 26.

Shenkman, Carey, Dhanaraj Thakur, and Emma Llansó. 2021. *Do You See What I See? Capabilities and Limits of Automated Multimedia Content Analysis*. Washington, DC: Center for Democracy and Technology.

Shepherd, Simon. 2019. "The Nation: National Cyber Policy Office's Paul Ash." *Scoop NZ*, September 28.

Sherman, Justin. 2019. "India's Digital Path: Leaning Democratic or Authoritarian." *Just Security*, February 4.

Shibata, Saori. 2020. "Gig Work and the Discourse of Autonomy: Fictitious Freedom in Japan's Digital Economy." *New Political Economy* 25.4, pp. 535–551.

Singh, Manish. 2021. "India Proposes Tougher Rules Following Complaints against Amazon and Flipkart." *TechCrunch*, July 21.

Sinha, Subir. 2021. "'Strong Leaders', Authoritarian Populism and Indian Developmentalism: The Modi Moment in Historical Context." *Geoforum* 124, pp. 320–333.

Sissons, Miranda. 2022. *An Independent Due Diligence Exercise into Meta's Human Rights Impact in Israel and Palestine during the May 2021 Escalation*. Palo Alto, CA: Meta.

Síthigh, Daithí Mac. 2020. "The Road to Responsibilities: New Attitudes towards Internet Intermediaries." *Information & Communications Technology Law* 29.1, pp. 1–21.

Slaughter, Anne-Marie. 2004. *A New World Order*. Princeton, NJ: Princeton University Press.

Soha, Michael and Zachary J. McDowell. 2016. "Monetizing a Meme: YouTube, Content ID, and the Harlem Shake." *Social Media+Society* 2.1, p. 2056305115623801.

Sonderby, Chris. 2019. "Update on New Zealand." *Facebook Newsroom*, March 18.

Squirrell, Tim. 2019. "Platform Dialectics: The Relationships between Volunteer Moderators and End Users on Reddit." *New Media & Society* 21.9, pp. 1910–1927.

Srivastava, Swati. 2023. "Algorithmic Governance and the International Politics of Big Tech." *Perspectives on Politics* 21.3, pp. 989–1000.

Srnicek, Nick. 2016. *Platform Capitalism*. Cambridge, UK: Polity Press.

Stanford World Intermediary Liability Map. 2017. "Information Technology (Procedure and Safeguards for Blocking for Access of Information by Public) Rules, 2009." *WILMAP*, November 3.

Stanford World Intermediary Liability Map. 2018. "Omnibus Bill, No. 524, Amending Provisions in Various Laws and Decrees Including Law No. 5651 'Regulation of Publications on the Internet and Suppression of Crimes Committed by Means of Such Publications.'" *WILMAP*, May 4.

State of California. 2022a. "Governor Newsom Signs First-in-Nation Bill Protecting Children's Online Data and Privacy." *CA.Gov*, September 15.

State of California. 2022b. "Governor Newsom Signs Nation-Leading Social Media Transparency Measure." *CA.Gov*, September 14.

Statista Research Department. 2016. "Social Network Memberships in Germany 2016." *Statista*, October 20.

Stefano, Valerio De. 2022. "The EU Commission's Proposal for a Directive on Platform Work: An Overview." *Italian Labour Law e-Journal* 15.1, pp. 1–11.

Steinberg, Marc. 2020. "LINE as Super App: Platformization in East Asia." *Social Media+ Society* 6.2, p. 2056305120933285.

Strange, Susan. 1991. "Big Business and the State." *Millennium: Journal of International Studies* 20.2, pp. 245–250.

Streeck, Wolfgang. 2009. *Re-Forming Capitalism: Institutional Change in the German Political Economy*. Oxford, UK: Oxford University Press.

Stuenkel, Oliver. 2020. *The BRICS and the Future of Global Order*. 2nd ed. London, UK: Rowman & Littlefield.

Subbaraman, Nidhi. 2021. "'Inspired Choice': Biden Appoints Sociologist Alondra Nelson to Top Science Post." *Nature* 589.7843, p. 502.

Sud, Nikita. 2022. "The Actual Gujarat Model: Authoritarianism, Capitalism, Hindu Nationalism and Populism in the Time of Modi." *Journal of Contemporary Asia* 52.1, pp. 102–126.

Sukhtankar, Sandip and Milan Vaishnav. 2015. "Corruption in India: Bridging Research Evidence and Policy Options." *India Policy Forum* 11.1, pp. 193–276.

Suzor, Nicolas. 2018. "Digital Constitutionalism: Using the Rule of Law to Evaluate the Legitimacy of Governance by Platforms." *Social Media + Society* 4.3, pp. 1–11.

Suzor, Nicolas. 2019. *Lawless: The Secret Rules That Govern Our Digital Lives*. Cambridge, UK: Cambridge University Press.

Suzor, Nicolas, Tess Van Geelen, and Sarah Myers West. 2018. "Evaluating the Legitimacy of Platform Governance: A Review of Research and a Shared Research Agenda." *International Communication Gazette* 80.4, pp. 385–400.

Sweney, Mark. 2022. "Facebook Owner Meta to Sell Giphy after UK Watchdog Confirms Ruling." *The Guardian*, October 18.

Szabo, Carl. 2021. "NetChoice Opposition to Florida SB 7072—Anti-Bias." *NetChoice Blog*, April 19.

Tankovska, H. 2021a. "Facebook: Average Revenue per User 2011–2020, by Region." *Statista*, February 1.

Tankovska, H. 2021b. "Leading Countries Based on Number of Twitter Users as of April 2021." *Statista*, March 12.

Tarnoff, Ben. 2022. *Internet for the People: The Fight for Our Digital Future*. London, UK: Verso Books.

Tarnoff, Ben and Moira Weigel, eds. 2020. *Voices from the Valley*. New York, NY: FSG Originals.

Tarrow, Sidney. 2005. *The New Transnational Activism*. Cambridge, UK: Cambridge University Press.

Täuscher, Karl and Sven M. Laudien. 2018. "Understanding Platform Business Models: A Mixed Methods Study of Marketplaces." *European Management Journal* 36.3, pp. 319–329.

Taylor, James. 2021. *Big Tech Censorship: Is Free Speech Dead, or Will Heartland Prevail?* Arlington Heights, IL: The Heartland Institute.

Thelen, Kathleen and Sven Steinmo. 1992. "Historical Institutionalism in Comparative Politics." *Structuring Politics: Historical Institutionalism in Comparative Analysis*. Ed. Sven Steinmo, Kathleen Thelen, and Frank Longstreth. Cambridge, UK: Cambridge University Press, pp. 1–32.

Thiruvengadam, Arun K. and Piyush Joshi. 2012. "Judiciaries as Crucial Actors in Southern Regulatory Systems: A Case Study of Indian Telecom Regulation." *Regulation & Governance* 6.3, pp. 327–343.

Thompson, Peter A. 2011. "Neoliberalism and the Political Economies of Public Television Policy in New Zealand." *Australian Journal of Communication* 38.3, pp. 1–16.

Thompson, Peter A. 2019. "Beware of Geeks Bearing Gifts: Assessing the Regulatory Response to the Christchurch Call." *The Political Economy of Communication* 7.1, pp. 83–104.

Todoli-Signes, Adrián. 2021. "Spanish Riders Law and the Right to Be Informed about the Algorithm." *European Labour Law Journal* 12.3, pp. 399–402.

Tusikov, Natasha. 2016. *Chokepoints: Global Private Regulation on the Internet*. Oakland, CA: University of California Press.

Tworek, Heidi. 2019. *News from Germany: The Competition to Control World Communications, 1900–1945*. Cambridge, MA: Harvard University Press.

Tworek, Heidi. 2021. "Fighting Hate with Speech Law: Media and German Visions of Democracy." *Journal of Holocaust Research* 35.2, pp. 106–122.

Urman, Aleksandra and Mykola Makhortykh. 2023. "How Transparent Are Transparency Reports? Comparative Analysis of Transparency Reporting across Online Platforms." *Telecommunications Policy* 47.3, p. 102477.

Vaidhyanathan, Siva. 2018. *Antisocial Media: How Facebook Disconnects Us and Undermines Democracy*. Oxford, UK: Oxford University Press.

Van Dijck, José. 2013. *The Culture of Connectivity: A Critical History of Social Media*. Oxford, UK: Oxford University Press.

Van Dijck, José, David B. Nieborg, and Thomas Poell. 2019. "Reframing Platform Power." *Internet Policy Review* 8.2, pp. 1–18.

van Doorn, Niels. 2020a. "A New Institution on the Block: On Platform Urbanism and Airbnb Citizenship." *New Media & Society* 22.10, pp. 1808–1826.

van Doorn, Niels. 2020b. "At What Price? Labour Politics and Calculative Power Struggles in On-Demand Food Delivery." *Work Organisation, Labour & Globalisation* 14.1, pp. 136–149.

van Hoboken, Joris and Daphne Keller. 2019. *Design Principles for Intermediary Liability Laws*. Philadelphia, PA: Annenberg Policy Center.

van Hoboken, Joris et al. 2023. "Putting the Digital Services Act into Practice: Enforcement, Access to Justice, and Global Implications." *SSRN Scholarly Paper 4384266*. Rochester, NY.

Vasagar, Jeevan. 2014. "Transcript of Interview with Heiko Maas, German Justice Minister." *Financial Times*, September 15.

Veale, Michael. 2019. "Governing Machine Learning That Matters." PhD thesis. London, UK: University College London.

Veale, Michael, Kira Matus, and Robert Gorwa. 2023. "AI and Global Governance: Modalities, Rationales, Tensions." *Annual Review of Law and Social Science* 19.2, pp. 1–30.

Verdier, Pierre-Hugues. 2009. "Transnational Regulatory Networks and Their Limits." *Yale Journal of International Law* 34.2, pp. 113–172.

Verheecke, Lora. 2022. *Uber Files 2 in Brussels: Driving EU Lobbying*. Paris, FR: L'Observatoire des Multinationales.

Vernon, Raymond. 1977. *Storm over the Multinationals: The Real Issues*. Cambridge, MA: Harvard University Press.

Vogel, David. 2003. "The Hare and the Tortoise Revisited: The New Politics of Consumer and Environmental Regulation in Europe." *British Journal of Political Science* 33.4, pp. 557–580.

von Notz, Konstantin. 2015. " 'Hate Speech': Bundesregierung muss gegen Internet-Hetze vorgehen." *Handelsblatt*, December 15.

Vowles, Jack and Jennifer Curtin, eds. 2020. *A Populist Exception? The 2017 New Zealand General Election*. Canberra, AU: ANU Press.

Wagner, Ben. 2013. "Governing Internet Expression: How Public and Private Regulation Shape Expression Governance." *Journal of Information Technology & Politics* 10.4, pp. 389–403.

Wagner, Ben. 2016. *Global Free Expression—Governing the Boundaries of Internet Content*. Cham, CH: Springer.

Wagner, Ben et al. 2020. "Regulating Transparency? Facebook, Twitter and the German Network Enforcement Act." *Conference on Fairness, Accountability, and Transparency in Machine Learning (FAT*)*. Barcelona, ES.

Walby, Kevin and Mike Larsen. 2012. "Access to Information and Freedom of Information Requests: Neglected Means of Data Production in the Social Sciences." *Qualitative Inquiry* 18.1, pp. 31–42.

Walby, Kevin and Alex Luscombe. 2017. "Criteria for Quality in Qualitative Research and Use of Freedom of Information Requests in the Social Sciences." *Qualitative Research* 17.5, pp. 537–553.

Warren, Elizabeth. 2019. "Here's How We Can Break up Big Tech." *Medium*, October 11.

Warzel, Charlie. 2022. "Is This the Beginning of the End of the Internet?" *The Atlantic*, September 28.

Wawro, Gregory J. and Eric Schickler. 2007. *Filibuster: Obstruction and Lawmaking in the US Senate*. Princeton, NJ: Princeton University Press.

Weigel, Moira. 2023. *Amazon's Trickle-Down Monopoly*. New York, NY: Data & Society Research Institute.

Weir, Margaret. 1992. "Ideas and the Politics of Bounded Innovation." *Structuring Politics: Historical Institutionalism in Comparative Analysis*. Ed. Sven Steinmo, Kathleen Thelen, and Frank Longstreth. Cambridge, UK: Cambridge University Press, pp. 188–216.

Weiss, Martin A. and Kristin Archick. 2016. *US-EU Data Privacy: From Safe Harbor to Privacy Shield*. Washington, DC: Congressional Research Service.

Wells, Chris et al. 2020. "Trump, Twitter, and News Media Responsiveness: A Media Systems Approach." *New Media & Society* 22.4, pp. 659–682.

Wenguang, Yu. 2018. "Internet Intermediaries' Liability for Online Illegal Hate Speech." *Frontiers of Law in China* 13.3, pp. 342–356.

West, Sarah Myers. 2017. "Raging against the Machine: Network Gatekeeping and Collective Action on Social Media Platforms." *Media and Communication* 5.3, p. 28.

Westerwinter, Oliver. 2021. "Transnational Public-Private Governance Initiatives in World Politics: Introducing a New Dataset." *Review of International Organizations* 16.1, pp. 137–174.

White House. 2004. "Promoting Innovation and Competitiveness: President Bush's Technology Agenda." *Bush Administration Digital Archive*, June 24.

Winterton, Robert. 2023. "NetChoice v. Bonta." *NetChoice Blog*, March 21.

Witt, Ulrich. 2002. "Germany's 'Social Market Economy': Between Social Ethos and Rent Seeking." *Independent Review* 6.3, pp. 365–375.

Wood, Alex J. 2021. *Algorithmic Management Consequences for Work Organisation and Working Conditions.* Seville, ES: Joint Research Centre.

Woodcock, Jamie and Mark Graham. 2020. *The Gig Economy: A Critical Introduction.* Cambridge, MA: Polity.

Woods, Lorna. 2019. "The Duty of Care in the Online Harms White Paper." *Journal of Media Law* 11.1, pp. 6–17.

Wray, Ben. 2021. "Gig Economy Project—Reaction to the Platform Work Directive." *Brave New Europe*, December 9.

Wu, Tim. 2018. *The Curse of Bigness: Antitrust in the New Gilded Age.* New York, NY: Columbia Global Reports.

Yackee, Jason Webb and Susan Webb Yackee. 2009. "Divided Government and US Federal Rule-making." *Regulation & Governance* 3.2, pp. 128–144.

Yackee, Susan Webb. 2019. "The Politics of Rulemaking in the United States." *Annual Review of Political Science* 22, pp. 37–55.

York, Jillian C. 2021. *Silicon Values: The Future of Free Speech under Surveillance Capitalism.* London, UK: Verso.

York, Jillian C. and Corynne McSherry. 2019. "Content Moderation Is Broken. Let Us Count the Ways." *EFF Deeplinks Blog*, April 29.

Zaeem, Razieh Nokhbeh and K. Suzanne Barber. 2020. "The Effect of the GDPR on Privacy Policies: Recent Progress and Future Promise." *ACM Transactions on Management Information Systems* 12.1, 2:1–2:20.

Zhang, Lin and Julie Yujie Chen. 2022. "A Regional and Historical Approach to Platform Capitalism: The Cases of Alibaba and Tencent." *Media, Culture & Society*, 44.8, pp. 1454–1472.

Zingales, Nicolo. 2015. "The Brazilian Approach to Internet Intermediary Liability: Blueprint for a Global Regime?" *Internet Policy Review* 4.4, pp. 1–14.

Zuckerberg, Mark. 2018. "A Blueprint for Content Governance and Enforcement." *Facebook Newsroom*, November 15.

Zürn, Michael. 2004. "Global Governance and Legitimacy Problems." *Government and Opposition* 39.2, pp. 260–287.

Index

AirBnb 17, 19, 169
Algorithmic management 40, 41, 42, 53
Alibaba 18–19, 38
Amazon
  in India 154
  Logistics 40
  Marketplace 23–4, 34, 36
  Web Services 17, 19
American Legislative Exchange Council
      (ALEC) 136–7
Apple
  App Store 25, 26, 34
  Fines 35, 37–8
Application Programming Interface (API) 25,
      34
Ardern, Jacinda 96–8, 106, 108, 110; *see also*
      New Zealand
Australia
  Abhorrent Violent Material Act (AVM) 99,
      104–5, 111–12
  Brisbane Summit 101–2, 106, 111
  eSafety Commissioner 99–101, 103, 196
  Green party 104
  Labor party 105, 106
Austria 3, 48

Biden, Joseph 33, 118, 121, 123, 125, 127
Bolsonaro, Jair 161–2, 163; *see also* Brazil
Brazil
  'Fake News Bill' (PL2630) 163–4
  Marco Civil 161, 163
BRICS 160

Censorship
  in the German context 84, 192
  in US policy debates 117, 133, 137–8,
      139, 162

Child abuse imagery/material 51, 57, 99, 196
China
  Chinese Administration of Cyberspace
      (CAC) 150–1
Christchurch Call to Action (To Eliminate
      Terrorist and Violent Extremist Content
      Online)
  Paris Summit 106, 108
  Signatories 108, 110
Codes of Conduct 62–3, 74, 80–1, 88, 92, 94,
      103, 109, 191
  Digital Single Market 88, 91
Complementors (platform theory) 15, 24, 105
Computer and Communications Industry
      Association (CCIA) 133–4, 140, 167
'Community Standards' 80, 100
Conservative Political Action Conference
      (CPAC) 129–30
Content moderation
  automated/algorithmic 22, 23, 26, 49,
      109, 161
  commercial/professional 22, 26, 53
  community-managed 20–1
  policy changes 48, 85, 99, 137
  public outcry 79, 82, 97, 114
Co-regulation
  in the European context 61, 88
  in regulatory theory 28, 59, 61

Disinformation 5, 48, 115, 119, 126, 156, 161–2
Dorsey, Jack 110, 120; *see also* Twitter

eBay 13, 21
European Commission
  Clean IT Project 47
  DG Communications, Content, and
      Technology (DG CNECT) 88, 91

236   INDEX

European Union (*continued*)
  DG Justice (DG JUST) 88, 91
  Internet Forum 47, 109
  Technical Regulations Information System
    (TRIS) 87, 88, 89, 190
European Union
  Code of Conduct on Illegal Online Hate
    Speech 88, 92, 94, 109
  Code of Practice on Disinformation 48, 49
  Digital Markets Act (DMA) 35–6
  Digital Services Act (DSA) 2, 49, 52, 163
  e-Commerce Directive 44, 49, 89
  General Data Protection Regulation
    (GDPR) 31–2, 52
  Platform-to-Business Regulation
    36, 130
  Platform Work Directive 41, 52
  Terrorist Content Regulation
    (TERREG) 49, 51

Facebook
  Acquisitions 34, 39
  Fines 34–9
  FTC Lawsuits 123
  Oversight Board 27, 169
'Fake News' 83, 149, 163
Federalist Society 128, 137, 141–2
First Amendment to the US Constitution 43,
    131, 132, 134, 135, 137, 140, 141, 143
France 39, 48, 106, 108

Germany
  Alternative for Germany (AfD) party 83
  Christian Democratic party (CDU) 79, 82–3,
    85, 87, 90, 92, 187
  Hate Speech Task Force 78–81
  Interstate Treaty on the Protection of Minors
    (JMStV) 62
  Ministry of Justice and Consumer Protection
    (BMJV) 62, 78, 80, 81, 85–8,
    187–8, 199
  Network Enforcement Act (NetzDG)
    Key Provisions 84
    Negotiation with European
      Commission 87–90
    Parliamentary Debate 85, 93
  Social Democratic party (SPD) 82–4, 87, 91,
    93, 187
Global Alliance for Responsible Media
    (GARM) 50
Global Internet Forum to Counter Terrorism
    (GIFCT) 27, 50, 96, 101, 108–10, 111,
    113, 169
Google
  Android 37, 39

Search 17, 35
Shopping 34–5
Group of 20 (G20) 36, 39, 52

Hash-Matching (automated content
    moderation) 22, 27, 62, 109, 158
Hate speech 5, 8, 47, 57, 62, 79, 80, 88, 91,
    115, 126
Heartland Institute 132, 137, 141
'Hipster' antitrust 33
Human rights 7, 56, 70, 84, 89, 107,
    161, 192

India
  Bharatiya Janata party (BJP) 65, 156, 157
  Competition Policy 37
  Intermediary Liability 154–5
  Ministry of Electronics and Information
    Technology 155
  Supreme Court 158
Infrastructure 15, 18, 23, 25, 26, 29, 105, 160
Institutions 41, 53, 56, 59, 68, 113
International Business Machines (IBM) 32
Internet governance 27, 160
Internet Governance Forum (IGF) 149
InternetNZ 98
Internet stack 52, 64

'Jawboning' 64
Jourova, Vera 88, 91–2
Juncker, Jean-Claude 35, 88, 91

Khan, Lina 33, 123

LinkedIn 34, 154
Lobbying
  notable examples 42, 44, 91, 111, 128,
    141, 163
  in relation to regulatory demand 54, 56–7, 59,
    63, 71, 147
Lyft 17, 19, 169

Maas, Heiko 79–80, 82–3, 85, 86, 90, 94; *see also*
    Germany
Macron, Emmanuel 108, 117, 149
Market power
  in competition policy 32, 35
  in examples of global platform
    regulation 148, 188
  in regulatory theory 55, 67
Meta. *See* Facebook

Microsoft
  Azure 17, 19
  Codes of Conduct 46, 109
  Competition Investigations 32–5
  Labor Force 39–40
Modi, Narendra 154, 156, 157, 159
Morrison, Scott 99–100, 102, 103–4,
    106, 193
Multistakeholderism 27, 46, 62, 107,
    111, 136
Musk, Elon 25, 159
MySpace 46

NetChoice 132–4, 135, 139–40, 167
NETmundial Meeting on the Future of Internet
    Governance 160
Netscape 14, 30
New Zealand 8, 73, 97–9, 106–13
  Ministry of Foreign Affairs and Trade 198–9
North American Free Trade Agreement
    (NAFTA) 117, 1195

Open Markets Institute 120–1

Political will (demand for platform regulation)
    4, 54, 58, 70, 71, 85, 94, 111
Power to intervene (ability to supply platform
    regulation) 4, 54, 55, 66–70, 94
Platform cooperatives 18

Reliance Jio 154
Riots at the US Capitol, January 6 121, 129, 141

Singapore 3, 48, 148, 149
Smith, Bradford 97, 98, 101, 206; *see also*
    Microsoft
Standard setting 23, 52, 61

Tech Workers Coalition 42
Telegram 51, 90, 164
Tencent 18
TikTok 32, 51, 92, 153
Transparency reporting 49, 54, 103, 111, 115,
    140, 151
Trump, Donald 1, 2, 83, 116–18, 127–8, 129,
    135, 141
Trust and Safety (T&S) 1–3, 6, 20, 22–3, 24, 25,
    73, 78, 140, 153, 154

Twitter 2, 17, 19, 25, 46, 47, 78, 79, 80, 82, 85,
    92, 102, 108, 110, 116, 123, 129, 137

Uber 17, 19, 24, 41–2, 169
United Kingdom
  Digital Markets Unit 39
  Online Safety Bill 49, 51
United Nations
  Counter Terrorism Executive Directorate 111
  Special Rapporteur for Freedom of Opinion
    84
United States
  Institutions
    Federal Communications Commission
      (FCC) 117, 122, 123
    Federal Trade Commission (FTC) 31, 33,
      121, 123, 124
    House of Representatives 121–2, 124, 125,
      126, 127
    Senate 121, 124, 125
  Policies
    Allow States and Victims to Fight Online
      Sex Trafficking Act and Stop Enabling
      Sex Traffickers Act (FOSTA/SESTA)
      127
    Digital Millenium Copyright Act
      (DMCA) 44
    Internet Freedom Agenda 57
    Section 230 of the Communications Act
      44, 127, 137

Veto points 68, 93, 125, 138

'Weaponized interdependence' 153
Weibo 151
WhatsApp 34, 39, 90, 123, 154, 156–9; *see also*
    Facebook

X (microblogging platform). *See* Twitter

YouTube 15, 19, 154, 161
  Content ID 26–7
  European Co-Regulation 47
  Live-Streaming 95
  NetzDG Task Force 80–2, 86

Zuckerberg, Mark 1, 13, 15, 27, 65, 95, 120, 130;
    see also Facebook

The manufacturer's authorised representative in the EU for product safety is Oxford
University Press España S.A. of El Parque Empresarial San Fernando de Henares,
Avenida de Castilla, 2 – 28830 Madrid (www.oup.es/en or product.safety@oup.com).
OUP España S.A. also acts as importer into Spain of products made by the manufacturer.

Printed in the USA/Agawam, MA
March 21, 2025

884675.009